INTERNATIONAL DEVELOPMENT

INTERNATIONAL DEVELOPMENT:
Growth and Change

H. W. Singer

McGRAW-HILL BOOK COMPANY

NEW YORK   TORONTO   LONDON

International Development: Growth and Change

To my wife, Ilse Singer

1263673

Preface

Practically all the chapters in this book have been previously published, as indicated in each case. However, these previous essays are scattered through a large number of economic journals published in different parts of the world, many of which are not widely circulated among readers in any one country. The demand for reprints and other expressions of interest encourage me to think that this presentation of essays in a single volume may be welcome. I am grateful to the various journals involved for permitting me to make this presentation.

My interest in the problems of the poorer countries began in 1947 (although it may be said to have been implied in earlier work in the poorer areas and among the poorer population groups in an industrial environment). Throughout this period, my interest and experience in the problems of poorer countries were connected with work on the staff of the United Nations. This work was not limited to the headquarters in New York, but over the years took me into a number of the less developed countries as a researcher and technical adviser. It should be emphasized, however, that this volume contains the result of work done outside official duties in the United Nations. The views here presented, therefore, are my own and have no necessary relationship to any views held by the United Nations. At the same time I wish to acknowledge my debt of thanks to the many officials and others in the developing countries of Latin America, Asia, and Africa which I have been privileged to visit, as well as to my colleagues in the United Nations for the opportunities of observing and learning which work in and for the United Nations has provided.

No attempt has been made to present the essays in chronological order. It would be inhuman not to have changed one's mind on a number of points during the last sixteen years. (After all, the book is subtitled *Growth and Change!*). All the same, it is hoped that a certain degree of unity of thinking will be apparent. Those readers who wish to do so are, of course, entitled to look for inconsistencies but are also invited in that case to remember the chronology of the various chapters.

In the early years of the period during which the various sections were written, the subject of this book was considered, at least among the academic economists, as slightly exotic and only doubtfully worthy or capable of serious analysis. Since then, however, interest in the subject has increased tremendously, and the literature on it has correspondingly mushroomed. This last fact might have argued against adding to the literature, but it is hoped that the heightened interest in the subject will justify the present volume.

I owe a debt of gratitude to Mrs. Caroline Miles, a former colleague in the United Nations, now in London; without her encouragement and especially without her help in preparing the various chapters for publication —going far beyond the ordinary limits of editorship—this volume could never have been presented.

I also wish to thank Miss Shirley Fleischer and Mr. Man D. Chawdhury, both graduate students at the New School for Social Research, for assisting with the index and proofs; and Mrs. Vivian Bonano for much essential help in getting this volume ready for publication.

H. W. Singer

Introduction

Mankind today is facing its greatest challenge since the dawn of civilization. Two hundred years ago, through a combination of fortuitous circumstances, one nation got on the road to self-sustaining growth, opening up hitherto undreamed-of possibilities of material prosperity—the Industrial Revolution came to England. Within the next century, many other nations followed her example and embarked on the road to industrialization; but large parts of the world remained unaffected. The mid-twentieth century found three quarters of the world's population living in the conditions of stagnation and poverty which had characterized the lives of their ancestors, while the other quarter lived in an environment of affluence and steady material progress.

The world is realizing that such a state of affairs cannot be tolerated indefinitely. If lasting peace is to be won, the political emancipation of the underdeveloped world must be followed by its social and economic emancipation from bondage to poverty, ignorance, and disease.

With each passing day, economic planners have become increasingly aware that the ingredients of economic growth are more than mere physical quantities of labor, domestic capital, foreign exchange, and so on. A host of intangible elements affect the psychological and social climate of a nation, and these are of decisive importance.

It was the prior existence of these intangibles which enabled the phenomenally rapid recovery of Western Europe and Japan after the Second World War. The inhabitants of these countries not only had the skills to rebuild their lives; they also had the reserves of will, and the psychological and social attitudes—mirrored in social and economic institutions—which are necessary to provide a solid base for a modern economy. It is the absence of these elements in the poorer nations which makes the process of economic growth initially so difficult.

In *International Development: Growth and Change* Dr. Hans W. Singer carries the realization of this fact further than has usually been done in books on economic development. Built into his analysis is the conviction that development is a total process in which not one aspect of human life, education, health, and aspiration can be ignored. He accordingly gives due attention to the many aspects of public policies, always testing them on the touchstone of economic progress. Thus it is hardly surprising to find an implicit rejection of any effort to build a single neat model or theory of development.

Instead, this book offers to the practitioner of economic development a presentation of problems with which he is already familiar but considered here as part of the integrated whole which constitutes economic development. To a reader approaching the problem of economic development for the first time, these chapters offer a penetrating insight into the complex but fascinating process of development.

Among the numerous ideas and problems Dr. Singer has discussed, I would single out as worthy of special note three which, in my opinion, form guidelines to sound economic planning anywhere in the developing world. These are:

1. The crucial importance of undertaking preinvestment work prior to large-scale investment.

2. The necessity of differentiating quite sharply between "developing" and "truly underdeveloped" economies.

3. The need for planning the use of the total physical and human resources of an economy and not merely the planning of financial outlays in the public sector alone.

Preinvestment is the term used to denote a host of allied preparatory activities which are essential to laying the base for subsequent economic development. These include surveys of a country's natural resources; the undertaking of industrial feasibility studies; the inculcation of knowledge and new skills, both industrial and agricultural, in the working population; the building of national and regional institutions; and improving development planning. Such activities smooth the way for subsequent economic expansion and maximize the productivity of every unit of capital invested.

Unfortunately, because their effects are often not directly visible, but manifest themselves indirectly through the productivity of the subsequent large-scale investment, they are often neglected by developing countries, whose governments frequently—like these providing bilateral aid—are under pressure to show results quickly. The results have been dams that leak; irrigation works that water unsuitable soil; and factories without adequate transport facilities, supplies of raw materials, or trained labor. In underlining the importance of preinvestment activities, Dr. Singer has performed a service for development planners all over the world.

Dr. Singer's distinction between "developing" and "truly underdeveloped" economies is important, but so far it has generally been ignored in writings on economic development. A large number of the tenets of the theory of economic development are more pertinent to the "developing" countries than to the "truly underdeveloped" ones. These principles tend to assume the existence of a minimum of industrial infrastructure and administrative machinery as well as the capacity to mobilize a basic minimum of physical and human resources to initiate the developmental effort. Perhaps countries like India, Pakistan, and some of the Latin American nations fulfill these requisites; but there are a fair number of others for whom this minimum does not exist. In such countries the immediate need is less for some overall plan of development, than for an intensive examination of the existing state of the economy and study of its immediate possibilities to pick out the points where a little investment would yield the maximum results.

The need for planning total "real" resource utilization in the public and private sector, and not merely "financial" expenditure in the public sector alone, is especially urgent because of the adoption of the "mixed" pattern of economic organization in the majority of the developing countries today. When some industries are being developed by the public sector and others mainly by the private sector, concentrating exclusively on outlays in the former would incur the risk that resources might be diverted away from the industries in the private sector, where they would have been more efficiently utilized and contributed to a more balanced development of the economy. On the other hand, a financial "saving" made in the public sector by allowing a particular industry to be developed in the private sector, could also lead, under certain circumstances, to an inefficient use of scarce resources. Dr. Singer has brought this out clearly. He has also laid due stress on the integration of real and financial planning, specifically of the longer term development plan and the annual budget which has to provide the recurrent costs of running, maintaining, and replacing the capital projects included in the plan.

His warning against all but the most cautious deficit financing is also of great value. It is a lesson that many nations have learned painfully. Deficit financing may—when its inflationary effects are contained—reallocate resources; it can never create new ones. As a result, it can at best finance a single project if one disregards what happens elsewhere; it can never finance development as a whole.

These are only a few of the many ideas to be found in a book which, I am sure, will be of great value to all those who wish to understand or take part in the assault on poverty.

The first half of the United Nations Development Decade is gradually drawing to a close. In inaugurating it more than three years ago, the nations of the world took a solemn pledge to help each of the poorer countries raise its national income by at least 5 per cent per year by 1970. To this effort, I consider this book to be a valuable contribution.

It is evident that the leaders and the people of these countries have become increasingly aware of the immensity of the tasks ahead of them and are facing them with resolution and courage. Aiding them has been a major preoccupation of the United Nations in the seventeen years of its existence.

Dr. Singer has been associated with its activities in this field almost since its inception. He has been Economic Planning Advisor on behalf of the United Nations to the governments of Brazil, Turkey, the Philippines and the Sudan, and has participated in the framing and establishment of several United Nations economic organizations and programs. These include the Expanded Programme of Technical Assistance, the Special Fund, the African Development Bank, and the United Nations Development Decade.

In the following chapters, which present the essence of the lessons learned during his wide experience, Dr. Singer shows himself to be not only among the architects of economic development but also one of its very few philosophers.

Paul G. Hoffman
Managing Director of the
United Nations Special Fund

Contents

PART 1

The Prospects
for Development

The aim of this part of the book is to set the current prospects for development in perspective. It starts with a historical survey of theories of development from Adam Smith onward, which serves to illustrate how radically economists' ideas about the nature of the process have changed. To judge from the violence of some of the most recent swings of opinion, there is little reason to suppose that we have yet arrived at anything near a complete understanding of the phenomena of development. But since it is an issue of the most profound practical concern as well as a matter of considerable theoretical interest, it may be helpful to review some of the problems and approaches that seem important in the early 1960s. Three important topics which are currently receiving much emphasis are considered in the remaining chapters of this part of the book.

This bird's-eye view of the prospects for development suggests that we can be moderately optimistic about the economic trends in underdeveloped countries as a whole in the generation or so to come—although on grounds rather different from the more dogmatic or philosophical optimism of the classical economists. The world's conscience is thoroughly aroused, and the concept of an "interdependent world economy" is beginning to be more than an abstraction of the textbooks. This arousal of world conscience seems to be finding expression in much larger and more systematic exploration of investment opportunities in underdeveloped countries by preinvestment aid, as well as the development of a more systematic framework for public aid in new forms and conditions which will be really helpful to the underdeveloped countries. At the same time, the underdeveloped countries themselves have learned a great deal about rational approaches to the right use of scarce resources, and also about the overwhelming importance of such "noneconomic" factors as the establishment of a more appropriate structural and institutional environment and the need to develop their human resources as rapidly as possible.

All this is an optimism of gradualism. A generation may be a short time *sub specie aeternitatis,* but it is a long time during the revolution of rising expectations. Our hope must be that sufficient time will be given to us to let some of the positive forces we have identified work themselves out, but of this there can be no certainty.

1

Recent Trends in Economic Thought on Underdeveloped Countries

BEFORE WORLD WAR II: D-PESSIMISM/U-OPTIMISM

If, in looking at the great sweep of economic thinking from Ricardo to Keynes, we focus on the thinkers' broad attitudes toward the respective future of already developed and underdeveloped countries, we make a rather surprising discovery. In spite of their enormous doctrinal differences and the great diversity of their interests, background, and experiences, they all seem to agree that growth in already developed countries will sooner or later succumb to some kind of obstacle or come up against some kind of ceiling. The reasons which they adduce are as different as one would expect from their diverse general opinions, but they all seem to agree that for one reason or another economic growth will gradually create conditions which will make it grind to a halt. Conversely, in underdeveloped countries, where economic progress has not yet dug its own grave, conditions will be propitious to start the cycle of progress and decay. We may describe this illustrious school of thought which held such long sway as being D-pessimistic/U-optimistic, where D stands for continuation of development in already advanced countries, and U stands for starting development in underdeveloped countries.

It will be noted that we do not include Adam Smith in this D-pessimism/U-optimism school of thought. Adam Smith, writing as he did at the dawn of the industrial revolution (or the beginning of the "take-off," to use more fashionable language), did not give much thought to where it might all end—and who can blame him? He was too impressed by the beginnings of the process. He is not easy to classify. Sometimes, because of his flush of enthusiasm about the development of markets,

Nearly all the material in this and the following three chapters was originally published in Spanish, under the title "Tendencias recientes del pensamiento económico sobre los países sub-desarrolados" in *Revista de economía latinoamericana*, vol. 1, no. 1, 1961. A shorter version of this article appeared in *Social Research*, vol. 28, no. 4, 1961.

the increased skill that comes with specialization, the economies of scale, one can read into the *Wealth of Nations* a belief that a self-sustaining process has been created here which will feed upon itself. In such passages Adam Smith seems a curiously up-to-date forerunner of the modern "take-off into self-sustained growth." At other times, Adam Smith seems dimly to visualize and argue that once the whole nation is a fully developed market, once mechanization has been developed to correspond fully to the degree of specialization in a full market economy, once the economies of scale have been achieved, the movement will lose its momentum and reach some kind of ceiling. It is not easy to say what he argued or would have argued, and it is best not to classify him at all.

But from Ricardo on there can be no quarrel about classification. With impressive unanimity the great economists tended to be *D*-pessimists. It will be instructive to list the divergent reasons for their *D*-pessimism because it results in an interesting conclusion to which we will come a little later.

Ricardo's great worry and gravedigger of progress was, of course, the Law of Diminishing Returns in agriculture. Malthus's great worry and gravedigger was population. Karl Marx's gravedigger was collapse of markets and insufficiency of purchasing power. Schumpeter's chief worry and gravedigger was the undermining of the entrepreneurial spirit, whether from public hostility or from a "Buddenbrook complex," under which the sons and grandsons of successful entrepreneurs become poets or collectors of art or give their money away. In Keynes's view, the villain of the piece and gravedigger of progress was the "falling marginal efficiency schedule of capital": as capital accumulation proceeded, new investment opportunities were gradually used up; and as the rate of interest could not, for various reasons, continue to fall in step with the falling marginal efficiency of capital investment, capital accumulation and progress would come to a stop.

In the more dismal versions of *D*-pessimism, some kind of dramatic *Goetterdaemmerung* (twilight of the gods) atmosphere surrounded the prediction of the end of progress (especially, of course, with Malthus and Marx if we disregard the Marxian forecast of a new era in which progress would restart itself on a higher plane). In other versions, the petering out of progress is pictured as comparatively painless and accompanied with a great flowering or golden age for civilization, once peoples' minds are no longer dominated by the desire to expand and acquire more goods.[1]

One could, of course, add to the list of economists and to the reasons

---

[1] In an essay entitled "Economic Possibilities for our Grandchildren" (reprinted in *Essays in Persuasion*, London, 1931, pp. 358–373) Keynes quotes an inscription on the tombstone of a charwoman who has slaved hard all her life: "Don't mourn for me, friends, don't weep for me never, For I'm going to do nothing for ever and ever!" Galbraith's *The Affluent Society* (Houghton Mifflin, Boston, 1958) is also much concerned with this theme.

which were adduced for the petering out or collapse of progress; thus Jevons thought that the exhaustion of coal or other natural resources would bring things to a halt. It is more important, however, to look at the reasons which make the great economists *D*-pessimists and to realize why this list sounds so familiar now to us who worry about the underdeveloped countries. Worries about lagging productivity in agriculture (Ricardo)—worries about population growth (Malthus)—worries about lack of markets and purchasing power (Marx)—worries about the failures of, or interference with, entrepreneurship (Schumpeter)—worries about the absence or exhaustion of productive investment opportunities (Keynes): why has this list such a familiar ring about it? Of course! These are precisely the things that we are worrying about now when we think of the underdeveloped countries! It is an instructive and perhaps chastening thought to realize that all the things that we are worried about in relation to the underdeveloped countries, and that have made so many contemporary economists into *U*-pessimists, were far from unknown to the great economists of earlier days. Quite the contrary: these things were in the forefront of their minds. But they were worried about these things, not in relation to the poor or underdeveloped countries, but rather in relation to the conditions created by economic progress. This is certainly one of the most curious and dramatic reversals of thinking.

Keynes held that there were two barriers to continued economic growth, constituting between them a real trap, in the sense that as one of these barriers was overcome, the community would, *ipso facto,* run into the other. The first barrier was, of course, the inherent tendency of the system toward unemployment, insufficient investment, and a resulting low-level equilibrium of low consumption, low savings, low investment, high unemployment, plenty of idle resources, and slow progress. To this Keynes himself provided the answer by showing that successful investment via the multiplier would create sufficient effective demand. But to the extent that the problem of deficient demand was solved, the community would run into the new problem of falling marginal efficiency of capital. And the more successfully the problem of unemployment was tackled, the faster the marginal efficiency of capital would fall, precisely. Keynes held that in a fully employed community the marginal efficiency of capital would fall "approximately to zero within a single generation."[2] According to Keynes, if the postwar era is described as one of full employment and full employment is successfully maintained, the marginal efficiency of capital should be zero by 1980 at the latest. Certainly (writing halfway through the period of this forecast) there is not the slightest evidence for this.

By contrast, the great economists of the Ricardo-to-Keynes era tended

---

[2] J. M. Keynes, *General Theory of Employment, Interest and Money,* Macmillan, New York, 1936, p. 200.

to be *U*-optimists. This followed mainly as a direct consequence of their idea of economic progress being of the self-limiting or grave-digging variety. Since these self-limiting factors would only appear somewhere along the road of economic progress and were created by the force of economic progress itself, it followed logically that they would not operate in the early stages of progress in the underdeveloped countries. If we take Keynes as an example, the marginal efficiency schedule in underdeveloped countries would not have had time to fall very much; splendid investment opportunities would abound since they would not have been used up yet by previous capital accumulation; rates of interest could still in many ways be brought down, by improved financial institutions or otherwise, before they would strike rock bottom.

Apart from being the natural counterpart of their *D*-pessimism, the *U*-optimism of the great economists was also a reflection of the historical evidence of their day. They saw other countries joining in the march of progress, one after the other; first Belgium and Holland and France, then the United States and Germany, then Japan, then Russia, then Canada, Australia, New Zealand, and so forth. Like Adam Smith at the dawn of the industrial revolution, they saw no particular reason to picture any end to this march of progress. No great institutional difficulties were arising in these then "new" countries even though, as in Japan and Russia, their economic beliefs and policies might differ from those of the pioneers of progress. But it could not escape the economists that the march of progress seemed to be a little selective and seemed, in particular, to be hesitant in the tropical countries and in nonwhite countries. This was generally explained on noneconomic grounds: the effect of tropical climate on peoples' willingness or ability to exert themselves, the influence of fatalistic religions and philosophies, etc. The famous theories that the initiative in economic progress could only come through Protestants (Weber), or through Puritans or Calvinists or Jews or religious minorities generally (Sombart) or Prussians (Sombart again)—what were all these theories except an attempt to combine an inborn *U*-optimism with the facts of life? In economic principle the *U*-optimism was general, but in sociological application it tended to be limited to the white, or European-style, world.[3]

THE FIFTIES: D-OPTIMISM/U-PESSIMISM

The change-over from what we may perhaps now call the "classical" view of *D*-pessimism/*U*-optimism into its exact opposite has been startling and unmistakable. The prevailing view in the fifties was a combination of *D*-optimism (a belief in the powers of developed countries to continue self-

---

[3] The Japanese always gave trouble in this scheme, but this could be got over by describing them as "Prussians of the East" or "Puritans of the East"; and in any case, did they not live in a temperate climate?

sustaining growth indefinitely) with U-pessimism (a rather gloomy view of the formidable obstacles and vicious circles standing in the way of the progress of underdeveloped countries).

What are the reasons for this reversal? Take the change from D-pessimism to D-optimism first. In the first place, the Depression of the 1930s was over; war had shown the great power of industrial countries to expand their production even under conditions of great labor and raw-material shortages; the widely predicted postwar slump in the industrial countries had failed to materialize; the effectiveness of Keynesian policies in avoiding inflation (at least of the galloping kind), depression, and stagnation had been impressively demonstrated. A great speeding up of technical progress had occurred, partly under the pressure of war necessities but by no means limited to wartime applications; the development of synthetic materials, in particular, removed part of the Ricardian nightmare of diminishing returns. Perhaps even more important, the immediate postwar period had most impressively demonstrated the capacity of industrial countries to overcome with unexpected ease the effects of even widespread war destruction and war dislocation.

All these developments served to direct attention, in developed countries, away from such factors as physical capital and dependence on natural commodities—in both of which the dangerous traps of falling marginal efficiency and diminishing returns were lurking—and toward the human factor in development: skills, training, attitudes, institutions, research genius, developing machinery for applying new research in production, etc. Once this shift had taken place, the idea of self-sustaining growth became much more plausible. The human mind and its products are not subject to diminishing returns in the sense in which physical capital, labor, or natural materials alone may be assumed to be. Quite on the contrary, there is good reason to assume something like a Law of Increasing Returns in research and human development. As research proceeds, each new discovery has an increasingly widespread and diversified impact on other lines of discovery; with the progress of knowledge unproductive lines of research are increasingly abandoned, and research is concentrated on more productive lines. Investment in education is not only highly productive but also yields increasing returns insofar as cooperating teams of skilled and educated people are worth more than the sums of the individuals of which they are composed. Wherever we look in this area of human investment, we find increasing returns at play.

To us it now seems clear that when Keynes forecast that the marginal efficiency of capital would fall to zero in a fully employed community "within a single generation," he was seriously in error in assuming simultaneously full employment, a high rate of investment, and a constant technology—almost by definition an inconsistent trio of assumptions. To us it would seem fairly obvious that with full employment and high investment the creation of new investment opportunities by concomitant technical progress would push up the marginal efficiency of capital as fast as, or probably faster than, it is reduced even by rapid capital accumulation. Moreover, such is the complementary character of investment that capital accumulations in sector A will raise the efficiency of capital in sectors B and C. This is true particularly if investment in sector A is part of the accumulation of "overhead capital"—but in a sense *all* capital is somewhat an overhead.

Finally, it should be noted that the cessation of capital accumulation resulting from a zero rate of marginal efficiency is by no means identical with a cessation of economic progress itself, although to Keynes these two things seem to have appeared as identical. We can have a cessation of capital accumulation—in technical terms zero *net* investment—and still have some amount of *gross* investment, i.e., replacement of older, worn-out capital by new capital. If there has been a sufficient rate of technical progress between the date of the old capital investment and the date of the new investment which replaces it, the superior efficiency of the new capital can produce a tolerable or even high rate of economic progress by itself— even with zero net investment!

On the more purely theoretical plane, the *D*-optimistic idea of self-sustained growth was impressed by the growth models of the Harrod-Domar type. For such growth models, each increase in output provides the basis for a further increase in output in the next period. The chief mechanism is by reinvestment of part of this increased output through additional savings into additional investment, at capital/output ratios which, in the simple model, are assumed to remain constant (presumably as a result of the human factors mentioned above offsetting any tendency toward diminishing returns). In the Harrod-Domar models, there is no intrinsic reason to assume diminishing returns or self-limiting growth, since additional savings should become progressively easier at rising income levels, and thus the marginal propensity to save may be assumed to rise rather than to fall. If no exhaustion of investment opportunities is presumed, this would make for accelerating or at least self-sustaining growth rather than self-limiting growth. It is, of course, debatable to what extent the intellectual creation of the Harrod-Domar growth models was the cause or merely the expression of the reversal in thinking which took place in the postwar decade—presumably a bit of both.

The watershed from *D*-pessimism to *D*-optimism is well illustrated by the difference in flavor between Domar's earlier and later essays. This is commented upon by Domar himself in the foreword to his collection of essays, *The Theory of Economic Growth.* "The present-day reader may also be amused (I certainly am) at the timidity with which our growth potential is treated in the four earlier essays. A potential rate of growth of a modest

two or three per cent a year is discussed with numerous apologies, reserva-
tions and what not. . . . And yet compared to prevailing opinion, mine was
optimistic."[4]

In the earlier Harrod formulation, which dates from the D-pessimistic
period before the war, the emphasis was still on the lack of probability that
the economy would in fact follow the straight and narrow path of exponential growth and on the virtual certainty that the diminishing profit rates,
chronic unemployment, and idle capital would in fact produce the
stationary state forecast in the literature from Ricardo to Keynes. The
neutrality—but a neutrality strongly leaning toward a stationary state—of
the Harrod-Domar approach in the earlier versions is well formulated by
Domar. "Economic salvation is not impossible; neither is it assured."[5]

Remarkable as the change-over from D-pessimism to D-optimism in the
postwar era was, those economists whose thinking was shaped in the prewar
era still found it difficult to make the turnabout. Thus we often find a gulf
between theoretical reasoning still largely determined by an expectation of a
stationary condition and descriptive and practical policy reasoning in which
the possibility of continued growth is clearly accepted. This gulf remains
something of a mystery to perceptive observers, such as Domar. "Why in
spite of remarkable rapid growth, the vision of the stationary state hung
so heavily over the thinking of the Great Masters of the last century and still
preoccupies many of our contemporaries, is more than I can explain. Even
my more broadminded colleagues who love growth, are willing to grant
her only a reprieve, but not a pardon. . . ."[6]

Yet another reflection, and perhaps also cause, of this change in
thought was the notion of the "take-off into self-sustained growth," most
popular in the form put forward by Walt Rostow in his *Stages of Economic
Growth.*[7] It is interesting to note that the metaphors of this school of
thought are drawn from aeronautics and space research. Once an airplane
has taken off into the air, it is much easier for it to continue in serene flight
than it was to take off and gain altitude; similarly, once a rocket has left
the atmosphere of the earth, it is much easier to keep it in a given orbit than
it was to fire it off and place it in orbit. The influence of this aeronautical
and space element on economic thinking is perhaps more than purely verbal
or fashionable. Since, as explained above, the change in view was largely
caused by and based upon developments of scientific research and its application to production, it is more than accidental that this should be reflected
in the language and approach of economists.

Now let us look at the other side of the coin, namely the change-over

---

[4] Oxford, Fair Lawn, N.J., 1957.
[5] *Ibid.*, p. 8.
[6] *Ibid.*, p. 14.
[7] Cambridge, New York, 1960.

from U-optimism to U-pessimism. In some ways this follows directly from the change from pessimism to optimism in views concerning the more developed countries. This is particularly clear if we look at the take-off theory proposed by Rostow. According to this theory, the underdeveloped countries stand at the beginning of the runway or are not even on it yet, and a terrific concentrated effort will be required to take them down the runway in exactly the right combination of circumstances and at very high speed so that they may become airborne. More directly, according to Professor Rostow, an underdeveloped country must first create a number of diverse preconditions which include changes in institutions and attitudes, the provision of social and economic overhead capital, raising of agricultural productivity and solution of land-tenure problems, etc. Even the successful solution of these tricky problems will only place an underdeveloped country on the runway; then before take-off is achieved, it is necessary for an under-developed country to increase its rate of net investment roughly from 5 to 10 per cent within a comparatively short time, to develop a leading manu-facturing sector strategically placed so as to have strong linkage effects on the whole economic system, and simultaneously to create the capacity to transfer this impetus to other leading sectors as soon as the first leading sector begins to slacken. It will be seen that these are very formidable require-ments indeed. In fact, one begins to wonder how any country has ever managed to achieve a take-off. At any rate, this view of the matter must certainly be classified as an expression of some innate pessimism about the frequency of future take-offs by the present underdeveloped countries.

Similarly, a pessimistic trend of thought concerning the underdeveloped countries can be deduced from the Harrod-Domar growth model. Given the right kind of parameters—particularly a high rate of population growth —lo and behold! the Harrod-Domar equation is converted from a descrip-tion of cumulative self-sustaining growth into a description of cumulative self-sustaining stagnation. Let the rate of net investment be 6 per cent, the capital/output ratio 3 : 1, and the rate of population growth 2 per cent per annum, and the Harrod-Domar equation describes a state of utter stagna-tion which will continue indefinitely, until a new element enters the situa-tion to change either the rate of investment or the capital/output ratio or to change the rate of population growth. In fact, many economists have come to assume that the tendency in underdeveloped countries is for the parameters of the Harrod-Domar-type models to bear exactly those relations to each other which will result in cumulative stagnation.

The general picture which has been developed in this postwar decade of pessimism concerning the underdeveloped countries is that of some kind of obstacle or barrier which makes modest initial growth self-sustaining rather than cumulative and which can only be got over by some kind of exceptional "big push." The most obvious illustration is that of population.

Small advances will simply be eaten up by a fall in the death rate and possibly even an initial rise in the birth rate. To overcome the population hurdle would require a terrific advance in living standards of such a kind as to change fundamentally the attitudes to large families. Yet the achievement of this fundamental improvement is made well-nigh impossible by the self-limiting nature of more modest, slower rates of growth. If only the big push could be achieved, there would then be downhill coasting—but how to get to the top of the hill?[8] The pessimistic turn concerning underdeveloped countries in the postwar decade clearly had a lot to do with the evidence of rapid declines in death rates, associated with simple sanitary precautions (often imported from abroad), and the resulting acceleration in the rate of population increase with its great demands on food, housing, and all forms of social (as opposed to directly productive) capital.

The theory of the big push, or else no progress, had many other implications, quite apart from population. The most important implication relates to the provision of overhead capital—transport and communications, housing, urban utilities, schools and educational systems, hospital and health systems, etc. The provision of this overhead capital is notoriously expensive, i.e., has a high capital/output ratio and a very long gestation period. If the provision of overhead capital is an essential precondition of growth, it is quite plausible that most or all underdeveloped countries may fail to achieve progress because they will never be able to assemble the initially required volume of overhead capital. Let it not be forgotten that the period during which overhead capital is assembled and not much final output appears is also almost inevitably a period of acute inflationary pressures. The impact of these inflationary pressures, as well as insufficiency of total funds required for assembly of the necessary overhead capital, will make it highly probable that underdeveloped countries will not successfully achieve self-sustaining growth, according to this line of thinking.[9]

Another variation of the "big push" theory is related to the theory of "balanced growth." Broadly speaking, this theory (proposed particularly by the late Professor Nurkse) held that while the isolated development of individual lines of production in underdeveloped countries is impossible for lack of a market, the simultaneous development of a number of lines of production will be quite feasible, since the incomes created in producing commodities A, B, and C will return as demand for commodity D. Unless one assumes that an underdeveloped economy has sufficient slack in it and a sufficient volume of unutilized resources to enable it to engage in the

[8] The economist who has done most to construct models of this kind, where population appears as a big hurdle for slow rates of growth which would disappear if growth were to be accelerated, is Harvey Leibenstein, particularly in his book *Economic Backwardness and Economic Growth*, New York, 1957.

[9] The theory of the big push in relation to overhead capital is perhaps most closely associated with the name of Prof. Paul Rosenstein-Rodan.

simultaneous expansion along a broad front required by the principle of balanced growth—and this is clearly not plausible—this theory is very bad news indeed for the underdeveloped countries. It means that the only road to growth which may be feasible for them is barred. Hence there can be no growth. On the other hand, for the already developed countries the principle of balanced growth is good news. Since expansion is in fact going on along a broad front, the advantages of balanced growth ensure that no market difficulties will be encountered and that growth will continue to sustain itself. It is not accidental that the theory of balanced growth should have been developed and become popular at the same time that pessimism concerning the underdeveloped countries increased.[10]

In reflection of this increasing pessimism, the situation in underdeveloped countries was frequently seen as a system of vicious circles. In the course of time more and more of these were discovered, so much so that someone has recently said, "The road to economic development is paved with vicious circles." A vicious circle, in more precise language, is a situation in which various factors are so interlocked that they mutually tend to produce a stagnant or stationary situation from which it is extremely difficult to move away. Perhaps the prototype of all vicious circles is the one which runs around as follows: low incomes—low savings capacity—low investment—low output—back to low incomes. There are many others, such as low production—no surpluses for economic investment—no tools and equipment—low standard of production (a fair description of subsistence farming), and the fact that an underdeveloped country is poor because it has no industry and has no industry because it is poor. This situation can be summed up in the statement, "One thing leads to another, but nothing leads to nothing."

Perhaps the clearest connection between the more optimstic view of the prospects for self-sustained growth in the developed countries and the opposite tendency toward pessimism about the underdeveloped countries has been provided by the so-called "backwash" theory. This theory—with which the name of Gunnar Myrdal is associated—states that the growth of the developed countries, apart from any beneficial, or "spreading," effects it may have on the underdeveloped countries, also has some harmful, or "backwash," effects. Examples of such backwash effects are the development of a premature desire for high-level consumption in the underdeveloped countries caused by the demonstration effect of conditions in more developed countries; the spreading of premature ideas in underdeveloped countries about the welfare state, social insurance, minimum-wage legislation, etc., also caused by imitation of conditions in more developed countries; technical

---

[10] It will be remembered (see the first section of this chapter) that the difficulty of finding markets or purchasing power for additional output was precisely what worried Karl Marx, except that he attributed lack of purchasing power to changes which accompanied economic progress in its later stages.

progress in the developed countries may have a backwash effect on the underdeveloped countries because modern technology becomes more and more capital-intensive and laborsaving and hence less and less suitable for the underdeveloped countries.

In the classical scheme up to the Second World War, the spreading effects were more emphasized. Thus Alfred Marshall observed that the available stock of technical knowledge at the disposal of newcomers was increasing, and general emphasis was placed by economists on the increasing amount of capital available for newcomers from the wealth of already developed countries. But in the postwar decade the backwash effects received more attention. For instance, in relation to the availability of capital, it became clear that the financing of self-sustaining growth in the developed countries and the utilization of the many new investment opportunities opened up by technical progress would leave very little over for the underdeveloped countries—at least as far as the orthodox mechanism of private foreign investment was concerned.

Another example of a backwash effect is provided by the possibility that the technical progress in the developed countries, which has taken such forms as economizing in the use of raw materials, the development of new synthetic materials, and changes in their industrial structure, might recoil to the disadvantage of the underdeveloped countries in the form of a chronic tendency to weakness in their terms of trade, i.e., the price relationship between primary products and manufactured products. This line of inquiry has been particularly closely explored by Raul Prebisch. Recent years have lent force to his arguments and have justified his concerns, although during the Second World War and the immediate postwar period it seemed temporarily as if there were no cause to worry about primary-commodity prices.

Finally, the emphasis on the human factor in explaining progress in the more developed countries also had pessimistic implications for the underdeveloped countries. The development of human skills, institutions, and change in attitudes is a trickier and more complex affair than the mere injection of physical capital. It may possibly be cheaper, but it is certainly more difficult. Thus, whereas in prewar thinking human difficulties appeared more as exogenous and sociological, they now became endogenous and to that extent more emphasized.

In a way, the change to *D*-optimism can be represented as a return to a yet earlier school, preceding Adam Smith. This is the idea of rectilinear progress or even exponential growth, obviously congenial to the age of reason and enlightenment of the earlier eighteenth century. Thus it is stated that ". . . for William Goodwin, man was the master both of himself and of nature and could wield a cumulative control of the universe. Man, by taking thought about his condition, could progressively improve it subject to no inherent check whatsoever."[11] There are certainly traces of the possibility of continued progress even in the thinking and writings of the great economists themselves. Such speculations are sometimes inherent when they wonder at the marvels of science and technology, but the surprising thing is still that these wonderings failed to shape their views, as economists, of the future of society more than they did. In Schumpeter's writing, traces can certainly be found of the view that the progress of society may survive the demise of the functions of the capitalist entrepreneur on which it originally depended and that progress itself might be mechanized and acquire an independent existence, being embodied in scientists and teams of trained specialists instead of entrepreneurs.[12]

The growth of science and technology is such that it assumes a life of its own, that it can be depended upon to make available new ideas on a scale sufficient to create investment opportunities to offset any flagging tendencies of the marginal efficiency of capital. In fact, the growth of science and technology, combined with the basis of education and training on which it depends, is such that it may even be said to help to produce the social attitudes and institutions which will make the rapid introduction of new capital not only possible but actual.

THE SIXTIES: THE PENDULUM SWINGS BACK

As the decade of the 1950s rolled on to its close, it became more and more apparent that the facts of life did not really bear out the strong pessimism about the underdeveloped countries which had developed in reaction to the previous optimism. Although there has been much talk of "an increasing gap between the developed and the underdeveloped countries," the actual facts of the postwar decade are not so clear on this point. The national income of underdeveloped countries as a group increased at about the same rate as the national incomes of more developed countries as a group. If on a per capita basis the rate of progress among the underdeveloped countries was slightly less than that of the developed countries, this was due to differences in population growth and in economic structure rather than to any inherent failure of production to increase in the underdeveloped countries. Industrial output in the underdeveloped countries *taken separately* increased just about as fast as in the developed countries, and the same was true of agricultural output *separately*. If total output rose less in the underdeveloped countries, this could be attributed to the fact that agricultural output, with its slower rate of increase, had a heavier weight in the underdeveloped countries in relation to industrial output than was the case in the developed countries. A number of underdeveloped

[11] S. G. Checkland, "Theories of Economic and Social Evolution: The Rostow Challenge," *Scottish Journal of Political Economy*, November, 1960, p. 174.
[12] *Ibid.,* p. 178.

countries developed quite rapidly during the postwar decade; the growth of the Latin American region as a whole, for instance, compared quite favorably with the more developed countries. Perhaps the impression of "an increasing gap" was due to the conspicuous failure of some of the underdeveloped countries and regions to join in the march of progress and also attributable to the understandable concern about the continued existence of world mass poverty. It is also a fact that even satisfactory relative increases in the poorer countries look puny compared with the sums represented by the same relative increases in the richer countries. Perhaps one of the most startling facts of life in the contemporary world is that the average income for an inhabitant of the United States *increases* each year by not so very much less than the *total* income of the average inhabitant of India or Pakistan.

The terms of trade of underdeveloped countries also presented a rather mixed picture during the postwar period. The more pessimistic assumptions of a steady long-term deterioration in the terms of trade were not borne out; the terms of trade of underdeveloped countries throughout the postwar period have been more favorable than during the 1930s. On the other hand, the pessimists have been proved right against such people as Colin Clark and also to some extent Arthur Lewis, who both forecast a sharp improvement in the terms of trade of primary producers.[13] The fact is that commodity prices did show a weakening tendency from their Korean boom level throughout the 1950s. Thus it was possible for both sides to claim some confirmation of their views, although the balance of the argument seemed to be more with the pessimists.

In brief, then, the facts of the postwar decade did not really lend themselves to any general pessimism or optimism. The picture was mixed. Other elements were present which might make the picture more hopeful. For instance, as the decade went on it became increasingly clear that a far-reaching and probably long-term change had occurred in the attitude of the more developed countries to the question of aiding the underdeveloped countries. The concept of a single world economy began to rise on the horizon. In a remarkable degree, the developed countries recognized a responsibility to assist the underdeveloped countries, and by means which only a few years ago they might have rejected as too heterodox. Even the ill wind of the cold war blew some good for the underdeveloped countries. A great new international movement has arisen under the banner of "technical assistance" to transfer and adapt mankind's enormous stock of technical knowledge and expertise to the underdeveloped countries.

It was discovered that even though the difficulties of finding productive

[13] Colin Clark, *The Economics of 1960*, London, 1942, and W. A. Lewis, "World Production, Prices and Trade," *Manchester School of Economic and Social Studies,* 1952.

investment opportunities stressed by the pessimistic school might all be real, they were not unalterable, and that investment opportunities could be created even where they did not naturally exist.[14] It was also discovered that such planning techniques as had guided the war economies of the more developed countries could be applied successfully to the underdeveloped countries and that it was possible to make progress even with limited resources by concentrating them at strategic points where the maximum linkage effect could be obtained. Doubts came to be felt as to whether the complete assembly of economic and social overhead capital was really a necessary precondition in point of time for progress in increasing actual production or whether it would not be possible by judicious strategic use of resources to create limited shortages of such overhead facilities as transport and power, sufficient to cause an increase in their supply but not large enough to disrupt production.[15]

Historical analyses of the development of such countries as England, the United States, France, and even czarist Russia suggest that they did not experience a distinct "take-off" period, with the tremendous concentrated effort and rapid increase in the investment ratio that this implies. In fact, economic growth seems to have been quite steady, gradual, and organic in those countries, and there now seems to be no compelling reason why this could not also be the case in the underdeveloped countries.

While there was thus enough in the general picture to justify the abandonment of earlier optimism—much evidence of stagnation, weakness of primary commodities, increasingly capital-intensive technology, etc.—yet there also seemed to be a lot to relieve the gloom—evidence of progress, development of international aid and technical assistance, progress in development-planning techniques, etc. In the sixties, the complexity of the real world makes a mockery of any preconceived universal optimism or pessimism. There is a lot of good as well as a lot of bad. The better approach—better than a preconceived optimism or pessimism—seems to be pragmatic, to try to build on the more hopeful elements in the picture and strengthen them while reducing the impact of the unfavorable elements.

The change in the climate compared with the pessimistic postwar decade is perhaps best illustrated by a statement made by W. A. B. Iliff, Vice-president of the International Bank, in his opening speech to the 1960 annual meeting of the Bank in Washington. "The historic transformation which is going on in the under-developed world today defies any general 'solution'; but it does offer infinite possibilities to the practitioners of economic development."[16]

[14] This is described in more detail in Chap. 2.

[15] This was emphasized particularly by Albert O. Hirschmann in his *Strategy of Economic Development*, Yale, New Haven, Conn., 1958. This point is developed in greater detail in Chap. 3.

[16] See *International Financial News Survey*, Sept. 30, 1960, p. 519.

In other words, the difficulties in the path of economic development pointed out by the early students of the postwar decade are by no means neglected or considered to be nonexistent. Their spadework has made us much more aware of the problems and difficulties which we have to face. But these difficulties are now felt to be much more in the nature of a challenge which it is not beyond human wisdom and human efforts to cope with. They are not so much felt as immutable and probably insurmountable obstacles. It will be seen that this change is not a return to the general optimism, more implicit than argued, of the earlier economists. In the terms used by Iliff, we may describe the new approach as generally neither optimistic nor pessimistic but as a search for possibilities, whether they be numerous or few.

In general, we may define the new trend in thinking by saying that more emphasis tends to be placed upon the availability of an unutilized potential of labor, human talent (including entrepreneurial abilities), resources of all kinds, savings capacity, fiscal capacity, directions of technological research, etc., and upon the possibilities of activating such unutilized potentials. Whereas the pessimistic postwar decade had emphasized the need for growth by sacrifice and the small (and diminishing) capacity of underdeveloped countries for the big sacrifices required, the new thinking emphasizes the possibilities of growth by a sort of pump-priming process—the creation of a new dynamic setting in which, by good strategy, resource availabilities can be improved, difficulties temporarily bypassed or softened, and a broadening forward movement initiated.

2

An Example of
the New Pragmatism: Toward a
Theory of Preinvestment

In underdeveloped countries physical-supply shortages stand out so strongly as impediments to investment that they cannot be ignored. This applies specifically, of course, to the shortage of capital and to the low savings capacity inherent in low incomes. Economists have a habit of being *recherché* rather than obvious and perhaps it is because supply limitations are too obvious to be ignored that many economists have also looked to the demand side for limitations to investment in underdeveloped countries. Characteristically, for instance, Nurkse starts off his classical book *Problems of Capital Formation in Underdeveloped Countries*[1] with a chapter dealing with deficiencies, not in the supply of investment goods, but in the inducement to invest.

One can question Nurkse's specific reasoning and his specific conclusion that the lack of sufficient inducement to invest should lead to emphasis on "balanced growth." But it would show a lack of perception to hold that physical-supply limitations are the whole story in the underdeveloped countries. However *recherché* economists may tend to be, in this case their hankerings for finding deficiencies on the demand side are too strongly supported by practitioners and empiricists, casual and otherwise, to be ignored. Perhaps there *is* an essential deficiency on the demand side, although it does not necessarily lie in the absence of complementary projects —to be remedied by the "big push." The matter deserves more examination.

THE INVESTMENT CONTRAST

What else, besides a lack of complementary capital, could account for a low inducement to invest? Ignorance, uncertainty, and unfamiliarity are obviously crucial deterrents to investment. If surveys and the growing literature on investment decisions were not sufficient proof of this, it could be found in the predominance of domestic investment over foreign investment. The industrial countries invest about 20 per cent (gross) of their national products at home even though their own markets form only a

[1] Oxford, Fair Lawn, N.J., 1953.

small fraction of the total world market.[2] Yet they invest less than 1 per cent of their national products abroad (if we limit ourselves to normal profit-motivated and "commercial" investment, as we should) even though the foreign market is much larger. Some part of this discrepancy, no doubt, can be explained by legal obstacles of all kinds. But all evidence goes to show that the removal of legal and political friction alone does not make any essential changes in this startling discrepancy. Some understanding of the difficulties of investment in underdeveloped countries can be gained if we visualize that in underdeveloped countries *all* investment, whether domestic or foreign, is surrounded by the same aura of ignorance, uncertainty, and unfamiliarity with which in more developed countries only *foreign* investment is surrounded. In fact, foreign investment by industrial countries is about the same in absolute figures as *total* investment by the underdeveloped countries.

The Capacity to Create Wealth: A Key Factor. The real trouble with the classical view which focused on the falling marginal efficiency schedule of capital—and hence, as we have shown, tended to pessimism about developed countries and to optimism about underdeveloped countries—is that it concentrated only on one aspect of development, and that a secondary one, namely the production of wealth. It disregarded a primary factor—in terms of both importance and timing—namely the capacity to produce wealth. The fundamental problem of development is not to create wealth itself but to create the capacity to create wealth. Given that capacity, we have seen that even major disasters and long depressions will interrupt, but not essentially interfere with, cumulative growth. Now, in creating the capacity to produce wealth as distinct from the production of wealth itself, there is no falling marginal efficiency schedule. Quite the contrary: additions to the capacity to produce wealth mutually fructify, support, and stimulate each other; they are subject to increasing rather than diminishing returns.[3] It is only when comparing the developed and underdeveloped

---

[2] The United States, of course, is an exception to this, but even in its case the domestic market is only half the world market.

[3] This point comes out very clearly in the following quotation from Sumner H. Slichter's article "The Industry of Discovery," *Science*, Dec. 26, 1958, pp. 1610–1611: "A third significant characteristic of research is the fact that an increase in its output does not tend to reduce the marginal value. Hence, the greater the output of research, the stronger tends to be the demand for still more output.

"This peculiarity of research is a result of the fact that its output is knowledge. One may think of knowledge as consisting of a body of tested propositions. When two things are known, there is a possibility of seeing significant relationships between them which will yield practical applications. The larger the number of tested propositions, the more numerous are the cases in which the addition of a new tested proposition to old propositions will yield new useful applications and, in addition, will suggest hypotheses useful in adding still more tested propositions to the body of knowledge. Thus, the greater the body of existing knowledge, the greater is likely to be the value of the new discoveries."

countries in respect of the secondary problems of the conditions of wealth production that one may be led to be more optimistic about the under-developed countries than about the developed countries. Introduce the primary element of additions to the capacity to create wealth, and there is no doubt that the developed countries are better off than the under-developed countries. It may be that capital accumulation destroys invest-ment opportunities at a faster pace in the developed countries than is the case in the underdeveloped countries where capital accumulation is very slow. But the significance of this fact has been overrated. It is completely overshadowed by the rate at which technical progress and improvements in the capacity to create wealth create new investment opportunities in the developed countries, ahead of the rate at which opportunities are used up by capital accumulation. There is nothing comparable to this in underdeveloped countries.

The Mutual Stimulation of Science and Industry. Moreover, there is a further factor which would serve to produce increasing rather than diminish-ing returns in research and development. This is the mutual cumulative propagation of science and industry. The point can best be illustrated by a statement made in connection with the Tercentenary of the British Royal Society:

> Science and industry are now allies and history has proved that this alliance is as necessary for science as it is for industry. Indeed technology is often the pace-maker for scientific advance. In the nineteenth century, for example, the pace of research into the structure of animal and plant cells was set by the firms which designed microscopes. More recently the production of an electron microscope may be regarded as a major contribution to scientific thought. In biology alone it has opened up a new and fantastic world of the infinitely small; it has already illuminated subjects as diverse as human heredity and the synthesis of sugar in leaves. . . . [4]

The optimistic classical view about investment opportunities in the underdeveloped countries was that investment of capital there must have high productivity since capital was so very scarce. This view was embodied in the Keynesian falling marginal efficiency schedule of capital. As we have seen, this view was then superseded by the "sophisticated" postwar view in which things are the other way around. The long-term marginal effi-ciency schedule is now assumed to be rising, not falling. The very processes which lead to capital accumulation, primarily technological progress, also create a situation in which capital becomes more and more productive and

[4] "Science and Society," essay presented by Associated Electrical Industries, Ltd., *The Times* (London), special number on the Royal Society Tercentenary, July 19, 1960.

the capital/output ratio tends to fall. As a natural corollary, this view led to pessimism about the underdeveloped countries; their capital/output ratio would be less favorable as a result of their failure to accumulate capital and because of their remoteness from technological progress.

But nowadays this "sophisticated" postwar view, while closer to the facts of life than the classical view, is not entirely satisfactory either. Perhaps the time has come to resurrect some important elements of truth contained in the classical view. *Other things being equal,* the marginal efficiency schedule of capital *does* tend to fall, i.e., it does tend to be high when capital is scarce. The trouble is that other things are not equal. Among these other things which are not equal, there certainly is the amount of complementary capital providing economies of large scale. But where capital is short, other things also are lacking which are perhaps as important as supporting capital. Predominant among these other lacks are cooperative factors in the form of trained and skilled people, technical experimentation and knowledge suitable to the resource endowment of capital-poor countries, and the power to identify and formulate concrete opportunities of productive combination of factors of production.

IMPORTANCE OF THE PREINVESTMENT INFRASTRUCTURE

The now prevailing postwar view, according to which the efficiency schedule of capital is rising as capital accumulates, emphasized almost exclusively the importance of the capital infrastructure. It failed to take account equally of the importance of the human, technological, and data infrastructure, which we may call for short "preinvestment infrastructure." There is much empirical evidence to support the view that, given equality of conditions in respect of preinvestment infrastructure, the natural capital shortage of the underdeveloped countries will in fact make its effect felt; and the optimism of the classical school concerning the productivity of investment in underdeveloped countries may then turn out, after all, not to have been entirely wrong.

Technical progress is the main factor which has reversed the previous pessimistic view (for the developed countries) that capital accumulation destroys more investment opportunities than are currently created. But technical progress is no longer to be considered as an accident or essentially the product of some isolated brain waves. Rather, it is now the result of systematic and concentrated activities. Technical progress can be treated as the product of a separate industry, the research industry.[5] The activities of this industry are so widespread that the law of large numbers applies; the total output of the industry in terms of technical progress becomes predictable, however hazardous and unpredictable each individual research activity taken

[5] See Slichter, *loc. cit.*

by itself.[6] But technical progress creates investment opportunities. Hence it follows that investment opportunities do not "exist" in some mysterious or accidental fashion. They are made, a point which Schumpeter saw clearly. Economists have had very little to say about the way in which investment opportunities are made; they have " . . . pretty much taken the volume of investment opportunities as given."[7] But the industry of creating investment opportunities is strategic in the development process.

The more recent "sophisticated" view—that investment opportunities are greater in developed countries—truly describes the situation as it exists. However, that does not mean that the older classical view was wrong. Rather, this view—which held that investment opportunities must be greater in the underdeveloped countries—did not refer to *actual* investment opportunities but to *latent* opportunities. It requires a great deal of activity and even expenditure to transform the latent opportunities into actual opportunities. This is the role of the preinvestment industry. The difference between the two views derives from the fact that the older unrealistically assumed equality of preinvestment status in the underdeveloped countries and hence was unduly optimistic about them. The newer view is realistic enough, but it is unduly pessimistic in that it overrates the importance of capital-supply inequalities (which are almost unavoidable) and underrates the importance of preinvestment inequality (which can be remedied more cheaply).

A related thought is developed by J. R. Hicks. Hicks explains that the optimistic view concerning a tendency for economic gaps between nations to close does not seem to apply as between developed and underdeveloped countries, while it does seem to apply to relations among the various developed countries. "One of the great advantages of 'advanced' specialisms is

[6] This point is illustrated even for an apparently extreme example of "purposeless" research by the following quotation: "Computers are becoming complicated enough for most purposes, but unfortunately they are still very big and expensive. So it is not yet possible to use computers for flying aircraft even though their great speed would be an advantage. The trouble is that the mechanical brains are so much more complicated than the natural ones. So mightn't it be that somebody could make a porpoise brain work as a kind of computer? In an anti-missile perhaps? The benefits are so great that it is worth spending something on finding out. Even if in the end it turns out that this bizarre idea is just a fantasy, somebody will have learnt something on the way in which animal brain tissue works, and that would be worthwhile.

"This is not an unfair reconstruction of the kind of argument which has led the United States Office of Naval Research to support a good deal of academic— and amusing—research into the behavior of porpoises. At some stage a daring look was taken at all the apparently absurd possibilities of porpoise research. As in the most adventurous kind of gambling, money was staked—modestly enough, it should be added—on the chance that some of these might be realized. But nobody's nerves are strained, for the bet is well hedged. Even if first expectations are not realized something else will be done." "Science in America Today," *The Guardian* (Manchester), Sept. 13, 1960, p. 6.

[7] Slichter, *loc. cit.*

that they carry with them the *capacity* of doing other things; thus, if an 'advanced' country is driven off one specialism, it does not find it insuperably difficult to grow another."[8] What this amounts to is that once a country is "advanced," i.e., in the terminology used in this chapter, has the capacity to produce wealth, one can more or less rely on economic challenges to produce an adequate response. Hence there will be a tendency for a moderately advanced country to begin closing the gap with even more advanced countries: Japan, the U.S.S.R., and Italy are recent examples which come to mind. But where this underlying capacity to create wealth is missing, neither economic challenges nor economic windfalls create the kind of response which will lead to a closing of the gap. Thus, the earlier view about the tendencies of the gap to close is not exactly wrong, but its validity is restricted to at least moderately advanced countries.

Like any other industry, the preinvestment industry depends on its market. The market for preinvestment is investment. Hence preinvestment will be developed in the natural way only where investment has reached a high level. Yet investment depends upon proper preinvestment. Here we have yet another of those vicious circles with which the road to economic development is paved. Stimulation of the preinvestment infrastructure ahead of its current market may serve to break this particular vicious circle.

It would be pushing at an open door to argue in detail that conditions concerning the preinvestment infrastructure are not the same in the underdeveloped countries. Human investment in education and training is extremely small and certainly below its optimum; technological research is strongly biased away from the problems of underdeveloped countries and toward other problems arising from the needs and resource endowment of advanced countries. Rarely have systematic attempts yet been made in underdeveloped countries to collect the elements of investment opportunities, combine them, and bring the power of modern analysis to bear upon studies of technical and economic feasibilities.

COST AND VALUE OF PREINVESTMENT

The provision of the preinvestment infrastructure in underdeveloped countries cannot be exactly cheap, although it will certainly be cheaper than the provision of the capital infrastructure. It is possible to make some rough estimates of what is involved. In Great Britain, expenditure on "research and development" (which roughly corresponds to what is discussed here as creation of new investment opportunities) represented 2.35 per cent of the gross national product; the corresponding percentage for the United States was 2.74. Some of this expenditure in both countries, of course, was directed to noneconomic purposes such as defense, but an authoritative estimate of purely civilian research and development has placed the expenditure

[8] *Essays in World Economics*, Oxford, Fair Lawn, N.J., 1959, pp. 173–174.

for both countries at 1¼ per cent of the gross national product.[9] To this should be added at least a share of expenditure listed as education, which in the United States is 5 per cent of total national income and in the United Kingdom is 4 per cent. A minimum of 2 per cent of the national income may be assumed as applying to the United States and the United Kingdom for preinvestment work; this would represent about one-tenth of the total gross investment, which is roughly 20 per cent of their national incomes.

If we accept for the moment an estimate of about 20 billion dollars per annum as the total gross capital formation which would be aimed at as a start in the underdeveloped countries of the world, it would therefore seem plausible to think that 10 per cent of this sum, i.e., 2 billion dollars per annum (excluding education and health expenditures), should be devoted to a systematic attempt to supply the lacking preinvestment infrastructure. Only a fraction of this is being spent now.[10] Since no systematic attempt has ever been made to measure the volume of preinvestment activities now going on in underdeveloped countries, one cannot quote precise figures. It would be surprising, however, if the figures would show a total expenditure (adding both domestic preinvestment expenditures and external preinvestment aid) of more than perhaps a third to a half of what is required. There is a gap of probably 1 billion dollars per annum or more here waiting to be filled.

While a really big push—if we may borrow this term from the field of investment—in providing the preinvestment infrastructure is not exactly cheap, it has the advantage of being comparatively riskless. No doubt there would be individual failures (although a negative result of a feasibility survey should not really be considered a failure: to avoid a waste of money is as productive as spending it well). But the provision of training and skill, the collection of the necessary data, the promotion of a technology suited

---

[9] *The Economist,* London, Oct. 8, 1960, p. 175.

[10] The following statement by Crawford H. Greenewalt, president of E. I. du Pont de Nemours & Company, is of interest. The 1:3 ratio for the chemical industry is, of course, exceptional, and a 1:10 ratio for the economy as a whole may be more realistic. "For our own Company, I can be somewhat more quantitative. We have reasonably good figures for research expenditures year by year since 1921. For the same period, we have a record of construction expenditures, and it seems to me the ratio of the two can fairly be taken as an index of cause and effect. The ratio of research dollars to construction dollars has averaged about one to three—for every dollar we have spent in our laboratories we have sooner or later spent $3 for new plants, products, and processes. This ratio, incidentally, has been reasonably constant over a period during which our annual research expenditures have increased from $1 million to something over $70 million. Or if one wishes to have an over-all look, we spent in the past twenty-five years approximately $600 million on research, excluding the cost of buildings and equipment, and over the same period, approximately $1.8 billion for new plant and equipment. The ratio of one to three, valid for both the short and long term, can, I think, be extrapolated into the future with reasonable confidence." (*The Uncommon Man: The Individual in the Organization,* McGraw-Hill, New York, 1959, pp. 129–130.)

to the underdeveloped countries as well as improved methods of transfer and adaptation of technological knowledge developed elsewhere, the collection of data and the promotion of the power of investigating opportunities—all these could not conceivably be wasted. One cannot be quite clear in advance, but one *can* be reasonably certain that such expenditure would open productive investment opportunities of a magnitude many times its own size.

We must realize, of course, that a money figure put upon the necessary volume of preinvestment services will not tell the whole story of the dimensions of the effort which is required. The kind of services required and the nature of the reorientation of research will put strain upon resources in scarce supply, and the nature of the problem is such that it cannot be solved overnight. "Systematic plodding" may be a better term for what is required than "big push." Nor will the results be very glamorous; it is the structure which attracts the eye, not the infrastructure. But we have here at the same time a problem which should be noncontroversial and feasible in its total dimensions, the solution of which might yet justify our earlier classical optimism about the underdeveloped countries.

3

Reassessment of the Capital Requirements of Underdeveloped Countries

In the preceding chapters we have described in detail some interconnected developments in the areas of preinvestment and human investment which suggest the possibility of creating conditions more favorable to development in the underdeveloped countries and thus reducing the required massive injections of capital which would be inherent in a more mechanical application of the Harrod-Domar growth formula. Turning now to the subject of capital requirements itself, even here we can trace developments which may make us more hopeful. There are some elements of relative strength on which we may gradually learn better how to build in the underdeveloped countries.

HOPEFUL ASPECTS IN POPULATION AND SAVINGS CAPACITY

To begin with, the vicious circles are never entirely closed. For instance, underdeveloped countries may be either too densely populated (overpopulated) or they may be too thinly populated (underpopulated). Now in the first situation, while prima facie the road to economic development and even to a rise of productivity in agriculture itself must lie through industrialization, yet this very same situation also presupposes the existence of unutilized and underutilized manpower. Hence, the social cost, at least the domestic social cost, of new investment and industrialization is drastically reduced, provided—this is, it must be said, a big proviso—that (1) we can manage to find ways and means of withdrawing people from the overpopulated countryside while at the same time organizing the food *supplies* (not only food *production*) necessary to accompany the transferred ex-farmers, and that (2) we find a technology which enables the underdeveloped countries to utilize this specific asset of theirs—abundant, cheap, possibly in the social sense free, labor power. This second requirement obviously takes us back to the subject of technical progress discussed in the previous chapter.

In the other type of underdeveloped country, the thinly populated country, the pressure toward industrialization will be correspondingly

26

less, and increases in agricultural productivity can be achieved without the added difficulties of land shortages and exhaustion of the soil. Hence, as far as population is concerned, the situation is never one of entirely unmitigated gloom, provided again that we learn how to meet the rather different challenges inherent in the different situations.

But let us concentrate for a moment on this problem of capital requirements and insufficient savings capacity which underlay postwar pessimism concerning the underdeveloped countries. Here again, experience has gradually brought to the fore a number of qualifications. The savings capacity of the underdeveloped countries is by no means nonexistent or even as small as it might sometimes appear. The presently developed countries had a respectable savings capacity at corresponding levels. Quite apart from the well-known accumulations of "noneconomic" capital in the form of gold, commodity hoards, exported capital, cattle, real estate improvements, etc., all the lessons of economic history and recent experience also tend to show that we must not think of savings capacity as something existing in the abstract, setting some kind of low absolute limit to investment opportunities.

The savings capacity of underdeveloped countries is capable of stimulation by means of information, education, development of attractive savings channels and proper savings institutions, and, in the case of public savings, improvement of tax systems, more specifically, tax collections. Furthermore, the desire to save is itself very largely a product of available investment opportunities. While discussion has often emphasized the limitations in the supply of savings as setting the limit to investment, the opposite relationship is also of great importance. Historically, investment has often largely financed itself, at least in the directly productive sectors such as industry and agriculture, not only by the well-known process of ploughing back profits or farm surpluses but also by the stimulation of general savings directly attributable to the widening opportunities for productive investment.

Insofar as investment opportunities to some extent also create the savings necessary to carry them out, added importance is given to the possibilities related to the discovery and development of latent investment opportunities in underdeveloped countries, as described in the previous chapter. The neglect of possibilities of this kind may perhaps be traced to the prevalence of Keynesian modes of thinking. In the Keynesian system, with income distribution given, the propensity to save is determined by income levels alone. This is a very reasonable model in the advanced countries where it is taken for granted that the investment opportunities existing at a given level of employment are more or less fully and rapidly acted upon.[1] But if we abandon this last assumption for the underdeveloped

---

[1] To be sure, a reduction of levels of employment and effective demand will destroy or at least submerge investment opportunities, and in this sense there are

countries, it follows that savings become also a function of the rate at which latent investment opportunities in underdeveloped countries are actualized. Thus, just as Keynes has shown that in periods of revival from a depression investment can be self-financed in the sense that the additional savings required will come from the increased income, so we may say for the underdeveloped countries that investment can be self-financed in the different sense that the opening up of investment will raise the propensity to save out of given incomes by providing previously nonexisting justification and outlets for savings. But the other facet of Keynesian thinking, that an excessive propensity to save may kill off the inducement to invest as incomes rise, obviously is not directly applicable in situations where the increase in savings is conceived as itself the result of the emergence of new investment opportunities.

THE SHIFT FROM POSTWAR PESSIMISM

During the pessimistic postwar decade it was generally pictured that the establishment of a more or less complete economic and social infrastructure was virtually a precondition of actual production. This was held to be true both in point of time (i.e., it was believed that the creation of the infrastructure must precede in time the take-off in actual production) and from a technological point of view (i.e., it was believed that without the creation of the infrastructure production would be hopelessly inefficient, wasteful, and noncompetitive). The natural deduction from this picture was that in the early stages of development the aggregate capital/output ratio must be high, i.e., unfavorable, because of the need to devote a high proportion of resources to not directly productive investment of a foundation-building type. This argument was further reinforced by the fact that infrastructure investment by its nature tends to be particularly capital-intensive, so that the effect on the capital/output ratio inherent in the lack of direct productivity of infrastructure investment would be further reinforced. The natural conclusion to be drawn from this state of affairs was that the start of economic development and its early stages were obstructed by the tremendous hurdle of infrastructural capital requirements which could only be overcome by a "big push," which in turn would be beyond the resources of many or most of the underdeveloped countries.

The development of ideas of this kind after the war was justifiable and meritorious in opposition to the previous somewhat romantic optimism. Nothing should be said to deduct from the merit of these observations, which have led us to a deeper understanding of the processes of develop-

---

latent investment opportunities in an underemployed economy. But this is quite different from the problem of frustrated investment opportunities in the underdeveloped countries.

ment and of the required degree and nature of assistance to underdeveloped countries. The development of public aid[2] and its specific concentration in such infrastructural sectors as transport, power, education, health services, etc., testify to the degree in which these theories correspond to the realities of our time.[3]

However, now that the general point is so well established, many of us who have thought and argued along these lines are becoming aware of some of the modifications and qualifications which should also be borne in mind. Even if the intellectual truth of the proposition that a more or less complete infrastructure is a necessary precondition be accepted, it is not beyond the powers of development planners in the underdeveloped countries to adjust themselves to this situation to some degree. For instance, it is at least possible to limit the impact of the enormous infrastructural capital requirements in the geographical sense. Thus, infrastructural investment can be limited to development regions, often coincident with river-valley systems. Once such regions have been developed, the additional output can then serve as a springboard for the subsequent development of other regions. Regional planning and the creation of efficient interrelated investment packages in regions with particularly favorable development prospects have been much furthered and hold out hopes for the future.

Investment in infrastructure can also be lessened by invoking labor-intensive technologies utilizing abundant factors of production. The building of feeder roads by using rural manpower through community development schemes is one illustration; the development of rural or small-town industry with the avoidance of some of the cost of new urban public utilities and housing is another. Such tremendously important developments (unfortunately mainly still in the future) as the use of sunpower and windpower, or for that matter animal power, for the generation of energy furnish yet another illustration. Some parts of the social infrastructure can be economized by methods which, however difficult to introduce, are at least not expensive in the sense of capital expenditure. For instance, improved health education can lead to the avoidance of disease, reduce the impact of epidemics, and reduce the need for hospital and medical services.

Beyond such possibilities of economizing on infrastructural investment either by geographical concentration or by the use of labor-intensive technologies are possibilities of developing the infrastructure to some extent simultaneously with, or possibly even subsequent to, the development of actual production rather than before this. Economists have increasingly drawn attention to the possibilities of running a "disequilibrium economy" in which deliberate pressure is put on resources generally or on strategic

---

[2] Discussed in the following chapter.
[3] Though one cannot exclude the possibility that economic teachings about the importance of infrastructure had something to do with the distribution of aid.

resources specifically in order to provide the incentive for their development. This is really an extension of the argument presented above about savings, namely that one does not necessarily have to have a supply before proceeding to utilization but that the demand arising from utilization may quite often create its own supply. To some extent, this may be true of infrastructural investment resources, as it is of the smaller direct capital requirements of industry and agriculture. As already mentioned, the economist who is particularly associated with the development of such ideas is A. O. Hirschmann, in his *Strategy of Economic Development*.

While the pessimistic postwar decade set up a picture of heavy capital requirements, low savings capacities, bad savings habits (gold, real estate, etc.), and bad entrepreneurial habits (speculation, hoarding of goods, capital flight, etc.) as tremendous obstacles to investment, the view now gaining ground, without denying the accuracy of the analysis, presents these obstacles in a rather less formidable light. It now appears that the great problems are the lack of an adequate inducement to invest and the lack in efficiency of much of the investment that does take place, both of which can be remedied by a combination of preinvestment activities, a more realistic approach to the potentialities for increasing domestic capital resources, and a growth of international aid. The obstacles now appear not so much as autonomous and immovable but rather as naturally derived from the stagnant nature of the economy. There is in fact a good deal of empirical evidence that where the economy begins to move forward, entrepreneurial habits rapidly adjust themselves, and productive long-term investment begins to be preferred to short-term speculation; that savings begin to flow out of money lending and gold hoards into productive investment and bank accounts; that the rate of saving itself begins to increase as savers acquire trust and economic foresight.

Thus, the problem begins to look more amenable. There is one further element which will also have to be considered in explaining the more activist and optimistic element in recent thinking. This is the remarkable growth of public aid to underdeveloped countries, to which we now turn.

4

Public Aid: A New Factor

A major recent development which could not have been foreseen has been the spread of public financial aid from developed countries to the underdeveloped countries. The most striking thing about this is not the giving of aid itself but the degree in which the *idea* of giving has established itself—the degree in which giving has become a recognized responsibility of the more advanced countries and an institution which they recognize as being in their enlightened self-interest. Although it was precisely the purpose of some of the pessimistic thinkers of the postwar decade to point out the necessity of some kind of international aid mechanism of this kind, their rather unexpected degree of success in this direction could not fail to modify some of the more pessimistic conclusions which they had formed.

THE AMAZING GROWTH OF AID

It would not have been easy, ten or fifteen years ago, to forecast a present situation which may be broadly described (although with some exaggeration) as "aid, not trade." When commodity prices were lifted by the booms of the Second World War and then the Korean conflict, the talk was all of "trade, not aid."[1] Even granting foresight of the kind which Raul Prebisch displayed as to the subsequent decline of commodity prices, I think most observers—including myself—would have forecast that any concessions by the industrial countries to the underdeveloped countries would take the form of trade concessions; or if capital transfers, then capital transfers linked with the movements of trade and commodity prices, in the form of some kind of compensatory payments. In fact, the earlier 1950s were full of discussions and ideas of this kind.[2] One might have

---

[1] It may be recalled that a prominent elder statesman, when asked what he thought about this slogan "trade, not aid," is reported to have replied, "I agree with the second part of it." One wonders what he would think of the present situation!

[2] See, for instance, the report of a United Nations committee, *Commodity Trade and Economic Development* (UN Publication Sales No. 1954 II.B.1), including a proposal by F. Garcia Olano on compensatory transfers depending on movements of terms of trade. Interest in ideas of this kind is reviving again, and it seems likely that in the next few years the trade problems of the underdeveloped countries will be to the fore in international discussions, starting with the United Nations Conference on Trade and Development, which commenced in March, 1964.

thought that the idea of helping underdeveloped countries to *earn* the finance for development would have been more appealing to the general public in advanced countries than the idea of *giving* or *soft lending* them this finance. But the general appeal of trade as against aid in the industrial countries seems to have been more than offset by a combination of regard for domestic vested interests, on the one hand, and a desire to maintain the general principles of a free market economy (at least in external dealings), on the other. On the surface at least, aid mechanisms seem to involve less apparent interference with allocative market mechanisms than would stabilization of commodity prices or compensatory payments based on commodity prices or commodity trade. Perhaps there was also the consideration that if one gives, one might just as well be *seen* to be giving and get moral credit for it.

Whatever the reasons may have been, the fact is that aid has developed much more vigorously than trade as far as concessions to the underdeveloped countries are concerned. Unhappily, aid is such a comparatively young institution that, in spite of its vigorous increase, it is still insufficient to compensate underdeveloped countries fully for the losses they suffer when commodity prices are really weak, as they were during the 1956–1960 period.

It is truly remarkable that public aid to underdeveloped countries— entered into so reluctantly, exposed to such heavy criticisms as a "giveaway," developing entirely on an *ad hoc* and unplanned basis, with its multiplicity of institutions and sources—should have developed into such an important and, in the aggregate, steady and steadily growing source of foreign exchange for the underdeveloped countries. As a matter of fact, in the last five or six years the flow of resources to the underdeveloped countries by the medium of public aid has been a more dependable element in the flow of foreign exchange and resources to them than export earnings, service payments, flow of private capital, or any other balance-of-payments item. Foreign aid has steadily and year by year increased at the rate of about 15 per cent per annum, from about 2 billion dollars per annum in the mid-fifties to around 5½ billion dollars per annum now, without a single setback in any year. Since public aid has grown at a faster rate than export proceeds or other components among the foreign exchange earnings of the underdeveloped countries, its importance has grown from 9 per cent of the total export earnings of underdeveloped countries around 1954 to 20 per cent now, and from 1 per cent of their national incomes to 3 per cent. Since a rate of increase of 15 per cent per annum is also higher than the rate of growth of the money national incomes and higher than that of the export proceeds of the industrial countries, it also follows that industrial countries have allocated increasing percentages of their national incomes and export proceeds to aid to underdeveloped countries. The figures are 0.3 per cent of the national incomes of industrial countries around 1954 and 0.5 per cent now, and 1.9 per cent of their total export proceeds in 1954 and over 3 per cent now.

At the same time, the percentage of national income of industrial countries devoted to public aid for underdeveloped countries is so small even now that public aid is still well below the point where it would impose real sacrifices on the industrial countries; hence its growth potential is still very great. The fact that the national incomes of the more industrial countries of Europe—with their outward-looking trade conditions, their dependence on trade with underdeveloped countries, and their special commitments to underdeveloped countries—are rapidly increasing is also a good omen for the continued growth of public aid policies. So is the fact that the growth of public aid to date has coincided with tremendous armament expenditures by the industrial countries. If at any time this burden should be alleviated, industrial countries might not only be willing but in fact anxious to devote part of the resources thus set free to public aid. Countries have set forth their willingness to do so in solemn international declarations. Since even now public aid does not represent more than at most 5 per cent of the total armament expenditures of the industrial countries, here is obviously another enormous growth potential for public aid.

Moreover, the forms in which public aid is rendered have also shown considerable flexibility and capacity of adjusting themselves to the conditions of the underdeveloped countries. Particularly striking are the growth of soft-lending facilities and the rapidly growing acceptance of the principle of soft loans. Some years ago, the principle of soft loans was considered subversive. It was argued that salvation lay either in hard commercial lending—loans at 5 or 6 per cent repayable in hard currency over a reasonable period with strict repayment schedules—or else in open grants-in-aid. Any "bargain basements" in between were considered to be the work of the devil.

The situation is unrecognizably different now. New institutions specializing in soft loans have sprung up: the United States Development Loan Fund, the International Development Association affiliated with the International Bank, the Inter-American Development Bank, etc. Soft loans, i.e., loans at concessional rates of interest or with concessional repayment provision in local currency, are in fact ideally suited to the job in hand. Grants-in-aid are not popular among the receivers, are destructive of sound project analysis, induce a highly political element into the relationship between giver and receiver, and fail to reflect the inherently commercial purpose of the transaction, namely the development of the receiving countries with its manifold, although indirect, benefits to the world community and hence to the giving country. The commercial loan defeats its own purpose by placing excessive burdens on the country to be assisted, by limiting its absorptive capacity for such hard loans to a ceiling which in many cases has now been reached, and by distorting development strategies and investment patterns in order to maximize its repayment capacity for foreign loans and thus its absorptive capacity for further aid. A public aid program based on hard loans alone results in a distribution of aid among various countries which reflects neither their economic needs nor their economic prospects.

All this has sunk in very thoroughly and surprisingly quickly. The subversive doctrine of yesterday has become the orthodoxy of today. The confusion between soft loans and "lax lending" which was in the earlier debate so frequently insinuated against the advocates of soft loans has virtually disappeared; indeed, everybody now is busy explaining the vital difference between the two.

PRESENT PROBLEMS AND THE OUTLOOK FOR THE FUTURE

At the same time public aid displays all the teething troubles of a young creature. In some ways, the present situation is positively chaotic. To begin with, and most obviously, there is no agreement on what the various countries are doing in the field of public aid and what the standards of measuring their performance should be. The area is thick with conflicting claims and statistics. Country A maintains that it is doing "three times as much" as country B, while country B equally plausibly shows that it is doing "twice as much" as country A. Some confusion would not be too surprising, since public aid is in so many different ways intermingled with private sources, trade credits, short-term flows, etc. Nor are the lines of division between economic aid, military aid, "defense support," general administrative subventions, war-reparation payments, etc., very clear. Even so, the present degree of confusion is rather excessive. The previously quoted figures of public aid of underdeveloped countries are based on a rather restrictive definition, and many countries claim to be doing more in fact.

Not only is the measurement of performance itself in dispute, but also the standard against which performance should be measured. What is the relevant standard? Should it be the percentage of national incomes? Should it be the state of the balance of trade or the balance of payments? Should it be the size or movement of foreign reserves? Should it be the volume of trade? Should it be the fiscal strength of the individual country? There are obviously many possible standards against which performance could be, and is being, measured.

Perhaps more serious than these problems of measurement and standards, however, is the absence of any rational standard of allocating foreign aid to individual receiving countries. Here again, a great many standards could be, and are being, advocated. To mention only some of the more widespread and more plausible standards: Should foreign aid be concentrated on the poorest countries, so as to relieve mass poverty as quickly as possible, or should it rather be concentrated on the semideveloped countries which are already near their "take-off," to make a start on reducing the number of potential recipients? Should economic aid be concentrated on those countries where the marginal efficiency of capital is high? Should it be concentrated on countries which are most likely to make effective use of aid because they have stable governments, efficient development programs, etc.? Should it be allocated on the basis of fair shares, and if so, should it be fair shares by countries or fair shares per capita? Should public aid be concentrated on one or more certain areas, such as training and education, infrastructure, agriculture, and industry? Should it be allocated to individual projects or to overall resources of the receiving country? Should it be allocated as an untied-money program or in the form of commodities, whether in the shape of tied loans or as direct distribution of surplus commodities of all kinds? Should grants be allocated differently from soft loans and hard loans? Should allocation be by bilateral agreement between giver and receiver, or should it be by a multilateral mechanism of some kind?   1263673

Answers to many of the questions posed here have not yet emerged. The one thing that is certain is that the present situation does not satisfy any of these possible rational standards. The distribution of public aid among the various underdeveloped countries is extremely uneven, not to say haphazard. It seems to reflect past history, historical accident, and practical bargaining strength rather than any recognizable economic principle. No wonder then, that in spite of its quite impressive aggregate, the total effect of public aid is widely felt to be disappointingly difficult to define.

However, there are also signs that in spite of these and other teething troubles, this youngster on the economic scene is beginning to become more rational. The distribution of sources of public aid becomes wider and more secure, as the "second string" of industrial countries, i.e., Europe (East and West) and Japan, begins to catch up with the "first string," i.e., the United States. There is growing evidence of concerted action, so that the sum total of public aid is maintained or steadily increased even though the aid-giving capacity of individual industrial countries fluctuates with their changing balance-of-payments positions. The share of multilateral aid (which is on the whole preferred by the recipients and which holds greater assurance of continuity) is gradually increasing. Perhaps the most striking and promising evidence of order beginning to be infused into a somewhat chaotic growth is the increasing importance of "package deals." Package deals, of which the annual rounds of concerted aid to India are the prime example, are an attempt to bring together the aid efforts of different countries and international organizations on behalf of individual underdeveloped countries and at the same time set this combined aid into proper relation with the requirements and priorities of the receiving country and with the specific preferences and possibilities of the various sources of assistance. Perhaps it is from a generalization of such package deals that a rational system embodying elements of both bilateralism and multilateralism will ultimately emerge.

Growth potential for public aid may also be seen in the fact that so far it has been predominantly a monetary problem. With the exception of surplus-food disposal, mainly under United States Public Law 480, the possibilities of tapping the physical production reserves and unused capacities of the industrial countries in order to promote the development of under-developed countries have as yet hardly been explored. Public aid in terms of surplus commodities and mobilizing surplus capacities is bound to be more popular than public aid in terms of money. To the citizens of the giving countries an aid program in terms of money appears as the taxpayer's enemy; surplus-food disposal appears as the farmer's friend. A possible future aid program in terms of unused engineering products, secondhand machinery, structural steel, etc., may well appear as the worker's friend as well as the businessman's friend. If such possibilities have so far been less utilized than financial public aid, this is perhaps explained by the greater difficulties of organizing aid in terms of commodities and also perhaps by a somewhat irrational feeling that to deal with commodities rather than money would be a throwback to precapitalistic "stone age" economies. One must, of course, hope that an aid program in terms of commodities would be *additional* to more conventional money programs and by no means in substitution. The whole point would be to exploit *additional* sources, those not covered by the monetary approach.

To sum up, even as it is, public aid already adds one-third to the domestic investment resources of underdeveloped countries; and its growth potential is considerable. In the perspective of history, perhaps not the least effect of the Marshall Plan was its demonstration effect—the demonstration that the acceptance of a responsibility by the economically strong for the economically weaker may in the end benefit all by helping to create a viable world economy.

PART 2

Some Current Issues
in Development Theory

Many of the arguments about the content and shape of development plans have centered on the concept of balance, and the first and second papers are devoted to this theme. The term "balanced growth" is used to mean various things: the two papers printed here deal with, respectively, the classical technical usage—the balance between the size of markets, the volume of supply, and the demand for capital—and the balance between obstacles to development and the forces of progress.

The third and fourth papers in this part deal more specifically with the human factor in economic development. These two papers were originally prepared for two conferences separated by a number of years, the third paper for a more recent conference of African Ministers of Education held in Ethiopia under the auspices of UNESCO, and the fourth paper for the earlier World Population Congress held in Rome under the auspices of the United Nations. In spite of the difference in time, the two papers taken together represent a more general approach to what has since become known as the question of "human investment" and recognized to be basic to economic growth.

5

Balanced Growth
in Economic Development:
Theory and Practice

QUESTIONS OF DEFINITION

The concept of "balanced growth," or of the maintenance of some kind of equilibrium during the process of growth, means different things to different people. Broadly, we may distinguish three classes of usage: a nontechnical usage, a general technical usage, and a specific technical usage.

1. In the *nontechnical* usage, the term is often used to describe such ideas as growth without too much social disruption, broadly based growth, growth which spreads its benefits widely among different classes, sustained growth, i.e., growth which is neither of such a kind nor of such a rapidity that it turns out to be a flash in the pan. In its most watered-down versions this nontechnical usage comes pretty close to identifying balanced growth with the kind of growth with which the observer agrees or with growth which is considered *ex post* as having turned out to be successful and which is then retrospectively given the laudatory epithet of "balanced." For some economists, of course, there can be no higher term of praise than "balance" or "equilibrium," and the bestowal of this praise on a certain growth process may then merely amount to a general accolade for a certain country or period. Needless to say, we shall not be concerned with this non-technical usage, even though the problems with which we shall deal will not be found entirely unrelated to these more emotional roots of the concept.

2. In the *general technical* sense, balanced growth may refer to the balance between ambitions and the resources available to satisfy the am-bitions or, more narrowly, the balance between intended savings and in-tended investment. Investment is balanced if it fits in with available re-sources and in this sense can be carried out without inflation or at least with

This paper was originally delivered at the Conference on Economic Development organized by the department of economics of the University of Texas on the occasion of the seventy-fifth anniversary of the foundation of the University, and published in E. Nelson (ed.), *Economic Growth-Rationale, Problems, Cases,* University of Texas only that amount of inflation which serves a useful pump-priming function and brings itself to an end. The latter qualification is necessary, although many observers would agree that in underdeveloped countries he who primes the pump will often find that he has a tiger by the tail instead. Still keeping within the class of general technical usage, the term "balance" may refer, not to the equilibrium between aggregate resources and aggregate demands, but to specific resources. It is well understood among the practitioners of economics that the balance of resources and ambition may be upset not only by excessive demand in the aggregate but also by bottlenecks, i.e., a failure to match the "mix" of resources with the "mix" of demands or claims upon these resources.

The third balance referred to in general technical usage is the external balance, the interrelationship between the pressure of domestic demand and the need to equalize the incomings and outgoings of foreign exchange after taking account of intended changes in foreign reserves. It is well understood that developmental investment may be brought up short by the barrier of external balance even before the barriers of bottlenecks and of the limitation of aggregate resources are reached. Again, underdeveloped countries may have special reason to worry about the external balance because of their chronically low foreign exchange reserves, their chronically high import demand as a result of demonstration effects and of the facts of technological life, and their chronic difficulties of achieving the desirable degree of export promotion. But although these problems are coming nearer home to our present subject than those indicated by nontechnical usage, they are not the problems with which I shall be concerned.

3. So now we come to the *specific technical* sense of the concept. In this usage, the term refers to the balance between the size of markets, the volume of supply, and the demand for capital. It is the same balance between the division of labor, the extent of production, and the extent of the market which worried Adam Smith. In the more modern literature on underdeveloped countries, this concern with the balance of markets and supplies often takes the form of a discussion of the balance between different sectors of the economy, e.g., agriculture and industry, or of the need to create the necessary improvements in the efficiency of production which create new markets by a simultaneous expansion of the economic infrastructure of health, education, transport, power, housing, etc., together with the more direct expansion of supplies of final goods; or it may take the form of achieving these necessary improvements in the efficiency of production by broadly based simultaneous investment so that the infrastructure, external economies,

Press, Austin, Tex., 1960. It was also printed, almost exactly as delivered, in *The Malayan Economic Review*, vol. 3, no. 2, October, 1958. A Spanish translation appeared in *Revista de economía política*, September–December, 1962.

economies of large-scale production, and the total supply of final goods should go forward together all along the line, and in such a fashion that at each step the increase in real incomes is such that it provides the market for the increased flow of final goods. The "big push," Schumpeter's "waves of investors," and the virtues of the "investment package" are all variations on this theme.

It is with this specific technical use of the term that I am concerned. Essentially, in spite of the rather different form in which this concept expresses itself now, the problem is still Adam Smith's $64 question—the question of keeping the growth of markets and the growth of supply in balance. As if to emphasize the continuity of the problem from Adam Smith to Nurkse and other more modern writers, we have the celebrated article by Allyn Young in the *Economic Journal* forming such a clear bridge between the two.[1]

STRUCTURAL CHANGE AND THE MARKETING PROBLEM

What then, precisely, is this problem of balanced growth, in its specific technical sense of the problem of markets? To help our understanding of the problem, we have to construct some kind of fundamental structural picture—model, if you like—of an underdeveloped country. An underdeveloped country has a clearly defined employment structure: 70 to 90 per cent of the employed population is engaged in agriculture. In a developed country, which has reached the national income levels of northwestern Europe or North America, about 15 per cent of the population is engaged in agriculture—more if the country is a net exporter of agricultural products (or accumulates agricultural surpluses), less if the country is an agricultural net importer. However, even those developed countries which are heavy net exporters of agricultural produce—Canada, Australia, New Zealand, Denmark, and, yes, even Iowa and Texas[2]—have an employment structure which sets them well apart from the underdeveloped countries.

An underdeveloped country then may be defined as a country with 80 per cent of its people in agriculture and a developed country as one with only 15 per cent of its employment in agriculture, in both cases give or take a little according to foreign trade. Arthur Lewis has defined the process of economic growth as the problem of transforming a country from a 5 per cent saver into a 15 per cent saver. We can, with equal justice, define the process as one of transforming a country from an 80 per cent farmer to a 15 per cent farmer. Note that we are speaking here of the employment structure, not of the structure of foreign trade or of the composition of the national income.[3]

[1] "Increasing Returns and Economic Progress," *Economic Journal*, vol. 38, 1928.
[2] Iowa 28 per cent, Texas 16 per cent of total employment in agriculture.
[3] I emphasize this because there is frequent confusion on this point.

The 80 per cent farmer economy, or underdeveloped economy, has this specific employment structure because this specific employment structure corresponds exactly to its low level of productivity. The low level of productivity in farming decrees that the bulk of the people must be in farming in order to feed and clothe themselves and that they have little to spare over and above their own needs. The low level of incomes decrees, by writ of Engel's law, that a very high percentage of the low incomes is spent on food and essential clothing. The demand for other things, particularly manufactured goods and services, is thus limited to a very small percentage of a very small income. This compound effect of low incomes and Engel's law means that the market for nonagricultural goods is exceedingly small. Productivity in agriculture, level of incomes, Engel's law, and employment structure form an interdependent equilibrium system. The equilibrium which they determine by their interaction in an underdeveloped country is a low-level equilibrium.

The above brief description is subject to a significant but not fundamental modification arising from the existence of foreign trade; in that case the employment structure is not in direct harmony with the level of the incomes and productivity, and the "rest of the world" account must appear as a further determinant. Normally, underdeveloped countries are net exporters of agricultural products and net importers of other products. Overpopulated countries or mining countries can be significant exceptions to this. But the rule remains. As we shall see later, the existence of domestic markets for manufactures presently satisfied by imports from abroad is a significant factor in applying the doctrines of balanced growth. For the moment, however, it is better to stick to fundamentals, and we may think of the world as a whole or of a closed economy or of an underdeveloped country, the foreign trade of which is balanced in respect of farm and other products.

At this point a second feature should be introduced into our simple model of employment structure. The output-labor ratio in agriculture appears in the statistics almost invariably as lower than the national average ratio. Caution is advisable in connection with this statement. First, there are one or two exceptions to it among the more developed countries (Australia seems to be one of them), yet it remains one of the best-founded generalizations we can make for underdeveloped countries and developed countries alike. Second, the published figures may understate agricultural output, especially in connection with subsistence farming and agricultural capital formation; hence my proposition refers to what appears in the statistics rather than what *is*. Third, my proposition has doubtful applicability in welfare terms: it is doubtful whether the lower value of output per employed person in agriculture is not largely or wholly offset by lower prices, lower cost, and less need for keeping up with the Joneses or other nonpecuniary factors. But when cautiously interpreted, I do not think that the evidence for the lower output-labor ratio in agriculture can be contested. In fact for a surprising number of countries the figures come remarkably close to a constant relation of the form

$$a = \tfrac{2}{3}\,n$$

where a is output per employed person in agriculture and n is output per employed person in the economy as a whole.[4]

From this differential between agricultural output per person and non-agricultural output per person, there follows with the force of an arithmetical identity a fact of considerable political and emotional significance: if an 80 per cent farmer economy produces only two-thirds of its national per capita average in the agricultural sector, the differential between the agricultural sector and the nonagricultural sector will be much larger than will be the case in a 15 per cent farmer economy which also produces two-thirds of its national average in the agricultural sector. In fact, in the underdeveloped country output per worker outside agriculture compared with agricultural output per worker would be in the ratio of $3\tfrac{1}{2}:1$. Thus, structural change in the sense of moving from an 80 per cent farmer economy in the direction of a 15 per cent farmer economy begins to look like more than a *symptom* or *measure* of economic development; it begins to look like a *method* or *instrument* of economic development.

This impression is understandable, but it is doubly fallacious. In the first place, any transfer from agriculture which is not justified by the level of productivity and the state of real demand or markets cannot possibly be maintained or beneficial. In the second place, the higher output per person outside agriculture is not in itself conclusive evidence of a more favorable capital-output ratio outside agriculture than inside, either in the average sense or in the marginal sense relevant for allocation of available capital. However the magic of this differential is understandable. Moreover, in spite of the basic fallacies involved, there is at least an element of truth in the idea that this differential could be utilized in economic development. Insofar as the greater output per person outside agriculture does in fact represent greater net productivity of labor derived from internal and external economies and not only a greater input of capital, a cumulative or multiplier effect is introduced into the process of structural change. As the levels of productivity and of real demand and markets rise, the structural change from an 80 per cent farmer economy toward a 15 per cent farmer economy made

---

[4] The form in which the equation is presented fails to bring out clearly the implied compound relationship, i.e., that the ratio of output per person outside agriculture to the one inside agriculture is a diminishing function of the importance of agriculture to the economy, as explained in the next sentence. From $a = \tfrac{2}{3}n$, it follows that $(x = 150 - y)/(100 - y)$, where x is the ratio of nonagricultural per capita income to agricultural per capita income and y is the percentage of the population in agriculture. I am indebted to my colleague, Mr. Martin Ekker, for pointing this out to me.

possible by this rise will in its turn generate forces which themselves tend to raise productivity and real incomes. In this fashion the effect may become the cause, and we are in the midst of a hen-and-egg riddle. Here we have the starting point of the doctrine of balanced growth in the more modern form developed by Rosenstein-Rodan, Nurkse, and others: the self-justifying broadening of real demand and markets, the investment which looks uneconomical *ex ante* but becomes economical *ex post*, the shipwreck which helps to set off the wave which will float it off the rock.

BALANCED GROWTH: A POSSIBLE SOLUTION, BUT OF DOUBTFUL APPLICABILITY

We have now established that a shift in the employment structure from agriculture toward nonagriculture, especially industry, can be considered as an inevitable accompaniment of economic development. This is certainly true for a closed economy and, with a certain time lag, almost certainly true also for an open economy. We have further seen that in a very limited sense it might even be said that the process of transfer itself can help to promote economic development. At the same time we have seen that the extent of the market—reflecting the state of real incomes, the institutional framework, and the state of foreign trade—sets strict limits to this required (and desired) shift in the employment structure. Industry cannot expand because it needs expanded markets in agriculture, and agricultural marketing, in turn, is limited by the absence of employment opportunities in industry which forces agriculture to feed too many people on the farms. Individual industries cannot expand because they lack markets as a result of the lack of development of other industries.

The doctrine of balanced economic growth, in its specific technical sense, offers a way of solving this marketing difficulty. Perhaps it would be more correct to say that it offers a way of bypassing the marketing difficulty. What it says, in effect, is this: "Let us leave the present system alone, deadlocked in low-level equilibrium. Let us superimpose upon this deadlocked system a second, self-contained system which provides additional markets at the same time as it provides additional supply. Let us create this second, self-contained system with emphasis on the sector which would in any case have to be expanded in the process of economic growth, and which is also the sector where simultaneous projects can most readily support each other. The way to do this is by a simultaneous wave of new plants, composed in such a way that full advantage is taken of complementarities and external economies on the supply side and of the complementarities of markets on the demand side." In this way, it is explained—to use a metaphor coined in a rather different context—a hundred flowers may grow where a single flower would wither away for lack of nourishment.

In other words, we are told that the marketing difficulty looks formidable only to our habit of thinking small, in terms of piecemeal projects. "Stop thinking piecemeal, start thinking big," we are told, "and the marketing difficulty which seemed so formidable will turn out to be a paper tiger."

Let it be said at once that this doctrine must command respect and sympathy. Advice to underdeveloped countries to stop thinking piecemeal and to start thinking big is sound advice. The programming approach is better than the project approach. In a good development program, individual projects can and should mutually support each other; if proper advantage is taken of such opportunities, the productivity of investment can be significantly increased. A widespread expectation among individual entrepreneurs that the demand for their product is going to increase can do wonders with the inducement to invest, and it can be self-justifying as far as the demand side is concerned.

Yet there remain several areas of doubt—indeed, of rather obvious doubt—about this approach. In the first place, it seems obvious that a purely nonagricultural system of additional markets can never be entirely self-contained. Engel's law may say that the demand for food increases less than in proportion to income, but it certainly does *not* say that the demand for food does not increase at all—and most particularly not at the low income levels of underdeveloped countries. Moreover, it is fallacious to think of the new system of additional markets and the old deadlocked system as unrelated to each other. Where you have the institution of family subsistence farming, as the employment structure changes and people are drawn off the land, the demand for food per capita of those remaining on the land will increase with their increasing real income. This increase in demand for food will be additional to the increase in the demand for food of those drawn off the land.

All this is well known and much discussed,[5] but the implications for the doctrine of balanced growth have not perhaps been fully realized. The implications are that the big push in industry may have to be supplemented by large-scale investments in agriculture additional to the "balanced diet" element in the package. But once this is admitted, two consequences follow: in the first place, the doctrine begins to look suspiciously like the more orthodox doctrines—with which Adam Smith would not have quarreled— that structural change must rest on a foundation of raising productivity within the existing structure (and in underdeveloped countries that means mainly agriculture) until real incomes have risen to a level which justifies structural change. Even more damaging to the doctrine, at least in its practical application, is a second consequence of the admission that the widening of markets must include major additional blocks of investment

[5] Indeed, Nurkse's linking of the balanced "investment" package with the need for a "balanced diet" gives telling recognition to this connection.

in agriculture. The total resources required for the big industrial push may already be too large for an underdeveloped country. But even they are not sufficient: we must further add to the required resources not only the investment which is needed in agriculture to make the new system self-contained and remove the market difficulty, but also further blocks of investment to cater for the higher real incomes of those not transferred from agriculture.

The reason why these difficulties are more clearly seen in connection with the problem of sectoral balance between agriculture and industry than in their implications for the specific doctrine of balanced growth lies probably in a lingering belief that the required changes in agricultural supplies could be brought about by institutional changes rather than by new investment. While it is true that reduction of population pressure may make it easier to introduce institutional reforms, such as consolidation of holdings, introduction of commercial crops, experimentation with better farming methods, etc., yet once the subject is brought out into the open, the need for agricultural investment will be fairly generally admitted. But at the same time, the argument is often conducted along lines which seem to neglect this need.

A second obvious area of doubt about the doctrine is already implied in what has just been said. We may put it in the words of Marcus Fleming: "The situation might be roughly expressed by saying that, whereas the balanced growth doctrine assumes that the relationship between industries is for the most part complementary, the limitation of factor supply ensures that that relationship is for the most part competitive."[6]

We may say that the resources required for carrying out the policy of balanced growth—particularly when the extension to agriculture just made is borne in mind—are of such an order of magnitude that a country disposing of such resources would in fact not be underdeveloped. A slightly different way of putting the same point would be to say that the doctrine may be more useful as a recipe for sustained growth in developed countries than as a recipe for breaking the low-level equilibrium deadlock in underdeveloped countries. To justify the doctrine as a recipe for breaking the deadlock, it would really have to be argued that the required resources, even though not initially available, would be forthcoming under the pressure of widened markets and balanced growth of demand. But this also would hardly be compatible with the assumed inelasticities of factor supply in underdeveloped countries. If pump priming were the answer, the problems of underdeveloped countries would not be as tough as they seem to be. This issue has been clearly brought out by Fleming in the article just quoted and his subsequent discussion with Nurkse in the *Economic Journal*.[7]

[6] "External Economies and the Doctrine of Balanced Growth," *Economic Journal*, vol. 65, p. 246, 1955.
[7] Vol. 66, 1956.

It may be tempting to try to vindicate the doctrine by some argument along the following lines: "True, the balanced investment package requires large resources, but these can be provided by a pump-priming process. The savings of underdeveloped countries may not be sufficient to provide the required resources *ex ante*. But if the balanced investment can be physically realized in the first place, the required savings will be provided *ex post*. So there is nothing to worry about, really." But this argument presumably must assume that the marginal rates of savings and taxation are sufficiently high to secure the *ex post* identity of savings and investment without too much inflation, unless it indeed refers to a fleeting identity brought about as part of a continued galloping inflation.

In any case, however, the argument cannot vindicate the doctrine. Insofar as the additional incomes are saved or taxed away, it is true that the insufficiency of resources no longer furnishes an argument against the approach. But this is only achieved at the price of removing the initial justification for the whole operation. For it stands to reason that insofar as additional incomes have to be saved or taxed away, these incomes are not available to provide the required markets. Supply can create its own demand, or it can create its own finance—but it cannot conceivably do both. Therefore, to recommend the balanced investment package as a device simultaneously to solve the marketing deadlock and to solve the deadlock of insufficient resources is to become the victim of a double-counting trick. Where pump priming *can* be successfully practised—probably not a frequent case in underdeveloped countries—that is fine; but there is no particular point about pump priming by means of balanced investment packages.

The argument proves the doctrine of balanced growth *premature* rather than *wrong*, in the sense that it is applicable to a subsequent stage of sustained growth rather than the breaking of a deadlock. It may well be better development strategy to concentrate available resources on types of investment which help to make the economic system more elastic, more capable of expansion under the stimulus of expanded markets and expanding demand. This would draw our attention to investments designed to strengthen the economic and social foundation, or infrastructure: health and education, transport and communications, energy and power, skills and knowledge of resources. Added to this general strengthening of the foundation, there would have to be investment designed to remove specific bottlenecks as they arise as a result of previous growth and recent economic history. As before, if we assume that such a system of investment could be simultaneously undertaken with the wave of directly productive projects described by the doctrine of balanced growth, all would be well. There is certainly nothing inherently contradictory about the two areas of investment. But by thus increasing even further the required size of the investment package so as to include the public foundation services required for expansion, we remove the whole idea even further from the realm of practical development policy in underdeveloped countries. And if a choice has to be made, it is difficult to avoid a sequence in which, during the early stages, foundation investment is bound to predominate. For such investment, which is essentially promotional and does not itself produce goods sold in the final market, the marketing difficulty in the normal sense does not exist. This investment also has the purpose of *creating* markets but by a different route than balanced growth, namely by creating conditions where subsequent individual projects become economically feasible as a result of lowering their real cost of production. Where the choice is between the simultaneous creation of complementary high-cost plants—high-cost for lack of skills, transport, power, etc.—on the one hand, and the improvement of transport, power, etc., combined with investment in such selected individual projects as have become economical as a result of lower real cost, on the other hand, who can doubt what the better resource allocation in an underdeveloped country is?

To summarize: In spite of its intellectually satisfying features, the doctrine of balanced economic growth has severe limitations in its applicability to underdeveloped countries. While it rightly insists on marketing difficulties as a cause of low-level equilibrium and rightly shows that the marketing difficulty can be overcome by a broadly based balanced investment program, it fails to come to direct grips with an even more fundamental problem of underdeveloped countries, i.e., the shortage of resources. It may be true that supply of goods—provided it is properly composed and properly balanced—will create its own demand. But supply of goods means demand for factors of production and especially for capital; and while supply of goods may create its own demand, unfortunately in underdeveloped countries demand for factors does not create its own supply. Worse, the demand for factors implied in the broadly based investment program must be in direct competition with other investment projects and other types of expenditure whose direct objective it is to increase available resources. If both types of investment could be undertaken simultaneously, all would be well, and the doctrine would be fully vindicated. But in that case the concept of balanced economic growth would have to be broadened considerably beyond what is normally implied. The doctrine would then come perilously close to saying, "If only the economic problem did not exist (i.e., if resources were not scarce and everything could be done simultaneously), then the problem of development could be solved." This is a somewhat unfair *reductio ad absurdum,* but it does bring out the severe limitations of the doctrine. The more urgent the problem of economic development is, the more the doctrine fails to apply. The more the doctrine applies, the more the problem of development is likely to take care of itself.

If the doctrine has merits in pointing out the marketing difficulty and in describing a way of making investment more productive, it also has dangers in that its inherent limitations may be ignored. The intellectual appeal of the doctrine, together with its direct association with the desired structural change, may lead countries to apply it even in situations of resource shortage and of resource inflexibility. In that case it will lead to policies which reduce rather than increase the productivity of investment. It will either lead to inflation, to a formulation of balanced investment packages on a very narrow geographical base, or to costly sacrifices of other types of investment on the altar of balanced growth. To return to our previous paraphrase: it is sound to advise underdeveloped countries to *think* big, i.e., in terms of aggregate national income accounts, but it may not be sound advice to tell them to *act* big or at any rate bigger than their resources permit.

It should be emphasized that the doubts that must attach to the doctrine of balanced growth refer to the applicability and operational value of the "wave of investments" or "balanced investment package" in underdeveloped countries, rather than to its intellectual validity or even to its operational value in the different circumstances assumed by Schumpeter in his *Theory of Economic Development*. Nurkse, for instance, who took a leading part in relating the Schumpeterian idea to the marketing deadlock in underdeveloped countries and thus evolved the idea of expanding markets by balanced investment packages, makes it abundantly clear that he is aware of the limitations here suggested. "There is no suggestion here that, by taking care of the demand side alone, any country could, as it were, lift itself up by its boot-straps. We have been considering one particular facet of our subject. The more fundamental difficulties that lie on the supply side have so far been kept off-stage for the sake of orderly discussion."[8] But our problem here is not orderly discussion: it is economic development. Our paper is called "Balanced Growth in Economic Development: Theory *and Practice*." The trouble with Nurkse's approach is that the remedy for the demand side that he proposes puts a particularly heavy strain on the supply side which in any case is the "fundamental difficulty," in his own words. It is perhaps a pity that the chapter entitled "The Size of the Market and the Inducement to Invest" should have been the first rather than the last chapter of his great book. This has given rise to some misunderstanding. Nor has this misunderstanding been confined to one side only. When Fleming raised the supply problem, Nurkse objected as follows: "The word 'growth' alone hints that something more is involved than, e.g., the rules of allocating a given factor stock (which, in their proper place, are not to be disparaged). This is all the more evident if attention is paid to the

[8] Ragnar Nurkse, *Problems of Capital Formation in Underdeveloped Countries,* Oxford, Fair Lawn, N.J., 1957, pp. 30–31.

context in which the balanced-growth idea has turned up in the literature. My own assumption, in Chapter I of my book, was that of a given labour force being equipped with an increased stock of capital."[9]

But Nurkse's assumption, so clearly stated in his last sentence, does not remove the objections. The fact is that even though we may assume that resources are available for net investment, so that "a given labour force is being equipped with an increased stock of capital," the additional capital still has to be carefully allocated, and the investment package will have to compete on its own merits together with other possible ways of utilizing "the increased stock of capital." It is by no means certain that the right strategy for an underdeveloped country is the "frontal attack of this sort—the wave of capital investments in a number of different industries"[10] that Nurkse writes about. Perhaps guerilla tactics are more suitable for the circumstances of underdeveloped countries than a frontal attack.

A BALANCED VIEW OF BALANCED GROWTH

We have described the doctrine of balanced growth as a possible solution and one with some educational merit for underdeveloped countries but, on the other hand, as an incomplete, implausible, and even potentially dangerous solution. Perhaps we should now amplify this judgement by standing back and taking a broader view of the problem involved. For this purpose, we may perhaps reintroduce the elementary sketch of an underdeveloped economy used before. Our little sketch tells us that there are several distinct roads to economic growth.

In the first place, and most obviously, there is the increase in productivity in agriculture. It is not unnatural that foreign missions to underdeveloped countries should emphasize this road to economic growth: any visitor to an underdeveloped country will observe, first, that the bulk of the population, about 80 per cent in our sketch, is employed in agriculture and, second, that agriculture is carried on at a particularly low level of productivity not only in relation to agriculture in more advanced countries but also in relation to other occupations in the same underdeveloped country. All this is described in our sketch. High productivity in agriculture must certainly be one of the main roads to economic growth. When it occurs, it would normally solve the marketing difficulty; the higher income of farmers will provide expanded markets for industries, and according to Engel's law, part of the additional demand is likely to be for nonagricultural products. Note, however, that the solution of the marketing difficulty through higher agricultural productivity is by no means automatic: where the high productivity results in a higher level of feeding for the extended

[9] "Balanced Growth on Static Assumptions," *Economic Journal,* vol. 66, p. 366, 1956.
[10] Nurkse, *Problems of Capital Formation in Underdeveloped Countries,* p. 13.

family of the subsistence farmer, it is still clearly a good thing—but it does not remove the marketing difficulty from the path of structural change. Where improvements in agricultural productivity occur in relation to commercial crops, and even more so where they occur in relation to export crops, we can be reasonably certain that such improvements will create preconditions for growth and enable us to dispense with the balanced investment package as a specific remedy for marketing troubles. Where agricultural productivity rises within a system of subsistence farming, it should normally be possible for an enlightened government to link this rise in productivity with institutional changes which would utilize it as a foundation of growth. For example, where the higher agricultural productivity is accompanied by the offer of "incentive goods" to farmers which will induce them to develop a propensity to "truck, barter, and exchange" as their output increases, growth becomes possible as a result. Furthermore, an increase in agricultural productivity, insofar as it releases labor from the farm, creates part of that elasticity of factor supply which makes the balanced investment package possible.

In the second place, there is improvement of productivity outside agriculture, and specifically in industry. There is plenty of evidence to show enormous scope for such improvement. It would indeed be surprising if it were otherwise, considering the lack of experience in handling capital, the scarcity of managerial skills, the absence of supporting managerial services and of external economies, the absence of maintenance and repair facilities, etc. We may perhaps add to this list the fact that the technology used is an alien growth imported from abroad, and has therefore not developed in line with the requirements and resource endowments of the underdeveloped countries. The pioneer study by the United Nations Economic Commission for Latin America[11] on cotton-textile industries may perhaps be mentioned as providing many illustrations of possible improvements in efficiency. Such improvements outside agriculture may be not so obvious, especially to the outside observer, as the need for higher productivity in agriculture. But even though agriculture may employ 70 to 80 per cent of the total population, it does not normally account for more than half the national income.[12] It follows that a given degree of improvement in the nonagricultural sectors will increase total real incomes by about as much as the same degree of agricultural improvement. Investments designed to raise nonagricultural productivity by lowering real cost curves will create markets where none existed before, and they do so without the need for a broadly based investment package.

[11] *Labour Productivity of the Cotton Textile Industry in Five Latin-American Countries,* UN Publication Sales No. 1951 II.G.2.
[12] In our structural sketch, agriculture provides 80 per cent of the employment but only 53 per cent (80 × ⅔) of the national income.

Third, the low-level-equilibrium deadlock of real incomes and markets exists only in a closed economy, or for the world as a whole. In any individual underdeveloped country with significant foreign trade—and that means nearly all underdeveloped countries—some of the markets lie abroad, and hence are not limited by the low domestic incomes. These markets are, of course, also limited: by real incomes abroad, by competition from possibly lower-cost competitors, by technological changes, by development of synthetics, etc. Furthermore, the notorious instability of world commodity prices may make markets abroad particularly hazardous for the specialized exporter. All the same, export promotion offers a historically and analytically most important method of bypassing the marketing deadlock, offering opportunities for economic growth without the balanced investment package.

Fourth, by the same token, a country engaged in foreign trade has established domestic markets presently supplied by imports from abroad. Import substitution, like export promotion, thus offers an opportunity of growth in happy disregard of the need for an investment package. The protective tariff has historically been a major alternative to the balanced investment package in the early stages of development. Arthur Lewis's *Report on the Industrialization of the Gold Coast* provides the *locus classicus* for this unbalanced yet effective approach.

Fifth, and related to the improvement of productivity, there is the approach to economic growth via the building up of the economic infrastructure. Here, investment in transport facilities is perhaps the most obvious alternative to the balanced investment package as a method of creating new markets. The absence of markets in underdeveloped countries is not merely a question of low real incomes; it is also a question of the specific economic framework and institutions in which the incomes are earned. If the division of labor depends on the extent of the market, the market in turn depends on the extent in which certain facilities are provided. Transport is the most obvious of these facilities. The doctrine of balanced economic growth is right in emphasizing the creation of markets as a key problem, but one can create markets by methods other than by inducing balanced demand. Infrastructure investment in underdeveloped countries is best considered as mainly of the "autonomous type" and as governed by final demand only in some rather vague, technological sense.

Sixth, and quite apart from foreign trade, it would be unrealistic to assume a state of perfect harmony—even the harmony of the deadlock—between markets and supplies. The doctrine of balanced growth seems to assume that in making decisions on the allocation of resources in an underdeveloped country, we start from scratch. That, of course, is not so. Rather, we start with a situation which incorporates the effects of previous investment and previous developments. This means that at any given point of time there are types of investment which are *not* in themselves balanced investment packages but which are complementary to existing investments, and thus bring the total stock of capital nearer balance. We must thus distinguish between balance as the end result at which to aim and balance as the method of approach. Where you start with imbalance, you need *further imbalance*[13] in order to come closer to balance.

It may be said that this still leaves the concept of the balanced investment package valid, only stretching it over several investment periods. The trouble is that life does not stand still. While we are aiming at better balance by unbalanced "bottleneck" investment, conditions change again and at the end of our investment period we are left with a new imbalance—with new bottlenecks which we then must try to remedy by a further set of unbalanced bottleneck projects. Thus, while we may be aiming at balance as an investment criterion, we achieve this objective by unbalanced investment. The ideal that we aim at constantly eludes us and has to be constantly pursued by methods which are not those recommended by the doctrine of balanced growth. The metaphor of the man chasing a rabbit from a point sideways to the path of the rabbit has been used in other branches of economics, but it is also apposite here. The hunter is governed by the path of the rabbit, but by directing his own path at each moment directly at the moving objective he will in fact describe an erratic path, quite different from that of the rabbit itself. It is suggested here that the path of economic development is more like that of the hunter than that of the rabbit streaking in a straight line to its refuge. The situations where the balanced investment package is appropriate would be at the two extremes: where investment starts entirely from scratch, on the one hand, and where development continues from such a high level that existing bottlenecks are relatively unimportant, on the other.

We have now described six alternative approaches other than those singled out by the doctrine of balanced growth. Each of these alternative approaches could conceivably, if successfully pursued, resolve the marketing deadlock which gave origin to the doctrine of balanced growth. Thus balanced growth should be judged not as the sole cure for the evil correctly diagnosed but as one of several possible cures. Which of the various cures will be the most appropriate will then depend on specific situations, more particularly on the total volume of available resources. In this respect, the specific cure of the balanced investment package does not compare well in the early stages of development because it requires large resources—in fact, larger resources than most expositions of the doctrine seem to realize. The balanced investment package cannot logically be confined to a group of projects which are self-supporting on the demand side; the package must include investment in agriculture and in the infrastructure. The cure is not

---

[13] Professor Lerner suggests to me the terms "re-balance" and "disimbalance"—by analogy with reflation and disinflation.

only far from being the sole cure; it is also an expensive cure and one which is most effective when taken as a mixture with other prescriptions.

But having thus defined the limitations of the doctrine, we are now perhaps in a better position also to appreciate its merits. The combination of self-supporting projects can serve to raise the productivity of investment. In particular, it can prevent the creation of white elephants—projects without a market—which dot the landscape in so many underdeveloped countries as standing monuments to folly and waste. As between alternative appropriations of *given* resources, the balanced investment package has an inherent superiority—wherever the available resources are sufficient for such a package.

There is another lesson which we can learn from the doctrine of balanced growth. The inducement to invest will be greatly increased by anticipation of expanding markets and expanding incomes. Inflationary expectations are one way of raising the inducement to invest; an expectation of real growth would be just as effective—perhaps more effective. It is not sufficient for complementary investment which will provide markets actually to go forward; it is also necessary that it should be seen or known, or at least assumed, to go forward. For this reason, in any development program of an underdeveloped country it is crucially important to create a general sense of moving forward. The very formulation of development programs may be helpful in creating such a sense of moving forward; more specifically, I believe that this is one of the most important effects of the community development movement in India. Balanced growth can play a part in improving what in trade-cycle theory is perhaps rather vaguely called "the state of business confidence." A low-level deadlock of incomes and markets can be due to excessive self-justifying pessimism concerning future markets, particularly where there is a long history of stagnation or economic troubles. It is, however, not so easy for excessive optimism to be self-justifying; the inexorable limitation of resources stands in the way. Where the low-level equilibrium has been determined by excessive pessimism rather than by resource limitation, the doctrine of balanced growth acquires considerable theoretical as well as practical merits.

Finally, let us remember that the objections to the doctrine of balanced growth will be greatly reduced and finally vanish as the available resources increase in the course of economic growth. Thus interpreted, the doctrine should stimulate underdeveloped countries to undertake the necessary sacrifices in the early stages of development; it promises them that one day when resources have become big enough, balanced investment packages will become possible. When they have labored to the top, the balanced investment package will help them to "coast down the other side of the hill," into the promised land of cumulative growth and compound interest.

6

Obstacles to
Economic Development

The one consistent body of thought which has so far been presented as a "theory of economic development" is, of course, Schumpeter's
book of that title. This theory is a good basis for a survey of the general
obstacles to economic development, not because it applies to underdeveloped
countries but because it fails to apply. The reasons why it fails to apply are
what is significant.

The differences between Schumpeter's theory and what can be
observed in underdeveloped countries have been strikingly summarized by
Prof. Henry C. Wallich of Yale University, in a paper entitled "Some Notes
Towards a Theory of Derived Development," presented in Havana in 1952.[1]
He finds the following three main differences, which will be used as the
springboard for the present analysis, though he should not be held responsible
for this use made of his classification.

First, the agents of economic development, in Schumpeter's
theory, are the innovating and pioneering private entrepreneurs, but in the
economic development of underdeveloped countries the agency is much more
likely to be the government. Innovating private entrepreneurs either are
conspicuously absent or are unable to operate within a framework in which
the public prerequisites—ranging from law and order to essential public
utilities—are lacking.

Second, the method by which development is brought about is,
according to Schumpeter, changes in production functions through the introduction of new pioneering techniques, used either for the development of
new products or for new ways of producing old established products. In the
present underdeveloped countries, however, economic development proceeds
not by way of new technologies but through the introduction and adaptation
of old established technologies to the production of old established products
familiar in the countries that are now developed.

[1] A paper presented at the Third Meeting of Central Bank Technicians
of the American Continent, Havana, 1952. Reprinted in A. N. Agarwala and S. P.
Singh, *The Economics of Underdevelopment,* Oxford, Fair Lawn, N.J., 1958, pp.
189–204.

This paper was originally published in *Social Research,* vol. 20, no. 1,
Spring 1953.

Third, the generating force of economic development, in Schumpter's thinking lies in the sphere of supply—in the supply of new goods, or in the increased supply of old established goods, or in the lowering of supply price in relation to market price, and the consequent opening up of profits for the pioneering private entrepreneurs. In the present underdeveloped countries, however, the generating force lies much more in the sphere of demand—in the desire for increased consumption, derived from the known gap between the consumption standards of the countries that are developed and those that are not. According to the Schumpeter system, the changes on the supply side are the cause, and the increase in consumption is the effect, almost the incidental effect. But in underdeveloped countries the desire for increased consumption is the cause, and the change in supply functions must result if the desire for increased consumption is to be fulfilled.

This is a useful picture to bear in mind for a first approach. We are faced not with the private entrepreneur adding to the supply of goods by the application of revolutionary technologies—the model of earlier economic development—but with the problems confronted by governments trying to give effect to a desire for higher consumption by introducing and adapting known technologies from other countries. Many of the handicaps to economic development are implied even in this simple model. It will now be considered more fully in its three main aspects.

GOVERNMENTS INSTEAD OF ENTREPRENEURS

The substitution of government for the private entrepreneur has obvious drawbacks. In the first place, where governmental resources are limited— whether in terms of trained personnel or in terms of financial resources or in any other way—the lack of innovating individuals to serve as agents may divert governments from their normal duties into "the promotion of economic development." Governmental resources may be too weak to shoulder simultaneously such duties—themselves essential for economic development—as the maintenance of law and order; the establishment of confidence in monetary, banking, and general economic institutions; the provision of continuity; impartial and uncorrupt application of laws and regulations; the maintenance of industrial peace; and on top of all that, the manifold duties of the main agent of economic development. Where this is the case, the one duty can be discharged only at the expense of the other—a self-defeating process. Where governments, in attempts to "promote economic development," fail to discharge their primary duties, the result will very probably be not economic development but its absence.

Moreover, the establishment of government as the main agency of economic development throws an enormous burden on the quality of administration, which unfortunately is itself largely a function of economic development. Here may be seen one of many vicious circles that impede development in underdeveloped countries. Development requires good administration, yet good administration is itself a result of economic development. It is not, of course, a necessary result, for some highly developed countries have very bad administration. The difference is that once development has been achieved, bad administration can be afforded as a luxury, while where administration is poor from the beginning, economic development is made more difficult if the government becomes its main agency, whether by choice or because of the absence of innovating entrepreneurs.

In any event, where government serves this function, the problem of drawing up development programs and plans becomes of great importance, but the preparation of a development program of the right kind and size and its implementation are themselves considerable administrative achievements. Thus the failure of administration to carry the enormous double burden placed upon it in the non-Schumpeterian world of underdeveloped countries, emerges as a serious obstacle to economic development.

One of the preconditions of that process is, therefore, the improvement of public administration. It is no accident that this plays a considerable part in international technical assistance programs. Unfortunately, however, there is only one way to improve administration: by administrative action. It takes good administration to improve bad administration. Here is another vicious circle that creates deadlocks and obstructions.

Still another, and perhaps an even more important, drawback in the substitution of government for the private entrepreneur is the fact that where government is the main agent of economic development, the immediate economic objectives are likely to become mixed up with national assertion abroad and with the distribution of political power at home. Government is the expression of the organized political will of the community, and in underdeveloped countries that often means it is the expression of a vigorous nationalism. But nationalism is ambivalent in regard to economic development: while it provides a driving force and a motivation, it contains within itself features that may be an obstacle.

Nationalism may take the form of clinging to established and traditional institutions, and thus prevent the reform or adaptation of institutions which may be a precondition for economic development. It may prevent the very taking over and adaptation of technologies developed abroad which, in the absence of new technologies, is the only possible method. It may distort the balance and sequences in economic development if particular sectors of economic life—the traditional steel mill perhaps—become imbued with special symbolic importance. It may result in the allocation of a high proportion of natural resources to the maintenance of large armies or police forces, or to the construction of monumental works, thus draining resources away from genuine economic development. In short, the association of national aspirations and economic development carries dangers that do not enter into Schumpeter's system, and at least some of the difficulties of non-Schumpeterian development are derived from this association.

The substitution of the state for the innovating entrepreneur is not always, of course, a matter of choice. It may be—and in the present underdeveloped countries it often is—a matter of necessity. The innovating entrepreneurs assumed in Schumpeter's system simply do not exist. And this brings up another reason why that system—and other theories of development as well—is not applicable to the present problems of underdeveloped countries: innovating entrepreneurs are in part the result of a different society from that which now exists in most such countries, for to some extent they are themselves the result and product of economic development. Thus the building up of a private sector, and thereby of private entrepreneurs, is a recognized goal of many governmental development programs. The declared intention is gradually to shift emphasis in economic development from the public sector to the private sector, from public initiative to private initiative, from public finance to private finance.

From this point of view the Schumpeter system is not really a theory of economic development, in the sense of a theory of how such development starts. Rather, it is a theory of how economic development continues and proceeds, once it has reached a certain stage characterized by the creation of innovating private entrepreneurs, and by the creation of the kind of society in which they can operate.

This is not a criticism of Schumpeter's system, since it was never put forward as a theory of how economic development starts from very low income levels. But in finding the reasons that explain why it is not applicable, we obtain valuable insights. Thus it becomes clear that the agents of economic development—whether public administrators of the required quality, or private entrepreneurs—are themselves to some extent the product and end result of such development. Here is truly a vicious circle for countries whose problem is to start development, rather than to continue it.

TRANSFERRED TECHNOLOGY INSTEAD OF TECHNOLOGICAL CHANGE

In their attempt to develop economically, underdeveloped countries have to make use of a technology that has been evolved, over a lengthy period of time, in countries that are much higher on the economic scale. This is most dramatically evident in the technical assistance programs, in which the transfer of technology from the more highly developed to the underdeveloped countries is explicitly organized. To say that the more developed countries have a practical monopoly of industrial and scientific research, and of productive experience with modern technologies, is true almost by definition.

Modern technology—which is equivalent to technology evolved by and for industrialized countries—is both deliberately and innately determined by the requirements and factor endowment of industrialized countries. In particular, it is shaped by the underlying assumption that capital is abundant, that labor is relatively scarce, and that wage rates are correspondingly high. This assumption of a relative abundance of capital has three major effects on the evolution of technology.

In the first place, it results in a rapid evolution of new and superior technologies, and in a correspondingly rapid scrapping of capital goods embodying only slightly inferior older technologies. In the second place, technology is strongly directed toward labor-saving devices, and toward a substitution of capital for direct labor. And in the third place, which is perhaps most important, the application of modern technology requires those levels of scientific training and understanding, and those levels of education, which have now percolated widely in industrial societies.

Even in industrialized countries this particular direction of technological development creates certain problems. This is true particularly in times of unemployment and depression, when the underlying assumption of a relative labor shortage is less true (although even at the bottom of a depression labor in an industrialized country still tends to be scarcer, in relative terms, than it is in underdeveloped countries). The leaning of technological research toward a rapid introduction of new technologies may create or intensify technological unemployment, because of its tendency toward labor-saving devices; similarly, the leaning toward a rapid scrapping of capital goods embodying slightly inferior technologies may lead to business losses and bankruptcies in times when effective demand is not sufficiently high to enable producers to amortize their capital equipment ahead of technical obsolescence. With these qualifications, however, the direction of technological research is by and large in accord with the conditions of the countries in and for which it has developed.

But this does not apply to the underdeveloped countries. For them, a different technology, and in many ways an older or "inferior" one, would be more appropriate. Their factor endowment is defined by an acute shortage of capital and a relative abundance of labor, sometimes an acute abundance of labor. In many respects the technology of a hundred years ago would be desirable for them, and would make their economic development easier. But that technology no longer exists. It has been scrapped, and rightly scrapped, in the industrialized countries—and the technology of the industrialized countries is the only existing technology.

It was possible for an old industrial country like Britain to start off with a cheap technology requiring few and simple capital goods, and to develop technically in step with its changing factor endowments. Thus technology and economic possibilities were kept in harmony throughout.

Countries next succeeding Britain in economic development, such as the United States or Germany, benefited even more, perhaps, in getting the best of both worlds. On the one hand, they avoided some of the inevitable blind alleys and experimental costs of evolving an industrial technology; on the other hand, technology had not yet sufficiently advanced to be out of line with their factor endowment in the earliest stage of their economic development. This is particularly true of the United States, where there was a relative labor shortage even in the early stages.

The countries that are now in a state of underdevelopment are in a worse position. Technology has reached a point far remote from those countries' natural factor endowment and natural requirements. It is not open to them to develop their technologies harmoniously with their degree of economic development. This is true as long as they do not have their own technologies—and absence of an original technology is, contrary to the Schumpeter system, a characteristic of underdeveloped countries. Up to a point, it may have been an advantage to be a latecomer in economic development, but by now it has clearly turned into a serious disadvantage.

A capital-intensive technology—which is the only one now existing—affects underdeveloped economies in a variety of ways. These may be summarily listed as follows:

First, the initial expense of any investment is very high, and thus the scanty resources of underdeveloped countries are insufficient for a balanced type of development, which is the only kind that is reasonably productive.

Second, the elaborate and highly expensive capital goods in which modern technology is incorporated are too difficult to produce in under-developed countries, and therefore have to be imported. This puts pressure on those countries' foreign exchange, and it makes equipment expensive to them, through the added cost requirements associated with dispatch, transport, and installation.

Third, the labor-saving faculty of modern technology is largely wasted in underdeveloped countries, because alternative employment opportunities are lacking—and are indeed prevented by the very expense of the tech-nological investment. This factor greatly reduces the social productivity of new investment in such countries.

Fourth, the effective life of the expensive equipment in which modern technology is incorporated is often much shorter in underdeveloped countries than in those that are industrialized. For this there are various reasons, such as that operation is less careful, that there are lower standards of maintenance and care in use, that repair facilities are inaccessible.[2]

---

[2] This may apply even to such simple equipment as ordinary ploughs. Often the ploughs manufactured in Britain, for instance, are not especially reinforced at the rear, as the farmers are expected to lift them when taking them around a corner; moreover, fields in Britain are supposed to be sufficiently large te reduce the rela-tive amount of curved ploughing. But in India or Pakistan neither of these assump-tions is satisfied, and ploughs may be ruined after a short time, through the farmers'

Thus the absence of a technology which is at the same time modern (in the sense of incorporating the latest contributions of scientific knowledge) and in harmony with the factor endowment of underdeveloped countries must be classed as another major obstacle to economic development. Those countries, in adopting the technology of industrialized countries, *faute de mieux,* place themselves at a great disadvantage from the very start.

Underdeveloped countries have often diagnosed this disadvantage as merely an ailment of infancy, and have applied the medicine proper to the ailments of economic infants: protective tariffs. But the trouble is thus only augmented. Protective tariffs may saddle underdeveloped countries with permanently high-cost projects which constitute a continuing drain on national resources and thus prevent the very development they are supposed to promote. Often, however, there is no real alternative. The only remedy would be the development of a different kind of technology, and this is beyond the resources of underdeveloped countries. This is indeed a formidable dilemma.

INCREASED CONSUMPTION INSTEAD OF LOWER PRODUCTION COST

In the Schumpeter model of economic development the rise in real incomes is originated by a lowering of real-cost functions, that is, by innovations on the supply side. With the increase in real incomes there is an increase in standards of living and in levels of consumption. In the non-Schumpeterian world of underdeveloped countries the increase in real incomes and in levels of consumption is the immediate objective. Changes in techniques of production and in the field of supply are accepted and introduced only as means to that end.

The first consequence of this difference is that the connection between the rise in real incomes and the necessary changes on the supply side is not always clearly recognized. Combined with the ardent desire to "develop" and to achieve higher levels of living, there is sometimes a refusal—incompatible with that desire—to accept the social changes and institutional reforms that are the preconditions of changed supply techniques, and even sometimes a refusal to accept the changed supply techniques themselves.

This obstacle to economic development—a desire for levels of consumption out of line with the actually achieved technology of supply—is

---

failure to lift them and through constant curved ploughing on tiny fields; small technical adjustments might, of course, make a great difference in the life of the equipment. The same situation is found in regard to self-lubricating bearings, for in many underdeveloped countries the standards of lubrication are low. As a third example may be cited the adaptation of machinery to tropical climates. Most equipment and fuel is designed for optimum performance in temperate climates, since those are the climates in which practically all industrial countries are situated.

closely related to the change in method from original to transferred technology, discussed in the preceding section. It is very much easier to transfer a knowledge of higher levels of consumption achieved elsewhere, and to instigate a desire to imitate those levels, than to transfer technologies, or knowledge of the things that are back of the higher levels of consumption. Moreover, while the higher levels of consumption are generally acceptable, the things back of them, even where recognized, are not always equally acceptable.[3]

Modern media of mass communication, such as films and magazines, have spread knowledge of "the American way of life" throughout the underdeveloped countries, and particularly through their middle and upper classes. But the image thus spread is one of high living à la Hollywood, rather than an image of the hard pace of work in the factories of Detroit and Pittsburgh, or in the fields of Iowa, or in the offices of New York and San Francisco. It is easy to show pictures of such end products as shiny cars, television sets, and the like, but it is not at all easy to show pictures of the skill of those who make these gadgets—not excluding the skill of owners of shiny cars in repairing and maintaining their cars themselves. Thus the receivers of the image, while admiring the end product, are likely to ignore what goes into it.

It is worth mentioning that this tendency is noticeable even in Western Europe, where attempts to reach American standards of real income are so much more hopeful, and where the desire to emulate American standards of productivity as well as of consumption is so much more clear-cut. There is little reluctance to emulate "the American way of life" in terms of its end products, but there is a good deal of reluctance to accept "the American way of life" on the supply side: the ruthlessness of competition, the hectic nature of life, the emphasis on material things. It would seem that desire for the ends should imply also a certain degree of acceptance of the means by which they are brought about.

The technical assistance programs, whether conducted under Point 4 through the United Nations, or otherwise, may be regarded as an attempt —and, so far, an attempt made with insufficient means and insufficient force in comparison with the media of mass communication—to spread knowledge of supply methods at the same time as knowledge of consumption standards. The more successful these programs, the more will the discrepancy be reduced between the awareness of consumption possibilities and the understanding of production possibilities.

Again, as in the problem of original versus transferred technology, the importance of this obstacle to economic development may be seen by

[3] This point of view strongly pervades the United Nations report (E/1986) *Measures for the Economic Development of Under-developed Countries* (New York, 1951); see in particular chapters III and IV, on "Pre-conditions of Economic Development" and "Economic Organization."

contemplating what British economic development in the early nineteenth century might have been if it had occurred under non-Schumpeterian conditions. Would that development have proceeded so quickly, would it have proceeded at all, if the population had known of another country full of dream gadgets à la Hollywood? If radios, television sets, vacuum cleaners, automobiles, films, mass-circulation magazines had existed? If Adam Smith, in Chapter I, Book I, of *Wealth of Nations,* had started off not with a description of a needle factory but with a description of a beckoning life of ease?

Much light has been thrown on this obstacle to economic development—although from a somewhat different angle—by Prof. Ragnar Nurkse[4] According to his view, the "demonstration effect" exercised by the high consumption standards of industrialized countries, through modern media of mass communication, has a discouraging influence on the rate of savings and domestic capital formation in underdeveloped countries. The pressure of a constant desire to enjoy standards of consumption in excess of standards of production accounts also for widespread inflationary pressure throughout these countries—itself disruptive of economic development—and tends to disrupt their balances of payments and their foreign-exchange stability.

If the argument of a preceding section is accepted, it would appear that the "demonstration effect" is part of the changeover from the Schumpeter model of economic development to the non-Schumpeterian world. Innovating individuals are not motivated by any desire to improve general standards of consumption. They desire only to improve their own standards, by means of profits, and there is only one way of doing that: by changes on the supply side. But the government of a country, and the individuals—not as innovating entrepreneurs but as voters and political animals—are greatly agitated by the spectacle of higher consumption standards elsewhere and the promise of higher consumption standards at home.

Increased concern with general consumption standards is by no means confined to underdeveloped countries. The tendency toward a "welfare state" is found in advanced countries as well, although in different degrees. The difference is that in the wealthier countries we now witness a process of "derived welfare," that is, welfare derived from previous and genuinely Schumpeterian development, whereas in the poorer countries we have a movement of "original welfare," not based on or derived from previous development. Where a trend toward "welfare" is the fruit of economic

[4] See particularly "Some International Aspects of the Problem of Economic Development," in *Proceedings* of the American Economic Association, Boston meeting, 1951, pp. 571–83, and *Some Aspects of Capital Accumulation in Under-developed Countries* (Cairo, 1952), especially pp. 36–52. Professor Nurkse's views are an application to the international plane of arguments developed in connection with domestic consumption and saving propensities in industrialized countries by James S. Duesenberry, in *Income, Saving and the Theory of Consumer Behavior* (Cambridge, Mass., 1949).

development, that trend is consonant with continued development, and to some extent even favorable to it. But where an attempt is made to start with welfare, the effort may inhibit economic growth and be a formidable obstacle to economic development.[5]

Where non-Schumpeterian development starts off with higher consumption, it puts the cart before the horse. In the Schumpeterian world the horse is before the cart, and it is not surprising that movement there is easier, and is indeed taken for granted.

[5] On the futility of treating social welfare as the seed rather than the fruit of economic progress, see H. W. Singer, "Economic Progress in Underdeveloped Countries," *Social Research,* vol. 16, pp. 1–11, March, 1949.

7

Education and
Economic Development

Up to the Second World War, economists—from Adam Smith to John Maynard Keynes—were practically unanimous in forecasting that economic growth in the more developed countries would first slow down and then come to a standstill. Although they were agreed in this conclusion, the reasoning which led them to it was very diverse, including diminishing returns in agriculture (Ricardo), demographic improvidence (Malthus), collapsing markets and purchasing power and growing inequalities of income distribution (Marx), the dying out of the entrepreneurial spirit or the environment in which entrepreneurs flourish (Schumpeter), exhaustion of natural resources (Jevons), and the exhaustion of investment opportunities and a fall in the marginal productivity in new capital into the bottomless pit of the liquidity trap (Keynes).

These great economic thinkers also disagreed in that some of them viewed the coming of the stationary state with satisfaction—as the dawn of civilization and a new golden age or as the birth of a new social order —whereas others viewed the coming of the stationary state with alarm—as a time of trouble, chaos, and possible collapse. The interesting point to note is how closely the various reasons given for a slowing down of progress in developed countries resemble the reasons which nowadays, in the postwar decade or two, give us so much concern, not for the continuation of progress in developed countries, but rather for the achievement or starting of progress in the underdeveloped countries: low productivity in agriculture, the population explosion, the lack of markets, the absence of managerial and entrepeneurial talent, low productivity of capital due to lack of infrastructure, etc.

It is surely one of the most dramatic reversals in the history of human thought that at present we have thrown overboard the belief in a coming stationary state for the developed countries and replaced it by a picture of a possibility of indefinite progress, whereas all the "dismal" elements have

This paper was prepared for a Conference of African States on the Development of Education in Africa, jointly organized and convened by the United Nations Educational, Scientific and Cultural Organization and the United Nations Economic Commission for Africa, held in Addis Ababa in May, 1961. It as printed in the final report of the conference, UNESCO Document ED-181.

become transferred in our thinking from the mature, developed countries to the underdeveloped countries. When we ask ourselves the reasons for this dramatic change of views, we are beginning to approach the heart of the matter which is the subject of this conference, namely the relationship of education and economic development.

BRAIN POWER, RESEARCH, AND PROGRESS

Broadly speaking, the new factor which has upset our belief in the coming stationary state and replaced it with a picture of continuing progress, once a certain "take-off stage" has been passed, can be summarized in the terms "technical progress" and "human capital." For instance, John Maynard Keynes—after demonstrating that given enlightened economic policies, deficiencies of effective demand need not be an obstacle to full employment—firmly believed that even if full employment were successfully maintained, the marginal efficiency of capital accumulation would continually fall and ultimately come to a standstill, and with it economic progress in the ordinary sense. In fact Keynes went as far as to predict that this would be the case within one or two generations. (Presumably he had Great Britain in mind.) If this belief has vanished from our thinking and been replaced by the opposite picture, it is because we now contemplate an economic system in which technical progress and the increasing efficiency of production constantly create new investment opportunities at the same or a faster pace than that at which existing investment opportunities are being used up by capital accumulation. In the mature industrial economies of Europe and North America, progress has become, as it were, a definite industry. Progress, as it is often put, has become a "built-in" feature of the economy, and as a result, economic "miracles" of growth abound and are sustained, especially in the European countries and Japan.

This new insight has been made possible by a shift in our whole thinking about the problem of growth and development. The fundamental problem is no longer considered to be the creation of wealth, but rather the creation of the *capacity* to create wealth. Once a society has acquired this capacity to create wealth, the creation of wealth itself becomes almost incidental; it follows quasi-automatically.

What is the capacity to create wealth? Essentially, it resides in the *people* of a country. It consists of *brain power;* it is based upon the application of systematic research to the problems of production and of the best organization of the economic institutions of a country—research systematically pursued and systematically applied. The history of postwar years has shown that given this underlying capacity and systematic application of research, economies can make up for gaps or destruction in their physical capital equipment in a surprisingly short time. The history of the postwar era also shows that systematic application of brain power seems to transcend in its importance for economic growth the distinctions between different economic and social systems, however important and fundamental these differences may be in other respects.

One facet of this development of research and brain power as a built-in growth element is the systematic expenditure of about 1½ to 2 per cent of the national income on "research and development" (excluding military research and development). Where this is done in a society in which a willingness and capacity to apply the results of this expenditure exists, and where the educational level of the population makes this application with its necessary adjustments possible, this level of expenditure seems to be sufficient to create a flow of new investment opportunities that can maintain the productivity of new capital accumulation at a high level, even though capital accumulation itself proceeds at the high rate of 15 to 20 per cent of the national income, i.e., ten times the expenditure on research and development. Thus, the rate of preinvestment expenditure on research and development (not counting the cost of education itself) in progressive mature economies stands to total investment in the general ratio of 10 per cent. In the underdeveloped countries, total new investment is presently of the order of magnitude of about 10 billion dollars per annum, but it ought to be of the order of magnitude of 20 billion dollars per annum to convert them into progressive economies. This means that preinvestment expenditure on the creation of new investment opportunities in the underdeveloped countries (not counting the cost of education) should be of the order of magnitude of about 2 billion dollars per annum. The actual figure is only a fraction of this sum, and so are the international resources available to aid the underdeveloped countries in this purpose.

Two points are important to note. First of all, such a systematic expenditure on brain power and the application of its results to production is not subject to the Law of Diminishing Returns. Quite on the contrary, it is governed by increasing returns. In any individual piece of research the early expenditure may merely serve to rule out certain possibilities. In that sense, money on "unsuccessful" research is wasted only if it is not followed up by further expenditure which can then be concentrated on the areas which the previous "failures" have shown to be more promising. It is typical of research expenditure that one can learn from one's mistakes. More important even is the second point, that as our total body of knowledge extends, the linkage effects of any new additions to our stock of knowledge are multiplied. New knowledge links up with previous new knowledge to produce quite unexpected new combinations of progress. Even more startling, new knowledge links up with previous failure and converts it into success.

Certainly, with the systematic pursuit of expenditures on new knowledge applied to production, the elements of the lucky break, the haphazard, and the "brain wave" are more or less removed. The law of large numbers begins to apply when thousands of research projects are going forward simultaneously. Although one *cannot* be certain at all in advance which projects in particular will bear fruit, yet one *can* be reasonably certain about the proportion which will bear fruit and about the approximate total effects. This is what is meant when we say that in a progressive economy the production of knowledge has become a more or less predictable annual industry. In fact, it has become the growth industry, or the "leading sector," par excellence.

This view of economic growth and progress is strongly supported by recent results of economic and statistical research. It has invariably been found that of the total increases in output over longer periods, only a minor part can be attributed to increased physical inputs, such as more labor, more physical capital, and more natural resources. The greater part of the increase is attributable to nonphysical factors, broadly described as technical progress or increases in the productivity of the physical factors. Different economists have expressed this result in different terminology. Some say that this shows the importance of the intangible and human factors in production; others prefer to say that the production function is not linear and homogeneous but that at certain stages of growth economies seem to enter upon an era of increasing returns which is due to both external and internal economies of production. This apparent controversy, however, really conceals an underlying identity of views, namely that the capacity of the economy to absorb and apply increasing knowledge rapidly and diffuse it throughout the economic system is capable of offsetting any tendencies toward the stationary state or toward diminishing returns and is able instead to produce considerable and comparatively frictionless economic growth.

In fact, the possibilities inherent in systematically produced and built-in technical progress are now so highly rated, as a result of the evidence which has come to light, that not only would very few economists now agree that the marginal efficiency schedule of capital is likely to fall and net investment therefore likely to decline or disappear, but even beyond this, most economists would now say that even if net investment should in fact disappear, this would by no means be the end of economic progress, as was taken almost for granted before the Second World War. Since most of the progress of the more developed countries is statistically attributed to nonphysical inputs (either changes in production function or increasing returns within the production function, according to the predilection of individual economists), it follows that *even without new capital accumulation,* rates of economic progress are still possible which are much higher than the rates actually experienced in most underdeveloped countries, even with increased labor inputs and capital accumulation.

In any case, technical progress via increased knowledge is embodied in *gross* investment rather than *net* investment. When a given piece of capital is replaced by value, this does not represent new capital accumulation; but the new piece of capital will represent a more advanced state of knowledge and be designed for operation in a more efficient organization and with a more efficient labor force. Hence, even without capital accumulation, technical progress is embodied also in capital replacement. The fact that in economies with technological progress, capital replacement does not wait for physical obsolescence but is undertaken as a direct result of technological progress adds further force to this line of thinking.

Of the total investment in research and development which in advancing economies amounts to about 10 per cent of total investment, or 1½ to 2 per cent of the national income, about one-third consists of the cost of training the scientific and other high-level professional personnel required for research and development. To that extent the problems of education and training, on the one hand, and of financing research and development, on the other hand, overlap. This means that about ½ to 1 per cent of the national income ought to be spent on the training of scientific and other highly technical research personnel. We may take this figure in conjunction with the estimated cost of training one such highly qualified person, which was calculated for Nigeria[1] as approximately $13,000 per person exclusive of capital expenditure and about $15,000 per person inclusive of capital expenditure. If underdeveloped countries, like developed countries, could spend ½ to 1 per cent of their national incomes on such training and did not encounter any other bottlenecks, it should be possible for the underdeveloped countries as part of a program of general expansion to double the number of such highly trained people in relation to the general population within the next ten years. While this would still leave the corresponding figure far below the present ratio in the more developed countries, it would at least be the beginning of a process of having progress "built into" the economic system of the underdeveloped countries.

Beyond the financing of research and development with its associated cost of training of scientific and related personnel there looms the much larger cost of general and vocational education and training. If the present United States figure be taken as a standard, the cost of elementary education in 1956 formed 9 per cent of the total cost of gross physical capital formation; the cost of high school education was 13 per cent of that of gross physical capital formation; the cost of higher education was 12 per cent of that of gross physical capital formation.[2] The total cost of education in all its forms therefore added up to 34 per cent of the cost of gross physical capital formation (the 1956 figure which would be higher now); 34 per cent of gross physical capital formation is equivalent to about 50 per cent of net investment or capital accumulation. In a progressive economy, this should

---

[1] "Investment in Education," report of the Ashby Committee based on the Harbison survey.

[2] Theodore W. Schultz, "Capital Formation by Education," *Journal of Political Economy*, December, 1960.

amount to about 7 to 8 per cent of the national income. This measures the burden of a full program of education and human capital formation in an underdeveloped country. It would be larger than the total domestic savings rate in most underdeveloped countries of today.

BUILDING HUMAN CAPITAL IN UNDERDEVELOPED COUNTRIES

Most of the cost of educational investment consists of the loss of time and hence of earnings by high school students, students in higher education, and full-time trainees. Considered this way, education is true investment in the pure sense, i.e., a sacrifice of production now for the sake of higher production in the future. A number of calculations have been made relating to the yield of the investment in education in terms of the additional earnings of individuals as a result of the educational investment made in them. Such calculations have invariably shown that educational investment is at least as productive as physical capital investment. Since the earnings differential of individuals after education is almost certainly an understatement of the contribution of educated persons to the national product—as they raise also the productivity of the less educated—the productivity of educational investment is in fact considerably higher than the average yield of physical investment.

In underdeveloped countries, where the loss of time of persons going through the process of education is less highly valued than in developed countries and the yield differential between skilled and trained people and others is much higher than in developed countries, the yield of educational investment is bound to be even higher than in developed countries. This, of course, is based on the assumption that the educational output is adjusted to the needs of the economic system and that the graduates and trainees will obtain jobs corresponding to their training and can make a proper contribution to national production.

The educational basis is an absolute precondition for the fruitful application of research and development to the process of production. It is only where the working force at all levels is sufficiently literate, educated, trained, and mobile to take advantage of new advances in techniques and organization of production that the creation of a built-in industry of progress becomes possible. Even so, a built-in industry of progress—involving as it does the expenditure of 7 to 8 per cent of the national income in educational investment, the expenditure of 1½ to 2 per cent of the national income on research and development, and the expenditure of ½ per cent of the national income on the training of scientific personnel, in addition to far-reaching adjustments in social outlook and adaptability—is evidently a matter which in underdeveloped countries cannot be achieved overnight. It is probably best thought of as a long-term objective to be achieved over three or four generations.

This, of course, leaves open many questions of more immediate educational policy. As in other branches of development planning, the problem is that so many things have to be done at the same time. The productivity of new capital investment has to be raised immediately by providing the complementary inputs of trained workers who are taken for granted in the more developed countries. The more obvious gaps in the ranks of business administrators and technicians, both private and public, have to be filled. The educational basis of literacy has to be created, or at least started. Educational institutions, especially in the field of secondary and higher education, have to be created. Above all, the essential first step of teacher training has to be taken.

This situation of a choice having to be made between many different things which all need doing is a familiar situation to the economist in underdeveloped countries. On the question of weighing the more immediate requirements against the necessary long-term planning no general pronouncements can be made. Where resources are limited, it makes sense—since a choice has to be made in any case—to select those projects in educational investment which make the greatest short-term contribution to economic output, provided this does not interfere with the long-term development of the educational system. This principle of selecting educational investment which, *other things being equal,* is also economically most productive does not seem in any way to deduct from the long-term importance of educational investment or from the fact that education is of great value in itself and that its role in a progressive society is not exhaustively measured by a direct cost/benefit analysis. To illustrate: where the introduction of general elementary education cannot be made in the whole country simultaneously, there seems no harm in selecting for priority development those regions and areas of the country where economic development is expected to be more strongly concentrated, e.g., in a river-valley region where a good deal of physical and agricultural investment is expected to take place.

The educational deficiencies of underdeveloped countries can, in the short run, be dealt with by measures other than the development of an educational system. Apart from the employment of foreign experts and technicians, which can provide temporary solutions, it is also possible to substitute for lacking skills by mechanization. Some economists have pointed out that while underdeveloped countries are short of capital, they are even shorter of skills, so that more capital-intensive or even automated methods of production which reduce the amount of skills required would be appropriate to the conditions of underdeveloped countries. Although on occasion it may be inevitable to follow this line in order to get something vital done or to get a crucial bottleneck removed, generally this is shortsighted advice. It is shortsighted because it perpetuates the disadvantage of underdeveloped countries which have low marginal productivity of capital because of the absence of skills. It prevents the underdeveloped countries from developing a technology of production appropriate to their resource endowment, developing the learning process, and adjusting their resource endowment and technique of production to each other harmoniously. Only in this way can an ultimate state of built-in progress he achieved by the presently underdeveloped countries. The substitution of skill by "foolproof" mechanical equipment may look like a convenient short-cut solution but is likely to prevent the only true long-term solution to the problem, which lies in the development of the required skills at all levels.

Another short cut often recommended is the transfer of existing technology by means of technical assistance to the underdeveloped countries. This is a much more hopeful approach than the introduction of foolproof equipment. But even this is not the fundamental solution. It is true that the stock of technological knowledge of all kinds is constantly increasing and that participation in this increasing stock of knowledge is one of the benefits of later development which should be exploited to the full. On the other hand, as our stock of knowledge grows, it becomes a stock less and less suitable to the needs and resource endowments of the underdeveloped countries. Since it is the developed countries which have a virtual monopoly of research and development, it is not surprising that the kind of research and the direction of progress should be based entirely on the situation and needs of these more mature societies. In particular, the prevailing direction of research is to save labor and substitute capital and also to develop lines of production suitable for a highly educated and sophisticated population. What the underdeveloped countries need is technological progress corresponding to their specific situation, meaning a relative shortage of capital and a population which is not so highly sophisticated and trained to begin with. Only in this way can a situation be created in which by harmonious interaction knowledge of a suitable kind can be assembled and diffused through the economic system and human investment can enable the population to take full advantage of progressively advanced and more complicated degrees of knowledge.

To be sure, there are areas of knowledge accumulated in developed countries which are capable of transfer or suitable application. Moreover, technical assistance can also be used to assist underdeveloped countries in making their own type of investment in human capital and in research and development. There are possibilities here in technical assistance which are by no means yet fully explored. Yet while technical assistance may help underdeveloped countries to achieve built-in progress, it can never be a substitute for it. True progress, based as it is on human investment, must always be a domestic product, even though it can be nursed, assisted, and stimulated from abroad.

8

Population and
Economic Development

DEFINING DEMOGRAPHIC FACTORS

Static Overpopulation. We may start off with simple statics. Overpopulation, by definition, lowers the national income per capita and is thus, also by definition, an antidevelopmental factor. The lower its per capita income, the more difficult it is for a country to achieve the rate of domestic savings which will enable it to pull itself up by its own bootstraps. This is true of low per capita income whatever causes it. We must beware of double counting here: having agreed that overpopulation lowers per capita income, we must adduce specific further reasons to show why overpopulation as such, i.e., not the increase in population, makes recovery from the low income levels more difficult than in other cases of equally low income levels.

It remains to add that the definition of static overpopulation may be more complicated than is sometimes assumed. It is possible for a country to be heavily overpopulated, and yet suffer from acute labor shortages at harvest time. In such a case the marginal productivity of labor need not necessarily be much below the average productivity—although both will be very low—and withdrawal of labor from the land without some mitigation of the seasonal nature of agriculture may reduce output, perhaps almost in proportion. Hence, even in the case of simple overpopulation, industrialization is not necessarily the answer. Changes in the nature of agriculture to reduce its seasonal character, expansion of available land, and other forms of agricultural development may be indicated. Seasonal overpopulation of this kind does not seem to contain any compensating advantages when industrialization is contemplated.

A provisional version of this paper was submitted to the United Nations World Population Conference held in Rome in 1954, and after revision is was reproduced in vol. V of the conference papers, UN Publication Sales No. 1955 XIII.8. In the course of revising the paper I benefited from discussion with S. Sioma Kagan and from the opportunity of studying his Columbia Ph.D. dissertation, "The Demographic Factor: An Obstacle to Economic Development with Special Reference to Japan."

73

Increasing Population. Turning now to what we may call comparative statics, i.e., an increasing population, but without taking into account the interactions between the rate of development and the rate of population increase itself, an analysis might proceed along the following lines; The increased population has to be equipped with capital merely in order to maintain existing levels of per capita income. With population growth, as in *Alice in Wonderland,* you have to run in order to keep in the same place. This investment that is required to equip the increase in population with the same amount of capital and resources as the rest must be considered as unproductive investment from the point of view of economic development, since it does not in itself help to develop a country but merely maintains the *status quo.* In other words, the higher the rate of population increase, the greater the required amount of unproductive investment of this kind. Hence the less will be left for truly developmental investment, other things being equal.

A reduction in fertility, *ceteris paribus,* is therefore of assistance to economic development.

But the reduction in the rate of population increase will not promote economic development, regardless of how it may be brought about. At this point it becomes vitally important to consider the *gross* rate of population change rather than the *net* rate of population increase. A decline in the rate of population increase brought about by an increase in mortality concentrated upon the adult age group, i.e., the active workers, can obviously do more harm than good. It may mean a greater loss in current production, proportionately, than in current consumption, and this loss may quite conceivably be greater than the corresponding saving in the amount of running to keep in the same place. In other words, the particular method by which population changes has also to be considered.

A decline in fertility, on the other hand, is unequivocally good in a dual sense: (1) there is less need for running to keep in the same place; (2) the age distribution of the population becomes more favorable—there are more producers and fewer consumers.

A reduction in the rate of mortality will have harmful effects on development—in a system of comparative statics— if it is equally spread over all the age groups. It can conceivably be helpful to economic development where the decrease in mortality is concentrated on the young productive ages or ages just preceding this (say twelve to thirty years). It is a matter of fact that mortality in this age group in underdeveloped countries is particularly high in relation to more developed countries.

In a system of comparative statics, a higher rate of population increase is prima facie harmful, because it means more running to keep in the same place. But its precise effects cannot be determined until the changes in the rate of population increase have been considered separately for birth rates and death rates and also specifically for the different age groups.

It is thus conceivable, although perhaps not likely, that an acceleration of population increase is beneficial for economic development. But this will normally require both falling birth rates and falling death rates, with the latter fall concentrated among the adult group.

The Dynamic Relationship between Population Factors and Development. Next we turn to dynamics, i.e., to a system where the factors which cause growth are also related to the general organization of production and economic life. The most important long-term dynamic effect, which has frequently been pointed out, is that economic development ultimately, on all available evidence, tends to lead to a structurally favorable combination of low death rates and low birth rates. This, however, may be an extremely long-term influence, and in the interval population may multiply, and development may come to a full stop with an era of static over-population. It is one of the tragedies of some underdeveloped countries that the stage of static overpopulation has already been reached or is close, and hence the long-range dynamic effect on birth rates cannot be realized.

There is, however, another dynamic factor from which some more hope may be derived. Technology could be adjusted to the changing level of population and to the changing rate of population increase. If technology could reflect the actual resource endowment and also change gradually with the resource endowment as development proceeded, development would be much easier and cheaper than where technology is rigid and reflects a resource endowment different from that where the technology is applied. Thus the effects of overpopulation with rigid technology will be different—and usually more harmful to economic development—than if overpopulation or population growth is combined with a flexible technology. It is at least conceivable that a country which, starting with a given technology, gradually adjusts that technology to utilize more labor-intensive or small-scale processes, to reduce urbanization, or to save capital in other ways, may make economic progress and largely offset the retarding effects of overpopulation or rapid population growth.

Insofar as in a dynamic system the resource endowment is able to shape the technology applied, the total impact of population factors on economic development will be correspondingly favorable. The evils of overpopulation or rapid population increase may be, in reality, the evils of overpopulation or rapid population increase combined with rigid technology. From that point of view, one may say that, other things being equal, it is either better or worse for a country to have a low income because of overpopulation than to have a correspondingly low income because of, shall we say, aridity of climate, absence of law and order, lack of natural resources, recurrence of natural disasters, or other causes—according to whether we may assume that there is more or less scope for an adjustment of technology to overpopulation than to aridity, etc. Hence the great importance of promoting labor-intensive methods of production where population is dense or rapidly inceasing, in particular small-scale production, rural industries, and community development works, as well as cheaper and simplified machinery.

PROBLEMS OF INCREASED POPULATION

The Need to Create Positive Health. There is undoubted concern that economic development will increase the rate of population increase and result in a greater amount of general misery rather than in economic improvement. This possibility of a population explosion is certainly the most worrying of these dynamic interactions. It is true that death rates are falling in a number of underdeveloped countries, in some of them spectacularly, but that is a long way from proving that the falling death rate has been caused by economic development. In fact, it is extremely difficult to establish a convincing correlation between the degree of decline in death rates and the degree of economic development. Death rates are declining in a number of underdeveloped countries which are economically practically stagnant or perhaps even retrogressive. It seems a better interpretation of the known facts to say that death rates tend to fall in underdeveloped countries, and hence the rate of population increase tends to speed up, almost regardless of whether or not there is economic development.

This interpretation of the facts focuses attention, not on the impact of economic development on the rate of population increase, but rather on those medical and general sanitary improvements which occur independently from domestic economic resources. Such independence from domestic economic resources may be due to three causes: (1) the improvements are so cheap that the resources needed are negligible; (2) the improvements are due to improved knowledge and medical technology rather than an input of resources; and (3) the improvements are due to international intervention, whether humanitarian or under the heading of "technical assistance."

All these explanations apply to some extent. The last one, in particular, is of great importance. We may assume that we have entered an era in which international collaboration in health matters—whatever its motives—has reached a degree in which the two old Malthusian devils (or remedies) of large-scale starvation and large-scale epidemics are chained. The World Health Organization will fly in cholera serum; loans at concessional rates of interest will be made to areas suffering from starvation to enable them to import food; disaster funds will be set up; at a cost of a few cents per capita, malaria is stamped out or reduced over wide areas; water is purified, etc.

It is surely misleading to describe all these things as the results of economic development. It is true that the resources created by economic development will, to some extent and legitimately, be spent on all these medical and sanitary improvements. But the main point surely is not this, but that these medical and sanitary improvements will happen even in areas where no or few additional resources are available through economic development. Thus it seems a better approximation to the truth to treat the fall in the death rate as a technical constant, as it were, rather than as a function of economic development.

Economic development will, of course, add to whatever medical technology and international humanitarianism will do by themselves. This addition will happen partly by way of further sanitary improvements and partly by way of better nutrition, better housing, and higher incomes generally. It may be noted that the latter kind of improvement, through better nutrition, etc., which is more characteristically a result of economic development, can hardly be said to result in "a greater amount of misery rather than in economic improvement." If better nutrition enables more people to survive, it also enables more people who would otherwise be sick to work; it enables other people who would only work intermittently to work more steadily; it enables yet other people whose productivity would otherwise be low to work harder and produce more.

If there is anything inimical to economic development, it would be an undue concentration of international humanitarianism and improvements in medical knowledge and technology on the prevention of death rather than the creation of health. Such a bias may exist. The appeal of a high death rate for international and domestic action is more dramatic and more direct than the appeal of low levels of productivity leading, among other things, to poor health and thus to vicious circles in underdeveloped countries. What is wanted, therefore, is not a cessation or reduction of economic development, but partly a reorientation of sanitary policies in the direction of good health and partly more *initial* economic development, which has an automatic tendency (as compared with "autonomous" medical improvements) to raise output faster than it increases population. The fault, if fault there is, lies in the nature of autonomous medical improvements, not in economic development. It would be tragically mistaken to imagine that the action required is a reduction of economic development.

No doubt it would be better for economic development—on a cold-blooded analysis—if sanitary improvements could be confined to creations of better health generally and prevention of death only in the productive age groups without a reduction of death in the older age groups. It is only in this restricted sense that it is true that population increase prevents economic development. Without going to the length of such cannibalism as to cause more deaths in the "unproductive" population, economic and health policy can do a great deal to restore the balance disturbed by the dramatic appeal of death prevention, by moving in the direction of creation of positive health.

Savings and Capital Problems. In many underdeveloped countries operating at low income levels the rate of voluntary gross savings is no higher than 10 per cent, and may be less. Much of this gross savings of 10 per cent may not be available for economic development at all; it may assume the form of hoarded gold, cattle money, palatial public buildings, or bank accounts abroad.

Assuming, however, that none of the 10 per cent is wasted in this manner, some 5 per cent, or half of total gross savings, will be required to replace the existing capital. It is true that there is very little existing capital in underdeveloped countries, but it would be fallacious to assume that the burden of replacing existing capital in relation to national income is any less than in developed countries. On the contrary, there are two reasons to assume it to be higher. In the first place, there is the fact that the capital/income ratio in earlier stages of economic development tends to be high because of the lack of "balance" and external economies in the system. Second, existing capital tends to wear out more rapidly than in developed countries because of lower standards of repair and maintenance and also because of the failure to adapt capital equipment to the specific conditions and requirements of underdeveloped countries.[1] Hence, it is a conservative estimate to assume replacement of existing capital at 5 per cent of the national income.

This leaves 5 per cent net savings. Before economic development can proceed, provision must be made for the increase in population. The increment in population must be equipped with capital at the prevailing standards. Development is an increase in per capita income. Insofar as an increase in income depends on an increase in capital, development, therefore, presupposes a corresponding increase in per capita capital. If the increase in population is not equipped with capital, the position will deteriorate. The existing housing, electricity, productive capital, etc., will have to be shared among a larger number of people, and hence per capita output will fall. A developing country with an increasing population has to run in order to keep in the same place.

How much of the 5 per cent net savings will be left over for economic development when provision for the increase in population has been made? Probably nothing at all. If the rate of increase of population is 1¼ per cent (a moderate rate of increase in underdeveloped countries at present) and the capital/income ratio is 4:1 (again a moderate estimate for underdeveloped countries, especially in the least developed category),

---

[1] Lack of lubrication equipment, on the one hand, and failure to provide self-sealing bearings, on the other, provide one illustration. A failure to lift ploughs when taking them around corners, on the one hand, and the failure to provide specially reinforced ploughs, on the other, provide a second illustration. The famous inverted Churchill slogan current in connection with the ill-fated groundnuts scheme in Tanganyika is a third illustration: "Give us the jobs and we'll finish the tools."

it takes 5 per cent of the national income to increase the national capital by 1¼ per cent, and it will take a 1¼ per cent increase in the national capital to maintain per capita capital—and hence, on our assumptions, per capita income.[2]

This looks like a gloomy picture, but a number of qualifications are in order. In the first place, the situation described above is a purely static relationship. In particular, it is assumed that the increase in population, while requiring capital for its productivity, will not in itself contribute to production and hence to capital formation. This, however, is unduly pessimistic. Even in the most developed countries, where dependence on capital-intensive techniques is great, it has been found that additional labor, even without additional capital, results in a significant increase in output, even though less than in proportion.[3] Thus, to some extent, the increase in population will help to create its own capital equipment. In the most tangible manner, this is true where labor and capital formation are directly linked, as in many forms of rural capital formation and in community development projects.

In the second place, it need not necessarily be true that output can only be increased if there is a prior increase in capital. Progress of technology can increase output over time without such an increase in capital; since the increase in population takes place over time, a simultaneous improvement in technology may also be allowed for. One could even imagine population pressure stimulating technological improvements.

Third, it is possible to increase output through better utilization of existing capital. Not all capital would have to be increased. The existing network of roads might be sufficient for the greater population, and better utilization of the existing network might result. Population increase may create external economies in the form of better utilization of existing capital. In most underdeveloped countries, there is considerable scope for more productive use of existing capital.[4] Population pressure itself may again form an inducement to better utilization of existing capital. In this direction, too, there are possibilities of brightening the gloomy picture.

Fourth, even if the *domestic* savings of an underdeveloped country would be completely used up in providing for the population increase,

---

[2] More recent estimates put the rate of population increase considerably higher—at about 2 per cent—and the capital/income ratio for underdeveloped countries rather lower, at about 2.5:1. The arithmetic of this paragraph is therefore unaltered. See the introductory footnote of Chap. 10, p. 117.

[3] According to Tinbergen and Polak (*Dynamics of Business Cycles*, The University of Chicago Press, Chicago, 1950, p. 128), the 1 per cent increase in the labor force in the United States, keeping capital and the state of technology constant, resulted in a 0.7 per cent increase in production.

[4] See, for instance, the very detailed data in this respect contained in the ECLA study *Labour Productivity of the Cotton Textile Industry in Five Latin American Countries*, UN Publication Sales No. 1951 II.G.2.

it would still be possible, with the help of foreign capital assistance, to accelerate the increase in production so as to result in an increase per capita and thus to generate economic development. Once generated with the help of foreign capital, development may create a sufficient margin over and above present production to permit of subsequent maintenance of the impetus of development from domestic sources alone.

When the above four qualifying considerations are taken into account, it would appear that there is no inevitable necessity for the increase in population to prevent economic development except in very extreme circumstances. It may also be pertinent at this stage to remember that contrary to a widespread impression, the rate of population increase in underdeveloped countries as a whole does not appear to be significantly greater than in developed countries. The figures are not complete and not easy to interpret, but as far as they go, they do not establish any clear difference between the two types of countries. The contrary impression is probably due to the focusing of attention on a few underdeveloped areas of rapid population growth (often islands). A contributory factor to the popular misconception of a rapid increase is the impression concerning the rate of population increase in a number of developed countries, which is based on the immediate past rather than on the present situation. Perhaps, also, the anticipation of rapid population increases in underdeveloped countries has been permitted to color assessments of the existing situation.[5]

BIRTH AND DEATH RATES AND UNDERDEVELOPMENT

The age distribution in underdeveloped countries is unfavorable to a high standard of production and hence to capital formation. The combination of high birth rates and high death rates is economically wasteful, since the high birth rate results in large numbers of children; and the high death rate prevents a sufficient number of these children from surviving to repay by sustained production throughout their working lives the investment made in them in terms of food, clothing, shelter, education, training, and other services. It may be said, perhaps somewhat paradoxically, that one of the troubles of underdeveloped countries is not so much that there is not enough investment but rather that *there is too much unproductive investment.* Practically all investment which occurs in underdeveloped countries is investment in the feeding and bringing up of a new generation for productive work instead of investment in economic development. If this spending on the young is included as investment—as it should be—it may well be found that investment in underdeveloped countries is higher in relation to national income than in the more developed countries with their low birth rates and low death rates, perhaps even higher on a per capita basis. The trouble is that so much of this

[5] The author would not now maintain this paragraph written a decade ago.

investment is unproductive because high death rates prevent the repayment, with interest, of the capital sunk in the younger generation; such repayment is a normal procedure in more developed countries.

Of the four possible constellations of birth rates and death rates that of high birth rates and high death rates is the most wasteful and antagonistic to economic development. When combined with a low death rate, a high birth rate leads to productive investment, although like all investment it involves a temporary sacrifice. A low birth rate combined with a low death rate leads to conditions favorable to high levels of consumption and capital formation and thus of economic development. A low birth rate combined with a high death rate leads to gradual extinction, which is one solution of the economic problem, and meanwhile leaves the age composition of the population fairly normal.

The proportion of the total population of working age, defined as the age group between fifteen and sixty-four, is shown for various countries and areas in the following table:

Percentage of Total Population between Ages 15 and 64
(latest available data—1947)

United Kingdom	68.8
United States	66.7
Underdeveloped countries of:	
Africa*	56.5
Asia†	57.5
Latin America‡	55.5
Europe§	60.4
All underdeveloped countries included	57.3

* Egypt, Angola, Cape Verde Islands, Mozambique, São Tomé and Principe, Mauritius, South-West Africa.

† Burma, Ceylon, India, Korea, Philippines, Siam, Turkey, Portuguese India, Portuguese Timor, Federation of Malaya, Palestine.

‡ Costa Rica, Cuba, Dominican Republic, El Salvador, Guatemala, Honduras, Mexico, Nicaragua, Panama, Leeward Islands, Windward Islands, Puerto Rico, Virgin Islands, Brazil, Chile, Colombia, Peru, Venezuela.

§ Bulgaria, Greece, Roumania, Yugoslavia.

SOURCE: *Demographic Yearbook of the United Nations.*

The figures show the distinctly lower proportion of persons of productive age among the populations of the underdeveloped countries. Taking the proportion of the United Kingdom as our standard, we find that the number of persons of productive age in the underdeveloped countries is 16.7 per cent, or one-sixth, less than it would be if these countries had the British age composition. The deficiency is 17.9 per cent for the underdeveloped countries of Africa, 16.4 per cent for the underdeveloped countries of Asia, 19.3 per cent for Latin America, and 12.2 per cent for the underdeveloped part of Europe. This means that even if we forget about different capital equipment, different levels of training and education, different efficiency, different climate, different natural resources, etc., and isolate the demographic factor of age composition, output in the underdeveloped countries would be one-sixth lower than it is in the United Kingdom, other things being completely equal. Thus, this demographic factor accounts for a *deficiency of national income in underdeveloped countries of one-sixth or so.* Such a differential, if steadily applied either to capital formation or to productive increases in consumption, would make a considerable difference. One-sixth of the national income used for capital formation at a rate of return of 10 per cent in total productivity would increase the national income by 65 per cent within a generation of thirty-five years.

It may be objected that in fact in underdeveloped countries working life begins earlier and possibly lasts longer than in more developed countries and for that reason such comparisons as the above are misleading. This does not, however, seem a valid objection. If people are shoved into the production process at an earlier age in underdeveloped countries, this is *a symptom of necessity rather than a virtue.* It is a result of the high death rate and of the poverty, particularly induced by a constantly unfavorable age composition, that it does not pay to invest in children, say of the ten-to-fifteen age group, further education and training and maintenance and that they must be used for current production *while they are still alive.* Such differences are induced but not germane to the comparison. The same applies to the differences between what constitutes the working age groups in agriculture and industry respectively. It is true that agriculture employs persons earlier in life and possibly also later in life than does industry and thus to some extent compensates for lower productivity. Industry in the England of Charles Dickens and earlier was started off by using child labor, and the later age of entry into industry, as compared with agriculture, is the result of higher productivity rather than the result of any ingrained technological differences between agriculture and industry.

The first approach through a comparison of the proportions of the populations of working age groups is somewhat crude, and more detailed and elaborate methods suggest themselves. The following table is based on a comparison of death rates at specific ages between the United States and the United Kingdom, representing highly developed countries, on the one hand, and a number of underdeveloped countries for which the required data can be secured, on the other hand. The assumption on which the computation is based may be set out as follows: The population is divided into 5-year groups, ranging from 0 to 90 years of age. A child living at age 1 represents a net liability of one year's maintenance, food, etc., without any corresponding productive return; his economic value is thus denoted as a negative figure of minus 1. A child at age 10 is presumed to represent a liability amounting to minus 10. A young boy at the age of 15, just before his presumed entry into production, represents a liability amounting to minus 15. In other words, the liability represented by

POPULATION AND ECONOMIC DEVELOPMENT 83

persons alive before presumed entry into production is assumed to be proportionate to age and to reach a maximum at age 15.

After presumed entry into production, the liability diminishes. At age 20, a person represents a net liability of minus 10, a liability of 15 at age 15 having been partly offset by five years of work, reducing it from 15 to 10. In other words, the assumption is that each year's work repays a previous year's maintenance. This seems equivalent to the assumption that each person at work produces enough to sustain himself and one dependent. That is, no doubt, a crude assumption; but since it is made for comparative purposes only, no great advantage seems to attach to more elaborate computations. Experimentation with different assumption will not affect the result very much.

The following table thus roughly shows, on the above assumptions, the economic value represented by 100,000 newly born persons, according to the survival rates applying in the various developed and underdeveloped countries. The figure obtained is in each case positive; that is to say, the net assets represented by persons living between the ages 30 and 100 outweigh in all cases the net liabilities represented by persons before 30 or surviving beyond 100.

Net Value Represented by 100,000 Persons Presently Born in Various Countries
(according to latest available survival rates)

United States...............	1,998,720
United Kingdom............	1,861,645
Brazil.....................	1,233,490
Bulgaria...................	1,366,760
Chile.....................	1,425,420
China (Formosa)...........	1,409,805
Colombia	1,449,445
Egypt.....................	1,172,527
Greece....................	1,389,980
Guatemala.................	1,254,325
India.....................	913,320
Siam......................	1,296,675

SOURCE: *Demographic Yearbook of the United Nations.*

What the table shows is very striking. The economic value of 100,000 births in the United States or United Kingdom at present survival rates represents a surplus to the community, on the assumptions described above, which is substantially in excess of the corresponding figures for underdeveloped countries. *Both the United States and the United Kingdom figures are over twice the Indian figure,* and the United Kingdom figure is about 40 per cent higher than the general run of figures for underdeveloped countries.[6]

[6] The paper originally prepared for the conference went on to describe the effects of this hypothetical difference in national income on potential capital forma-

High as a simple index of mortality in the underdeveloped countries is in relation to such developed places as the United States and Northwestern Europe, it tells only half the story. If the indices of mortality are weighted according to the economic significance of death in each age group, the differences between the developed and the underdeveloped countries become much more pronounced.

The incidence of excess mortality in underdeveloped countries for the particular age groups is shown in the table on page 85.

It will immediately be seen that in the highest age groups where death is economically less harmful, i.e., in the case of persons who have completed their productive life, the death rates of underdeveloped countries tend to be lowest in relation to those of the United States and in some cases even absolutely less.[7] Regrettably high as the infantile death rate is up to 1 year of age, it is not generally in this group that we find the peak of excess mortality. Thus, in Chile the peak is in the 1-to-4 age group (almost ten times the United States figure), and excess mortality falls steadily after the age of 25. The same is true of Egypt, Mexico, Nicaragua, Colombia, and Venezuela. In Burma, the peak of excess mortality is at ages 5 to 9, and excess mortality falls steadily from there onward. Thus, the figures display a well-defined pattern. In Burma, Palestine, Nicaragua, and Venezuela, excess mortality in the 15-to-19 age group is higher than excess infantile mortality.

Again, it is noteworthy that the demographic obstacle to economic development in the form presented above, namely an unfavorable age distribution produced by a combination of differentially high death rates and high birth rates, is common to underdeveloped countries generally, whether normally considered as overpopulated or underpopulated.

---

tion. However, the reasoning of Mr. Lorimer and Mr. Bourgeois-Pichat has conclusively shown that this difference disappears when the calculation is made, not in terms of equal-size generations of newly born, but per inhabitant. The figures for underdeveloped countries ought to be raised to allow for the fact that more than 100,000 births would be required to create a population of a size generated by 100,000 births in the more developed countries. The figure of "net value represented per 100,000 newly born" therefore has no direct economic meaning, and cannot account for differences in per capita income. It is the wasteful reproduction pattern as a whole which represents such an obstacle to capital formation. This conclusion seems to take us back to the earlier point that it is the demographic impact upon the *quality* rather than upon the *quantity* of consumption and investment which should be emphasized; in more developed countries a higher proportion of "consumption" represents social investment in human capital, since more people survive to produce; in the underdeveloped countries a higher proportion of "social investment" runs to waste before society is repaid in production. I am indebted to Lorimer and Bourgeois-Pichat for their demonstration.

[7] The absolutely lower level may reflect either statistical deficiencies or the fact that in view of the higher death rates at earlier ages, the survivors to old age in the underdeveloped countries tend to be of a tougher type—or a combination of the two factors.

Mortality Rates of Underdeveloped Countries as Percentage of United States Rates by Age Groups

Country	Under 1	1–4	5–9	10–14	15–19	20–24	25–29	30–34	35–39	40–44	45–49	50–54	55–59	60–64	65–69	70–74	75–79	80–84	85 & over
Chile.........	402	997	233	291	331	348	300	286	228	205	180	148	141	129	130	121	103	93	93
Burma.........	439	716	725	536	547	344		341		257		151		80					
Palestine......	182	1,064	383	309	189	159	258	181	133	101	99	58	49	70	67	65		61.5	
Egypt.........	416	2,758	708	464	305	300	284	284	214	196	139	145	100	120	101	112	100	123	230
Mexico........	353	1,539	658	382	326	344	352	343	302	248	203	161	137	133	127	124	103	97	109
Nicaragua.....	166	784	500	264	247	252	252	249	192	168	136	113	106	93	97	93	122	63	56
Colombia......	262	916	500	300	237	244	229	222	192	161		108		98		65			
Venezuela.....	170	677	453	240		241		253		176		131		62					

PART 3

Planning and Financing Development

9

Lectures on
Development Planning

BASIC PRINCIPLES

BASIC PRINCIPLES

In order to understand the relation of individual projects to the national economy as a whole we must get very firmly implanted in our minds two economic principles which are neglected only at the expense of a lack of understanding of the problems of planning for economic development. These two principles I shall call the principle of accumulation and the principle of interrelation.

The Principle of Accumulation. The principle of accumulation indicates that in economic life, in economic planning, we are dealing with a world which is rather different from the mechanical world. In the mechanical world you have relations of cause and effect between different factors. A causes B. This book is lying on this table and I push it along; it comes to rest again in a new position. The push is the cause of the movement of this book from here to there. Now many people, especially people with mechanical training, tend to think of economic development in this particular way. A push, and you come to rest in a new position! That is fundamentally wrong. In economics you have no cause and effect. What you have in economics is a movement of cumulation. If you do something, you do not come to a new position of rest; rather, the movement goes on and something else happens. A causes B, and B causes C, and C causes D, and in the end D causes a change in A again. The secret of development planning is to set in motion such forces of cumulation.

This essay is based on a course of lectures delivered at the Asian Centre on Agricultural and Allied Projects, held in Lahore, Pakistan, from October to December, 1950. The aim of the Centre, which was sponsored jointly by the government of Pakistan, the Food and Agriculture Organization of the United Nations, the International Bank for Reconstruction and Development, and the United Nations, was to provide a training course on development problems for economists and planners from Asian countries. The material is presented in a simple way, but it seems that not all of the points have yet been grasped by some of those concerned with planning for development, and I feel that it bears reprinting here. As printed in the United Nations volume *Formulation and Economic Appraisal of Development Projects, Book I*

I should like to give you a few examples of this principle. First, the relationship between capital formation and poverty. It is true, although only partially true, that underdeveloped countries are poor because of lack of capital. It would be very misleading, though, simply to calculate the amount of physical capital in a country like England or the United States and then to imagine that all you have to do is to build up a similar amount of physical capital per head in other countries in order to get the same standard of living. In countries like England and the United States the greatest proportion of national capital does not consist of tangible things; it consists of intangible things such as knowledge, scientific tradition, skill, a scientific organization that is conducive to economic progress. One direct application of this is that a development program which concentrates entirely on physical projects to the neglect of intangible forms of capital—high standards of education, good health, a scientific tradition, and so on—is not likely to be a good development program. People tend to think that what is not visible is not real. That is a dangerous confusion. What is invisible can be a very real factor in economic development. The danger is that development programs may concentrate too much on visible projects at the expense of the invisible.

As between remedying poverty and capital formation, which is cause and which is effect? Do we start providing for higher standards of living or by providing capital? Now obviously—if you have followed what I said about cumulative forces—neither the remedying of poverty nor capital formation is a cause of the other, but both are the causes of each other. As long as you try to ask such questions about a "basic cause" of underdevelopment, you are moving in a logical circle.

Another, more specific, illustration of this cumulative principle relates to combined river-valley development, the TVA type of development where a whole river valley is considered and its water resources are used, not for one single purpose such as irrigation or navigation or power or flood control, but for a combination of all these possible purposes. The relations between the various purposes of a combined river-valley development scheme are of a cumulative kind. If you have power development, you can have pumps and you can have irrigation, and your irrigation in turn can support your power development.

Finally, a word about the international aspects of this cumulative process. There is no competition between the development of one country and the development of another country. If one country now under-

(1951), the lectures extended to 110 closely printed pages, and it has been necessary to cut the text considerably and occasionally to go beyond revision to rewriting in order to compress them for inclusion in the present volume, though I have maintained the conversational style in which they were delivered.

developed starts to industrialize, utilizing domestic foods and raw materials that were formerly exported, the export demand now no longer satisfied by this country, A, will be met by another country, B. By exporting more, B will obtain more foreign exchange and thus be able to import more machinery and raw materials to start its own development programs. Thus you have a cumulative relation not only within the development program of each country but also between the development programs of different countries.

The Principle of Interrelation. I shall now leave for a moment this principle of cumulation and approach the problem of economic development programs from a different angle. Let us ask ourselves, "What does a development program contain? What should it contain? How can it be drawn up, and what is the place of the individual project within the program?"

To answer these questions it is important to have a number of subdivisions and definitions ready in mind. One important subdivision, that between "service," or "overhead," projects, on the one hand, and directly productive projects, on the other, contains in itself the starting point for many of the difficulties of planning for economic development. In more highly developed countries there may be no need for a systematic development program because development may proceed automatically. These countries have reached a stage where the principle of cumulation is really at work. They may, of course, decide to have a program for another reason, such as social justice, efficiency, or the dictates of their political philosophy, but development does not depend on the program or plan. In underdeveloped countries we are faced with a different situation. There the problem is not just to ensure appropriate conditions for the cumulative process to do its work but to arrive at a point where the process can begin to work. No automatic mechanism will bring a country to this stage; it requires deliberate action.

One of the major problems in beginning to draw up a development plan is to decide on the proportion of overhead facilities that have to be constructed in relation to directly productive projects. If you plan a certain increase in steel output, for example, it is fairly easy to select the best type of steel-making equipment for the job, given good technical data, knowledge, and advice. But it is much more difficult to determine whether the transport system of the country is adequate to meet the new demands that will be made on it. One must also ask whether outlets exist for distributing the finished product, whether sufficient skilled labor is available, whether housing facilities are adequate, and a host of similar questions.

Here you have the first difficulty in drawing up development programs. The general situation with which you are nearly always confronted in underdeveloped countries is that your basic overhead services are not sufficient for a particular new directly productive project or for a longer-range plan of increasing output. It is of course nearly always possible to economize, but this may lead to trouble later on. First of all, your project may not be able to expand—if, for instance, it is based on inadequate transport and shipping arrangements. The second trouble with this make-do approach is that if you improve the quality of your basic equipment, you not only improve the efficiency of your present directly productive projects but also create the preconditions for other projects. In drawing up a development program, it is most important always to have in mind not only, "What am I doing now?" but also, "What is the next step?" This is the principle of cumulation.

Another point to consider is that you cannot always postpone additions and improvments to basic services until development starts—until further productive projects are attracted to the area of your initial project. By that time it may not be possible to make the necessary changes. Once you have laid out your services in a certain way—enlarged a port, built a railway—it may be very difficult to make alterations, even though you discover at a later stage that it would have been better to have had your port or your railway in a different place.

You may ask, "What can economic calculations contribute to problems of this sort?" We shall consider the answer to that question in more detail at a later stage; there are certain answers to this kind of important question that emerge from cost and benefit calculations in relation to the economic system as a whole. But one point I want to make at the beginning is that fundamentally this is not a question of calculation. You cannot hope to sit down with a pencil and a sheet of paper and come up with an answer. It is a matter for political judgment whether it is better to get results in three years and then have trouble in ten years, or else to foresee all the difficulties now and spend a lot of money now without return but be reasonably certain that what is built will last and develop smoothly in later years. Are the population and the government willing to wait? Is the government strong enough to tell the people, "These things are necessary, but for a long time you must not expect any return"?

The technician and the economist have a great deal to contribute here, and ideally the political decision should be taken in the light of all the available evidence; but in practice there is always a limit to the number of alternative plans that can be prepared and, indeed, a limit to what it is wise to do in certain circumstances. If you produce too many alternatives for the people in charge to make up their minds about, they will suspect (although quite wrongly) that your planning is faulty because you do not come up with one single set of definite figures, definite time periods, definite suggestions. The technician and the economist may thus have to make some of the decisions; but the point is that if they do so, they are not acting as technicians and economists but making political judgments.

Relationships of Public and Private Projects in Development Programs.
So far we have only been considering public projects and public programs;
we should always remember, however, that in practically all countries a
good deal of economic development takes place under private direction and
private auspices. You must never forget about private development; in fact,
the relationship between public development projects and private development is, in a sense, the most important determinant of the efficiency and
quality of a development program.

One particular case I want you to consider is the establishment of
private service facilities in connection with a private directly productive
project. A private industrial firm, for instance, may want to set up its own
power plant. Your initial instinct might be to say, "That's fine—it saves
public money"; but let us look at this proposition from the point of view of
the economy as a whole, and we shall discover that there are disadvantages
as well as advantages in it.

Among the disadvantages are, first, that exactly the same amount of
resources will be consumed whether the project is private or public. There
will be a financial saving for the public authorities, but the community as a
whole will still need exactly the same resources of labor, materials, foreign
exchange (for importing equipment), etc. Second, you greatly increase the
cost of industrial activity if you expect firms to pay for their own power
installations, transport facilities, etc. You add to the initial capital cost and
therefore to the risk of industrial enterprise, and this is usually an undesirable thing to do in underdeveloped countries, where risks of operation
are already high and new enterprises difficult to establish. Third, if private
firms are allowed or expected to set up their own powerhouses, you create
conditions favorable to monopoly and so also make it difficult for new firms
to start. There are many other disadvantages to permitting private development of service facilities, but these three points indicate the kinds of objections that can be raised. Now I want to consider some of the advantages.

First, it may be that the public service system was well balanced until
new industrial demands upset it. In that case, and if you are already
engaged in other development projects of high priority elsewhere, it is perfectly possible that you may decide that it is in the interests of the economy
as a whole to let the private firm go ahead if it is willing to put its own
money into its own electric power supply. Second, if the firm is a branch
or subsidiary of a foreign enterprise, as is quite often the case, it may help
you with your general foreign exchange problem. The alternative to private
generating stations may be no generating stations at all if the government
is short of foreign exchange. And there are many other advantages which I
will not go into here.

From what I have said, it certainly does not follow that everything
should be nationalized or alternatively that the provision of general services
should be left entirely in private hands. What my arguments do tend to

show is that the activities of any private groups which provide basic services should be controlled in the public interest. It is not necessary that they be publicly owned. My argument is that in integrated development programs basic services, insofar as they are not public services, should be conducted in such a way as to fit in with the general outlines of the program.

It most certainly does not follow that directly productive projects must be public projects. The great problem in development planning, as I have said, is coordination between the public sector and the private sector. Apart from nationalization, which is an extreme solution to this problem, governments have other methods open to them. They can offer various fiscal and protective inducements, which can be used to discriminate between highly desirable and less desirable projects. And they can resort to direct physical allocation of scarce resources, including foreign exchange.

You may now discern more clearly the point that I am driving at. The development program of an underdeveloped country, if it is to be a real development program, must include the measures of inducement, on the one hand, and of control and penalty and prohibition, on the other, by which the government proposes to make the activities of the private sector reinforce its own development program, which will very largely be a public service program. A development program which includes public service projects and nothing else is not a real development program. It is a collection of projects, which may, indeed, be much better than no program at all. It is useful to put all your public service projects together and see what they add up to and how they fit in with each other. But you cannot possibly judge the real efficiency of a public service program unless you consider what will happen in the private sector. In the end, the success of a development program will depend on whether the government has made the right assumptions about what is going to happen in the private sector or has made the wrong guess.

There are several possibilities. Perhaps you—the government—have made the right guess, and private enterprise does by itself what you expect it to do. That, however, is an unlikely coincidence. In that case you have been very lucky, and can safely adopt a laissez-faire attitude to private enterprise, a live-and-let-live attitude. But if private enterprise does not do what you expect it to do, you cannot adopt this live-and-let-live attitude, though it does not follow that you must nationalize private enterprise. There are, as I have said, other ways of making private enterprise fit in with your development program, or else it may be open to you to change and readjust your public service program.

Of course, you can never accurately foresee what is going to happen, and if you have public service development of this anticipating kind, you will always make some mistakes. That is inevitable in the nature of things. It is not possible to have a perfect sense of what people in the private sector are going to do in the next twenty or thirty years. If you have strong central power and the desire to do so, you may possibly force people into doing what you had planned for them, but that is not necessarily the best way of planning economic development. Nor is it necessarily desirable to lie down like Buridan's ass between his two bundles of hay and do nothing because you can never be certain what is going to happen. Both these approaches, to my mind, lead to a waste of resources and retard development.

The Need for Research and the Importance of Timing. The only right course that I can think of is to make as certain as you can that your assumptions are right. If you want to build roads to open up an agricultural district, for instance, the important thing is to go through a great deal of detailed research to make sure that this particular area is actually the one that is most suitable for agricultural development. You must test the soil; you must determine what crops can best be grown in the area and investigate their production, price, and consumption prospects. That is to say, you should take a great deal of trouble and time over working out what could happen in that particular area, in the light of present circumstances, if everything went according to plan and the farmers (or industrialists) did what would be best. Then, when you are convinced that your assumptions are right and your plan is feasible, try to induce private investment to develop on the lines you have established. You will never be able to induce the private sector to conform completely to your assumptions and your plan. Prices may change, and crops which are profitable now may not be profitable in ten years time. But all the same, this seems the only feasible approach.

Some of these things may seem very commonplace—for instance, the need for careful preparation and research. But one could quote many examples of the failure of development projects which were based not on a detailed examination but rather on a wild guess in response to the pressure of needs of the moment, which may turn out to be very temporary needs. Undertaking careful and detailed research is not at all the same as doing nothing; it is an essential first step toward initiating a successful development program.

Probably one of the most common sources of mistakes in economic development programming has been to wait too long without having a program at all and then, having drawn up a program, to rush it through without sufficient research. Great mistakes are made and large sums of money wasted by not allowing a year or two for research after the outline of the plan has been prepared. The important thing is to be patient at the right time and impatient at the right time.

Another important principle about timing is that if there is a project that can wait without any harm to the rest of the development program, then it would be wrong to do it now. There are two reasons for this: first, in three or five years time you will have more data available, new knowledge to go on, and you are less likely to make a mistake; second, it is wasteful to apply present resources to something that will cater for demands in ten years time. The aim of development is to increase the resources that you will have available in the future; and if your plan is successful, you will find it easier to start new projects later on, as your resources grow.

I should like to turn now to the related problem of flexibility in development planning. In development it is bad to be too historical—to think too much of what has happened in the past. You have to take the situation as you find it, and if your original plan looks wrong in the light of the information you have now, you should always change it. As David Lilienthal, the famous Chairman of the Tennessee Valley Authority, put it from his experience, you should never have one plan, you should have a series of developing plans. By that he meant that you should revise your plans as you go along.

We should also be flexible in another sense; where we can make provisional arrangements and in that way avoid the need for making a decision now that we could make more usefully and more economically at a later stage, we should do that. But there is a word of warning, contained in the French saying "Rien ne dure que le provisoire." Many development projects have resulted in lasting and permanent installations of various kinds that started out as provisional arrangements—as makeshifts. In any development project there is what may be called a point of no return. There is a point where your opportunities for flexibility come to an end. At this point, even if the costs of the project turn out to be much higher than you had originally calculated or some of your other assumptions about the project turn out to be wrong, the right course of action will be to complete the project, because the cost of scrapping it or changing it radically may be much greater than the waste involved in not having done the right thing from the beginning.

It is one of the purposes of planning to postpone that point of no return, to give yourself maximum flexibility for as long as possible so that you can still change your project or your whole development program in the light of changing circumstances. But I think it would be futile to imagine that you can do that all the time. There comes a point in the economic life of a project or the economic life of a development program where you have gone so far that you have to go through with it.

Dispersed versus Concentrated Development. Now let me take up another problem arising out of this relationship between overhead and directly productive projects. Underdeveloped countries, particularly those with a large area such as India, Brazil, and Pakistan, are never equally underdeveloped in all their parts. In nearly all of them there are certain areas of urbanization, better facilities, or highly intensive industrial development. Parts of the country enjoy a higher standard of living than the rest. It is true, for instance, that the coastal area is usually more highly developed than the rest of the country.

You are faced with an important question. Your public services are concentrated in one part of the country. In Karachi, for instance, there is water, transport and electricity; there are port facilities and health services that are better than in the rest of the country. The question is this: in such circumstances, if you have to draw up a development program for your country, where do you start? It would be cheaper to build on what you already have, to go on adding to the development of the area that is already more developed. In the case of Pakistan it might be cheaper to concentrate further development in Karachi, where many of the required facilities are already available, than to try to reach into the interior of the country. On the other hand, if you are dealing with the problem of underdevelopment or lack of development, it seems logical to start where it is worst—where the real underdevelopment is—not to concentrate on urban areas which are already highly developed but to move into the interior where there is practically no development.

The first thing to be said in answer to this dilemma is that quite often the decision is not for the technician and not for the economist. There may be strong political arguments for dispersal, particularly in the big countries with a decentralized political structure, where the various states or provinces have their own parliaments, their own governments, their own budgets, and their own development plans. You, the planners, have to accept political realities, and you have to fit in with the political structure of the country with which you deal. It seems futile for an economist to go to a country that has a decentralized political structure and recommend that all development should be concentrated in the capital. The individual states or provinces may be very powerful and influential; it may be that they are the main agents of development work and simply would not stand for it.

But let us assume now that there are no political limitations, that you are free to answer the question as an economist or as a technician or as a planner. My own answer would be along these lines. In practically all underdeveloped countries the great difficulty is that national income is too low, that national resources are grossly insufficient even to make a start on continuous and cumulative development planning. We cannot plan properly until our resources have reached a level where we can spare from direct consumption sufficient resources to set the cumulative process in motion. The first important thing, then, is to raise the level of resources to the point where we can begin to plan intelligently. If this analysis of the problem is right, the answer to our particular question would be that in such conditions the best thing to do is to push ahead with development in the cheapest possible way. This often means you should start where the overhead facilities are already available, in the areas that are relatively more developed now, and move out into the hinterland at a later stage when you can utilize the additional resources you have created.

SOME PRACTICAL PROBLEMS

The Allocation of Resources. In drawing up a development program you must answer three key questions about your resources. You must discover what your present level of resources is, you must determine how these resources should be allocated between consumption and development projects, and you must decide how much of what you have available for development should be allocated for immediate improvements and how much should go into the kind of development that will yield an increase of consumption in the distant future.

Your plan must be based on the size of your present resources. It is a wrong approach to ask yourself first what you need. We can learn that principle from organizing war production, for war is very similar to economic development in some respects. Economists in underdeveloped countries may learn a great deal from the history of planning for war in countries such as England and the United States. The most common single defect of development programs is to try to start too much at once, to fail to adjust the program to the available resources. In some countries this has happened so frequently that the whole idea of planning for economic development has become discredited. Lots of things have been started, nothing has been completed, then everything has been stopped for three or four years, then something else has been started in the light of changing circumstances, and that also has not been completed.

It is instructive to study, from this angle, the reports that have been made by missions to underdeveloped countries. These missions have been sent by international organizations, by governments, and by private consultants. Time and again their reports say that too much has been started and too little has been finished. "We recommend that development expenditure should be more concentrated on fewer projects." "We recommend that instead of building twenty railway lines, the country should concentrate on finishing two missing links in railway lines that have previously been started." The reason for such recurring statements is that there is a tendency to draw up development programs that are based on needs. If you do that, you inevitably arrive at a program that is beyond your available resources. It is logical that this should be so, because if your resources were sufficient to cater for your needs, you would not be an underdeveloped country.

I am not saying, of course, that you should have a development program that bears no relation to your needs. The first step is to consider your available resources, but the second step is to consider what are the most urgent needs that you can satisfy with these resources. To have a development program that is unrelated to needs would be grotesque, but the first question dealt with should be the question of resources. For that reason I cannot stress too much the importance in underdeveloped countries of national income statistics. Some reliable statistics are a vital prerequisite for drawing up a development program.

This is a proposition that people find it very difficult to accept. National income statistics sound academic. It seems an elaborate business to work out the total value and volume of agricultural production and industrial production, the flows of income in different categories, the annual depreciation on your capital, etc. It seems a statistical luxury: the Americans can do it, the British can do it, but isn't it a waste of money to start it in underdeveloped countries? No, it is not a waste of money. It is essential for a good development program.

The Danger of Inflation. Let me now consider another aspect of our original question: what happens if your program is too big for your available resources? If you try to get out of your available resources, by way of development expenditure, more than they can support, there is only one way that the system can react, and that is inflation. You may succeed in financing your public development program by measures that undermine private capital formation, but on balance this may retard rather than advance the development of the whole economy.

At this point we come up against a financial problem for the first time —is it possible to finance development projects by inflation? My answer is that it is possible to finance *a particular project* by inflationary methods. If you want one particular project and you don't care twopence what happens elsewhere, you can always finance it unless the project is enormous and your resources are very small. If it is a public project and you are the government, you control the supply of money, money buys resources, and you can have your project.

But that is not economic development. You can finance a specific project by inflationary methods if necessary, but it is my conviction that you can never finance a *development program* by inflation. It is true that in industrialized countries, where you have unutilized resources, inflationary financing can be a good thing. By monetary expansion you can increase output, reduce unemployment, and achieve all sorts of other good effects. But the conditions we face in economic development are completely different. The trouble is not insufficient monetary demand. In underdeveloped countries production is limited by technical factors, by the absence of capital, by the absence of skills, by the absence of raw materials, by the absence of public services, and by the absence of machinery; and you cannot cure these physical deficiencies by monetary devices. The problem of economic development is to create the technical conditions under which output can be expanded—the skilled labor, the machinery, the materials, the factories, the enterprises, and the services that are required. *Demand* does not help; *supply* must be created.

I would like now to return to the earlier point that your development program must be based on your available resources, not on your needs, and to look at it from another angle. If your plan is too big for your resources, you will have inflation. But you should not rush to the conclusion that this inflation is all the fault of your too ambitious program. Many underdeveloped countries have not done everything they could to provide the maximum possible resources for development. The first inquiry should be whether your financial resources can be increased through taxation, borrowing, or savings, and if so whether your real resources can also be increased. But when you are satisfied that your resources are as large as you can possibly make them, then the important second step is to make sure that your total development program, including all your projects, does not add up to more than the resources you have available.

If the program is bigger than the resources available, it is no good making a start and hoping for the best. If you do that, not the best but the worst will happen. Nor is it wise just to cut everything by 20 or 50 percent. The right thing to do is to sit down and think again. To draw up a new program that is half as big, you do not just leave out some projects; you may change all or nearly all your projects completely.

The Case for Formulating More Projects than Can Be Executed. Having dealt with inflation, at least as regards its internal effects, I want to make a point which I feel is very important. It may seem, at first sight, to be contradictory to what I have just been saying, but I hope you will see quite clearly that it is not really contradictory. I have said that no country should try to *execute* a development program which is in excess of the resources available for it; the point I want to make now is that each underdeveloped country ought to *have* a development program which is greater than its available resources. The distinction I want to draw is between the program that you actually execute and the program that you have ready for execution. You should always have a reserve collection of projects that you know you cannot execute but that you have carefully worked out in detail. There are four main reasons for this.

The first reason is an obvious one on which I need not elaborate. It is that the first project you start on, the one at the top of your list, may get stuck. For instance, you will remember that at Rasul you were told that much of the work had been stopped for two or three months because they were waiting for some item of imported equipment. These things may always happen, and then it is important to have some other project that you can substitute.

A second reason is that your available resources will increase as development gets going; indeed, this is the aim of a development program. You must give some thought now to the problem of what to do with these increased resources when you have them—in three or five or ten years time. It is possible that the resources available for development may increase much more rapidly than you think. Suppose, for example, that your present resources are 100 and that you use 95 for subsistence, state administration, defense, amortization, and similar current demands and have only 5 to put into new development. Now suppose that in three years time your resources are increased to 125 and that you manage to keep the level of current expenditures almost constant—to 100. Then your resources available for development will have increased, not by 25 per cent, but by 500 per cent.

The third reason, which is rather similar to the second, is that it is always possible that you may be underestimating your present resources. They may be supplemented by foreign aid or in other ways. There will inevitably be a margin of error in your national income statistics. It is also possible that there may be a boom in the price of your export crops, and that again would increase your available resources.

My fourth reason is the most important; it is of a general economic nature, and concerns the application of the principle of "opportunity costs." If an economist is sent to study the development of a country, someone will probably come along and say to him, "We have this project. It will cost us 20 million rupees to irrigate 2 million acres of land. Is it worth doing?" To me this question is completely meaningless. My question would be, "What would you do with those 20 million rupees if you did not spend them on this project?" The latter question makes sense. But to answer it you must know much more than just all about the one project. You must know which other projects could be undertaken with the 20 million rupees. In other words, you can never appraise the economic development program of a country or the value of its executed projects unless you also study the other projects that the country has contemplated but not executed, and can compare the two sets. *You must always have rejected a project or a number of projects to be certain that the project you actually undertake is right.*

This point may be put in another way by saying that the costs of a development project are the sacrificed benefits from another project. To make comparisons possible, your cost and benefit calculations must, of course, be in identical terms, in money terms in your own currency. In deciding between two projects, however, you should bear in mind that the benefits of project A may reduce the costs or increase the benefits of project B. That is what I called the cumulative force in development. In a multipurpose river development project, for instance, if you have irrigation, it may be possible, without much extra cost, to have a second scheme for navigation or flood control or power or fishery development. If it becomes possible and cheaper for you to have a navigation system because of irrigation, it is absolutely essential that the reduction in the cost of navigation be taken into consideration as one of the benefits of the irrigation scheme. Otherwise your whole reckoning is wrong.

The costs of project A are also to some extent the costs of project B. If you incur certain costs for building a dam for irrigation purposes, that dam will also be part of the cost of your electricity scheme, and you are faced with the problem of spreading your costs over the two projects. One of the great problems in cost/benefit calculations for economic development is joint costs. In the present example, if you set all the costs of constructing the dam against irrigation, your hydroelectricity scheme will look much more promising than it really is; if you put them all down against hydroelectricity, your irrigation scheme will look much more beneficial than it really is.

Thus there are three questions to ask when you have a project. First, "How far are the costs of my project the sacrificed benefits of another project? In other words, what would I do with this money if I did not undertake this project?" Unless you can answer that question, you cannot appraise this particular development project. Never confine yourself to the project you are actually starting. The second question is, "How far does this particular project that I undertake here reduce the cost of some related project? In other words, how far have I got a condition of joint costs?" And the third question is, "How far are the benefits of my particular project part of the costs of another project? In other words, is my particular project a segment of a bigger project? How far does one thing lead to another, and then how does my cost/benefit calculation come out with the various segments of this big project, this combined project that I am undertaking?"

The Selection of Projects: Some Financial Considerations. How far should the priorities within the development program be influenced by financial considerations? Can you say, "I will simply pick out the project with the highest cost/benefit ratio and not worry about financial arrangements"? In a general way my answer would be yes. Priority selection among projects should be on technical grounds, not on financial grounds. Keynes once observed that it is the proper job of finance to see that nothing is ever done on financial grounds. That is a very true statement in our case. One of the most important jobs of financial experts in an underdeveloped country is to see that the true technical priorities within a development program are not upset or made impossible by financial obstacles. The priorities within a development program ought to reflect the real conditions and needs of the country.

The development problems of overpopulated and underpopulated countries, for instance, are quite different. For that reason many of the generalizations made about underdeveloped countries will not apply in particular cases. In an overpopulated country such as India or Pakistan, any project which takes people off the land, which leads to more non-agricultural employment, ought to have added priority. But the development program of an underpopulated country can be much more balanced, combining the development of natural resources, agriculture, and industry. In the ultimate sense the development program of a country must reflect its real economic position and not any financial considerations.

There are some important exceptions to this general rule. The first is that of a project which shifts the financial burden to another place where it is easier to carry. I shall discuss later the possibility of shifting the burden abroad by obtaining foreign financing. The point I want to make here is that there may also be advantages in shifting the burden from the public to the private sector domestically. It may be that in an underdeveloped country it is much easier to associate private capital directly with such projects as electricity generation or factory building rather than transfer this money into public ownership first and then have a public project. It may be that your taxation machinery is inadequate or that you will get undesirable effects if you try to tax these funds. In that case it is sensible to reconsider your priorities. If you find that there is a certain amount of private voluntary saving which you could not very well reach by taxation or borrowing, then there is no economic reason why you should not look at your projects in that light as well as look at your cost/benefit ratio.

The second case for accepting financial priorities exists when it seems that a project will result in salable securities; then it probably deserves some extra priority. The weakness of financial institutions in underdeveloped countries, particularly the weakness of their capital markets, is one of the obstacles to economic development. In the long run, when any country has gone through the process of development on a nonsocialist basis, it has a developed system of banking, companies established on a nonpersonal basis selling their shares and debentures, and intricate financial machinery for enabling people to invest their money in these securities and then to be pretty certain that they can sell them again when they want to. In underdeveloped countries anything is a good thing that helps the growth of a capital market, that gets people used to dealing in securities, to investing their money in this impersonal manner, that reduces hoarding, and that offers people an outlet for their savings. How much this intangible benefit is worth must be a matter for judgment, but it should always be borne in mind.

Third, when assessing projects in financial terms, a distinction must be made between projects that are revenue-producing, projects that are neutral in this respect, and projects that are revenue-consuming—that require more money after you have finished them to keep them going. If you build an electric power station, you get electricity that you can sell, and you get revenue from your project. Usually this revenue is much greater than the cost of operation or maintenance. At the other extreme, if you build a hospital, assuming that treatment is free, you get no return. On the contrary, your annual cost of operation, in the case of a hospital, may amount to about half of your initial capital expenditure. If you build this expensive hospital now but fail to provide funds for its operation, you have wasted your resources. It is one of the weaknesses of many economic development programs that they often make insufficient allowance for the cost of maintenance and operation.

Should Projects Be Self-liquidating? This brings us to one of the most important questions in our field, namely, "Should projects be self-liquidating?" This is not the same question that you ask in your cost/benefit calculations; I am not asking whether a project *could* be self-liquidating but whether it *should* be made to pay for itself. Should it be a settled aspect of development policy to cover the cost of development projects from their own proceeds if that is possible? There has been a good deal of economic discussion of this question, although not usually in connection with development policy. I would like to summarize some of the arguments for and against self-liquidating projects here and see which way the balance tips.

The first point for discussion is that the policy of covering the cost of development projects from their own receipts wherever possible amounts to a form of taxation. The revenue that you get from your development projects helps you to balance your budget. I want to get into the question of budgeting for economic development later; at this point I would just like to say that in my view a balanced budget or, if possible, a budget surplus is a desirable condition in underdeveloped countries. Once you reduce the problem to this point, it becomes a question of weighing the advantages and disadvantages of this particular type of taxation against other kinds of taxation. Is the money I take away from the users of my project by charging them a high price in order to cover my capital costs a greater help to my development program, in eliminating the competing demand for resources, than the money I could take away from people—not necessarily from the same people but from *some* people—in another way? For instance, you may find that the users of electricity are productive enterprises that you want to encourage. It may be that if you sold them electricity more cheaply, they would make bigger profits, and that if they made bigger profits, they would save them. On the other hand, you may find that if you collect the money by income tax, the tax will fall, shall we say, on landowners, and that these landowners will reduce their consumption in order to pay it. If the consumption they reduce is their consumption of imported commodities, you will get some relief for your balance of payments. Under these conditions, evidently the balance is in favor of not making your project self-liquidating but covering its costs from the proceeds of general taxation. There should be no economic case at all for insisting that your project be self-liquidating. You are only hurting yourself if you do it as a matter of principle. It is not a matter of principle; it is a matter of expediency.

It may be, of course, that there is no alternative. You have to take the administrative possibilities into account. It may be very difficult to have an income tax; the machinery may not be there, collection may not be possible. In that case it will probably be a good thing to make your project self-liquidating by charging the users a high enough price to cover your capital costs. If you have no alternative source of taxation and fail to recover the cost of the project from its users, you are following an inflationary policy, and this is an undesirable thing to do. Thus the result of our first argument is that you cannot tell whether it is good or bad policy to make your project self-liquidating until you know what (if any) the alternative possibilities for taxation are. If there are no good ones, it would probably be a sensible policy to make your project self-liquidating.

A second argument in favor of making projects self-liquidating is one of fairness. It seems fair that the people who benefit from particular projects should pay for them. Now let us look at this argument a little more closely. Presumably the project has been undertaken because it is a good project and benefits the economy as a whole; otherwise it should not have been undertaken. But if it benefits the economy as a whole, there is no reason why it should not be paid for through taxation or other forms of financing. If you argue that the beneficiaries must pay, you assume in your argument that it is right to restore the relative income positions of the various groups of the population which existed before you undertook your project—that no one should be any better off than before in relation to anyone else.

That is not necessarily good. It may be that the people who benefit are the people whom you want to benefit. The two decisions—whether to undertake your project and who should pay for it—are unrelated and must be taken separately. It might promote economic development more effectively to cover the cost of your project from general taxation and leave some groups to enjoy its benefits without specifically contributing to the capital cost.

A third argument that is often mentioned in favor of making projects self-liquidating is that unless you make the users pay for it, you cannot tell whether your project has been right or wrong. Now this argument is not very strong; a government which has a practical monopoly of the things produced by its projects can always make them self-liquidating by raising the prices of their outputs. But the only test of a good project is whether it adds more to national income than the total resources you put into it.

Whether you manage to cover the capital cost of your project by selling its output at a sufficiently high price has no direct relation to the quality of the project.

The real reason for this is that the extra money which you recover by raising the price of your product is not an extra benefit but a "transfer." The people who have to pay the higher prices transfer money to the government. It is a bookkeeping method of putting money from one pocket into another. In other words, when you calculate the cost/benefit ratio of an electricity project, it would be wrong to try to compute your benefits from that project by working from the prices consumers are going to pay for electricity. They may be low, in which case your project appears to be much less beneficial than it really is, or they may be high, in which case it appears to be much more beneficial than it really is. The proper thing to enter in the benefit column is the extra production that you expect will take place as a result of the increased provision of electricity.

The only way of telling whether a project is good or bad is to go very carefully into the details before you start work on it; to try to work out to the best of your knowledge the benefit and cost of the project in real terms, in terms of the extra output that you hope to get; and then to see if it seems to you not only a good project but the best project you can undertake. If it is better than any alternative project, then you can go ahead with it. The question of what to charge for the output, for the things that your project is going to produce, has to be answered separately, on its own merits. In certain circumstances it may be sound to keep your prices deliberately low, to encourage your industries by selling them cheap electricity, for example. In other circumstances it may be good policy to charge a lot for your electricity. It may be a very good form of taxation. In that case do not hesitate to charge twice as much for your electricity as you need to cover your capital cost. Make a big surplus on your project.

You can assume that something is wrong with the presentation of a project that tries to sell you the project only because you can recover more money from its users than you put into it. That is not an argument at all. It is equally wrong to listen to people who try to tell you that a certain project is not a good project only because you cannot recover the costs from the users. Whether a project is good or bad is one question and whether or not you should try to recover the money you put into it from its users is a different question that has to be answered by an entirely different analysis of the situation. If you keep these two problems apart in your own mind, I think you will make enormous progress in clarifying your thinking on this subject, in presenting the costs and benefits of a particular project in a logical manner.

The Appraisal of Projects in Real Terms. Now I would like to add one further step to our analysis of development projects—the importance of appraising projects in real rather than monetary terms. This is not a new point. It has come up all the way through our discussions. But I think it is always very important in considering a project or a development program as a whole to have in mind all the time the possible differences between real resources and the money items that you enter into your calculations. In our calculations we assume that money items represent the real resources, but that is not always true. In particular, I would draw your attention to three respects in which your money calculations have to be adjusted for an economic appraisal of a project.

The first is the case of "transfer items." A transfer item is a money transaction to which no movement of real resources corresponds. Some of these money payments are very important items in development projects. For instance, consider the item of compensation. You need the land, and you pay the landowners a certain amount of compensation. Suppose there is a certain amount of land that is not used, and you pay money to buy it. Perhaps it is land that will be flooded by a reservoir. Now if it was unused and unproductive before you bought it, you will not lose anything in the real sense by flooding it, and yet in monetary terms you will have the expense of compensating its former owners. This cost is a transfer item.

In any economic appraisal of a development project it is important that at each point you should ask yourself, "Is this item a real cost in the sense that it is using up current resources, or is it purely a transfer item, putting money from one pocket into another without any corresponding movement of goods?" If it is a transfer item, you should leave it out of your economic appraisal. It is not part of your real cost, and when you work out whether your development program fits in with your available resources or adds up to more than 100 per cent, you should exclude it. If you add in compensation payment to landowners as part of the cost of your program and then you find this particular program is too big and cut this particular project out, you are acting under an illusion because compensation payments to landowners do not have to be squared with your available resources. In other words, when I talked about fitting development program to available resources, I wanted to confine that statement to that part of the expenditure on development projects that represents the use of real resources. In the final summary of the project there should be a statement that sets out clearly what part of the total money cost represents the use of real resources and what part represents things that do not use up real resources. From the economic point of view this is a very important distinction and, I may add, a distinction that is very rarely made. Quite often there is great difficulty in the economic appraisal of development programs and activities because of a failure to distinguish between these two kinds of costs.

My second illustration is the case of a commodity that is taxed. Suppose you have a tax on cigarettes, and you want to consider the cost/benefit ratio of a combined project to grow tobacco and make cigarettes. The proper way to value the output of cigarettes is to take their price before tax. If you put down the tax as part of the benefit of the project, you are greatly overrating the value of the cigarettes—and of the project. The value of the goods and services you produce with the help of your project should always be put down at factor cost—at market prices exclusive of taxation.

Of course, having done that, it is perfectly proper to add another sentence or descriptive note to say that your project will enable you not only to produce so many thousands of cigarettes but also to collect so much tax on these cigarettes, and that this may be a most convenient way of collecting taxes. That is certainly an argument in favor of the project, but it is not part of the direct benefits of the scheme.

A third case where it is important to distinguish between real and money cost is the case of subsidized sales. This is the opposite case to taxation. Again I hope you all see that when you have an agricultural project which produces food that is sold at subsidized prices, you must enter in your calculations not the subsidized price but the true market price. You would underrate the benefits of the project otherwise. Where prices are controlled by law, I think the only sensible thing to do, from the economic point of view, is to try to form an opinion of what the true uncontrolled market price would be. In the case of subsidies you simply add the subsidy to the actual price to get the true market price. When you have a controlled price, it is much more difficult because you cannot tell exactly what the true price would be. You have to study the demand and supply curves for the product and then try to estimate what the price would be without control.

One more case I would like to mention here is technical obsolescence. In the economic appraisal of a project you must make a distinction between physical and technical obsolescence. You may buy a tractor which will last for ten years but which will be obsolete in five. But this does not mean that you must write off the tractor after five years. The thing to consider in the case of machinery or any other item you need for your project is physical obsolescence. If the tractor lasts for ten years on the project and the project goes on for ten years, then the only real annual cost to the project is one-tenth of the total cost of the tractor. If you decide after five years that there is a better tractor on the market now and that you will replace your existing tractor even though it will be serviceable for another five years, that is your own affair. If five years later you decide to buy the new tractor, it is presumably because, on the basis of the cost/benefit calculations you undertake at that time, you decide that it will be cheaper to have a new tractor than to go on using the old one. But at the present time, when you are making your initial calculations for the project, these future considerations do not enter in. Physical obsolescence is part of the cost of the project, and should be included in the economic appraisal of it. But technical obsolescence is something quite different, and physical and technical obsolescence should not be lumped together.

I would not want to leave you with the impression that technical obsolescence is not an important factor. It certainly is. Make it a separate item. You may, perhaps, decide to add a note to the presentation of your project, pointing out that although ten years have been allowed for the life of the tractor, it is quite possible and indeed likely, in view of rapid technical developments, that it may be wise to replace it in five years time and that this will mean extra expenditure in five years time. That is all right. But this is not part of the cost of the present project; it is part of the cost of a new project which you may decide to undertake in five years time and which must be assessed on its merits as they are evident then. To mix this future consideration up with your present project will only lead to confusion.

RESOURCES

In all I have said so far I have stressed the importance of keeping development programs within the limits of available resources. Of course this limitation should apply only to projects which are actually executed, not to those which are formulated and investigated. But the principle of keeping development programs within available resources does not suggest that development programs should be cut down. Rather, it suggests that the resources made available for economic development should be increased.

Avoidance of inflation is not an aim in itself. A country can always avoid inflation by failing to have any development program or development projects. Our problem is not how to avoid inflation but how to have the maximum possible development without inflation. The government of an underdeveloped country may have followed the soundest financial policies and may have an unbroken record of balanced budgets, absence of internal debts, stable prices, etc., and yet it may have failed in its essential economic duties.

Putting it in a different way, a government should not try to avoid inflationary pressure; such pressure is inherent in economic development, which means additional demand for labor, materials, and services of all kinds to go into development projects. Economic development *is* inflationary pressure. But if a government should not avoid inflationary pressure, neither should it give way before it. It should go out and meet it by making available additional resources to satisfy the claims of economic development.

Such additional resources can come from any of the following four sources: (1) taxation, (2) borrowing, (3) voluntary saving, (4) reduction of government expenditure for purposes other than economic development. There will be hardly any underdeveloped country where some additional resources cannot be mobilized from one or some or all of these four sources. Most countries, of course, can also obtain some money for development from abroad, and I shall discuss some of the features of foreign financing later on.

Domestic Resources. I have already suggested to you that the object of development programs and development projects is to increase the resources available for future development to the point where the principle of cumulation can begin to operate. I want to emphasize this point here by saying that the first development projects a country should undertake are projects designed both to improve taxation, borrowing methods, and savings facilities and to cut out inessential government expenditure by administrative or other reforms. Irrigation schemes, river-valley development schemes, electricity schemes—all these kinds of projects that were discussed earlier—come afterward. Resources are the horse and projects are the cart, and it does not make sense to put the cart before the horse.

Let me make it quite clear that the government's job in underdeveloped countries is to make resources available not only for the public development program but for private development projects as well. The government, not private developers, has the responsibility to see that development programs do not end in (and not frustrated by) inflation. Private people cannot do this; they have no power of taxation or control of money.

This point has two practical applications. First, a balanced budget may not be enough for an underdeveloped country. Second, there must be a group of persons in some government department or other official position who can examine the details of private as well as public development expenditures and look at them in relation to total resources and their wider financial and economic effects. The second of these two applications explains itself, but the first may stand in need of some elucidation. A balanced budget is not enough because taxation may have to be used to reduce consumption or inessential expenditures in order to find resources for public *and* private development projects. Inflation can start through excessive private development or excessive public development. It does not matter whether a specific project is public or private; either way it creates exactly the same demand for resources. The distinction between capitalism and socialism fades before the facts of inflation.

I think you will see now what I mean when I say that the normal condition in an underdeveloped country which relies to a large extent on private development and which does not get substantial aid from abroad in its economic development should be a budget surplus. Yet ninety-nine out of a hundred officials in underdeveloped countries concerned with government finance will sit back and think their job is done if they have related tax receipts to government expenditure. The question should not be, "What is the public expenditure for which I have to find revenue?" but, "What is the total development expenditure, public and private, for which I have to find revenue?" The answers to the second question would often result in a budget surplus. Yet how often is the question asked in that form?

The link between public expenditure and public revenue is traditional everywhere, not only in underdeveloped countries. But to have a good development program, I think it is important to abandon this link. The link should be between *total* development expenditure and public revenue, not between *public* development expenditure and public revenue. One way of seeing this is to realize that the yield of taxation may quite well be used in order to give subsidies to private development projects. Some underdeveloped countries have adopted this kind of policy.

I now want to deal with the question that looms large in many people's minds: "Is it necessary to fit development programs to *presently* available resources? Why should we not finance development from future resources—when we shall be so much better off?" This is a plausible question that reflects widely held views. But you can only shift the burden of development to the future in one way, and that is by borrowing from abroad. If you borrow from abroad and repay in the future, you do not have to use your present resources. Instead, you have committed some of your future resources; and if your resources are greater than your present ones when the time to repay the loan comes, both in terms of total production and in terms of foreign exchange, that may be a very sensible thing to do. Insofar as your program has to be domestically financed, however, you cannot shift the burden to the future in any way or by any device. You cannot build a dam today by using labor and raw materials in five years time. You all know that. Finance can never make possible what is physically impossible.

Yet the idea that it is financially possible to shift the burden to the future is deeply rooted and widespread. In nearly all underdeveloped countries people think that they must tax for current expenditure but can borrow for development expenditure; that there is no harm in running into public debt as long as we create tangible capital assets to balance the debts; and that as long as the revenue budget is balanced, there is no need to worry about the capital budget.

Now I wish to make it quite clear that I am in no way objecting to the idea of a capital budget. I think that in presenting its development program the government ought to distinguish between the revenue budget and the capital budget. But the value of the distinction is purely for purposes of information, for purposes of study, for purposes of estimation of future resources and requirements. My argument is that there is no economic case at all for financing the development budget, or capital budget, any differently from the revenue budget, as both budgets raise the demand for current goods and services in exactly the same way.

Having made this general point, let me modify it at once. There is, of course, a case for borrowing, but it must be put in the right way. If you borrow to finance development projects, you should do so with your eyes open and not under the illusion that by borrowing you are shifting the burden to the future. Borrowing serves other useful purposes. For instance, borrowing may be, in effect, a good form of taxation. If people are voluntarily willing to save their money and hand it over to the government for financing economic development instead of spending it on consumption goods, that is a thoroughly desirable thing. You have all the advantages of taxation, since it is not the purpose of taxation to "find the money for development" but to keep the development program within your present available resources. In certain circumstances borrowing may even be better than taxation. People may make voluntary subscriptions to bonds, but you might not have been able to tax them to the same extent. Your taxation system may not be good enough to reach into all the corners; or again, if you try to tax people, they may stop earning income.

The question of hoarding money and its relation to our problem has been raised. For eliminating competing demands on consumption, saving and hoarding are just as good as taxation and borrowing. But in actual administrative practice I think it would be very unsound to get the idea that hoarding should be encouraged. If people hold on to money, they give you a breathing space in which to work out how to persuade them to lend you their money instead of hoarding it. But a government faced with the knowledge that large hoards of money exist, and might be spent at any time, is in a very unsound position. When you try to get money out of hoards into better types of investment through taxation or borrowing, you are not doing it because the hoarding interferes with your present development program; you are doing it because dishoarding might interfere with your plans at some future date.

Let me add one further word that seems to me important in connection with this idea of having a separate capital budget that can be financed by borrowing. One of the dangers in holding to this idea of borrowing against tangible capital assets is to forget the proposition I made earlier that economic development consists of additions to intangible capital as well as to tangible capital. Now if you believe that you can always borrow safely as long as you are creating a tangible capital asset, you are creating a quite unreal distinction between tangible and intangible assets. For economic purposes there is no such distinction. The only question is whether or not the proposed expenditure benefits the future by contributing to economic development. Now you will see what I am driving at. If you draw a distinction between tangible capital assets that can be financed by borrowing and intangible capital assets that cannot, you not only are doing something that does not make economic sense but also are in danger of distorting your whole development program. You will put too much stress on tangible capital projects and you will tend to underestimate the importance of the other intangible things you should be doing. Your sense of priority is likely to be wrong.

The Contribution of Foreign Financing. If domestic resources can be supplemented by foreign financing, the development program may exceed the total presently available domestic resources. It is useful to distinguish the various uses of foreign finance; I would like to touch on seven of them.

In the first place, there are certain countries and territories which are so underdeveloped that there is no margin at all over and above immediate consumption needs. Any development, as well as capital formation of whatever kind, presupposes an influx of capital resources from abroad. We can broaden this case a little by including the many countries where the possibilities for domestic savings and capital formation are so small in scale that these countries cannot conceivably tackle some of the capital-intensive development projects that ought to be included in a sustained development program and without which continued development may not be possible.

The second function of foreign financing is to speed up capital formation. This may be important for a number of reasons. It may be politically necessary. The population may be impatient for a rapid increase in consumption. Another relevant consideration is that rapid capital formation may be more effective than slow capital formation; this is a case that has been much discussed in recent years. If we start off in a big way and undertake simultaneously a series of complementary investments, development becomes much more effective and can be made into a continuous process more readily, whereas by starting off in a small way, we may not get anywhere at all. The increase in output may be only just sufficient for the increase in population or for the increase in consumption that may be politically necessary, so that there is no cumulative development at all.

Third, through foreign financing it may be possible to plan capital formation over a longer range, provided that there is reason to expect a sustained influx of capital from abroad. There is no longer need to lay stress on those developed projects which yield immediately disposable output next year or in two years time; it becomes possible to look at the development program more on grounds of general efficiency and to include a number of slowly maturing projects if necessary. You can either speed up your development program, as explained before, or keep to your timetable, in which case you can broaden your program.

Fourth, an influx of foreign capital may be useful by enabling the government to maintain consumption at a higher level than would otherwise be possible. Some increase in consumption by improving efficiency and productivity may well be an element of capital formation; in other cases the maintenance of consumption may be a political or administrative precondition for development because the government is incapable of restraining the demand. The increase in consumption may also be desirable in order to maintain a certain fairness between different generations; there is no particular reason why development which will benefit future generations should be entirely financed from the sacrifices of the first generation. By borrowing from abroad (and only thus) it is possible to shift the burden of economic development from the present generation to future generations. This may be preferable on grounds of general efficiency as well as fairness because the future generation can be assumed to be better capable of carrying these burdens.

Fifth, apart from the maintenance of consumption, the value of the influx of foreign capital may lie in a reduction or elimination of inflationary pressure. In the case of imported consumption goods, the effect is fairly obvious. In the case of imported capital goods it is a little more complicated; but at least we may say that if the influx of capital goods is financed from abroad, there will be less inflation, other things being equal, than if there had been the same amount of investment and development without financing from abroad. Perhaps the best way of making the issue clear is to say that if an underdeveloped country uses foreign financing in the form of an influx of capital goods, it can have more development and investment with the same degree of inflationary pressure; alternatively, it can have the same amount of investment and development with less inflationary pressure than would otherwise have been the case. In practice the most likely combination is much more development and some more inflationary pressure.

The sixth use of foreign finance that should be distinguished is that of reduced balance-of-payments pressure. Foreign financing is not just money, not just additional resources; it is foreign exchange, command over foreign resources. Foreign credits naturally help to reduce the balance-of-payments pressure in a country which utilizes foreign finance. It may also improve its terms of trade and its bargaining position. What I have in mind is the fairly obvious point that a capital influx will relieve the balance-of-payments pressure on an underdeveloped country by putting it in a position in which it no longer has to pay for all its imports by as many exports. The bargaining position of the underdeveloped country is strengthened; it can hold back commodities that are in stock and wait for more favorable opportunities to sell. Thus, if we assume that the underdeveloped country concerned is determined to have its given degree of development and we then consider the alternatives—either to get loans from abroad or to finance the whole program by a domestic effort (and in the case of foreign exchange requirements that means *exports*)—I think it is very probable that the use of foreign credits would improve the country's terms of trade and raise its export prices in relation to its import prices.

Finally, the seventh and last use for foreign financing that I wish to list is that it increases the international division of labor. Foreign financing helps in the international specialization and international division of labor by enabling the underdeveloped country to import goods from abroad on credit now, paying for them later through increased exports of the goods it is presumably fitted to produce rather than being forced to attempt to produce goods, especially capital goods, which almost by definition it is not particularly suited to produce. Thus is removed the need for inefficient high-cost industries which may become a permanent drag.

SOME COMMON DEFECTS OF DEVELOPMENT PROGRAMS

A summary of the most common defects in development programs was drawn up at a United Nations Seminar on Formulation and Execution of Development Programmes held in Puerto Rico in 1950. I was privileged to participate in that meeting. To present this summary seems to me a fitting conclusion to my lectures, in the course of which I have discussed most of the eleven points mentioned in it.

1. *Lack of Consistency.* Development programs are not always consistent with the total financial resources available or with the particular requisite types of finance available. Sectional or regional programs tend to add up to more than available resources; this results either in starting more than can be completed or else in a cutting-down process which leaves an unbalanced set of measures.

2. *Priority for Public Works.* Development programs may tend to assign too much priority to public works projects relative to such needs as improvement of food production and general raising of productivity.

3. *Emphasis on Public Sector.* Since public investment is under much more direct control than private investment, development programs tend to give too much attention to the public sector and too little to the private sector. This should not be allowed to weaken development in the private sector unduly through diverting an excessive proportion of scarce resources into investment in the public sector.

4. *Paper Targets for Private Sector.* Development programs tend to establish paper targets for the private sector without providing for the measures required to assure that these targets are in fact attained. Alternatively, programs sometimes are faulty in trying to do by public expenditures what would be equally or more suitable for the private sector.

5. *Interest in Spectacular Projects.* Development programs tend to overemphasize investment which takes the form of concentrated, large-scale projects which are spectacular rather than basic, at the expense of

scattered, small-scale improvements not necessarily requiring big capital investment, which in the aggregate may be as important as, or more important than, a few big projects.

6. *Neglect of Short-term Requirements.* There is a tendency to neglect short-term requirements in the desire to draw up long-term development programs. A failure to solve pressing development problems may endanger the long-term objectives aimed at by the program.

7. *Insufficient Study.* Major schemes are sometimes started without sufficient prior study, sometimes under political pressure or in understandable impatience to get things started. In general, both the selection of projects and the examination of individual projects will require careful analysis. Time spent in such analysis is not wasted.

8. *Concentration on Creation of Tangible Capital.* Development programs tend to concentrate too much on specific expenditure resulting in the creation of tangible capital, to the neglect of improvements in institutions, in the domestic, economic, and social climate, and in the standards of the traditional government services.

9. *Multiplicity of Controls and Inducements.* In trying to secure attainment of private-sector targets, development programs tend to rely on a multiplicity of inducements and controls not sufficiently harmonized with each other. Such measures may create unnecessary conflicts between private and public interests.

10. *Insufficient Working Capital (for Productive Installations).* Development programs tend to concentrate too much on fixed investment and not to provide sufficient working capital for the productive installations they include. This may result in loss of productivity.

11. *Lack of Clearly Defined Priorities.* Development programs often lack clearly defined priorities. It does occasionally happen that without further inquiry one particular thing stands out as the supreme need at a particular moment, and in that case it is perfectly proper that such a particular project should be considered and promoted in isolation. This situation, however, will be the exception rather than the rule.

10

The Mechanics
of Economic Development:
A Quantitative-model Approach

This quantitative-model approach dates from 1952. It is tempting to improve the quantitative parameters which have been put into this model in the light of hindsight. Fortunately, the corrections which one would make happen to cancel out, in fact quite closely so. Thus the total picture and conclusions drawn from the model would not be affected. It is for this reason that the temptation to readjust the model has been resisted.

The two chief changes concern the rate of population and the capital/output ratio. As regards the first, I would now have written into this model a higher rate of population increase, perhaps 2 per cent per annum. When I assumed the lower figure of 1.25 per cent and maintained that this was typical, I was influenced by the official Indian figures and estimates of earlier UN committees. The higher rate of population increase would, of course, correspondingly raise the cost of transfer and capital requirements. On the other hand, the capital/output ratio of 6:1 which I assumed—also under the influence of the work of earlier UN committees—seems unduly unfavorable in the light of subsequent data and research. I would now assume a ratio of perhaps 4:1. As it happens, the burden to the economy of providing for 1.25 per cent of the population at a ratio of 6:1 is practically identical with the burden of providing for 2 per cent of the population at a ratio of 4:1. Thus the general picture is little affected, and the reader may be able to make his own adjustments.

Let us consider some of the important relations in development planning for underdeveloped countries, first with the help of a numerical illustration (hopefully thought of as reasonably realistic) and then with the help of a more general model of the type made familiar by the work of Domar, Harrod, and Hicks. It is hoped that this approach will lead toward an understanding of some of the problems involved in development planning and their mutual interrelation.

This paper was originally published in *The Indian Economic Review*, vol. 1, no. 2, August, 1952.

MODEL SCHEME

1,000 persons at $100 each = total "national" income of $100,000

Agriculture　　　*Nonagriculture*

700 persons at $57 each = $40,000　　　　　300 persons at $200 each = $60,000

Natural increase each year 12.5 persons = 1.25%

70% in agriculture　　　　*30% outside agriculture*

+8.75 persons		+ 3.75 persons
-8.75 persons	*Transfer from Agriculture: "Industrialization"*	+ 8.75 persons
+0.00 persons		+12.50 persons

Development Outline

A. "Industrialization" (transfer)

    Cost: $4,000 per worker transferred   Benefit: Increased annual net output = $2,333

        $1,600 per person transferred   (Yield 16%)

        8.75 persons = $14,000   (Capital/income ratio 6:1)

B. Agricultural investment

    Cost: $4,800   Benefit: 3% of agricultural production =

                                        $1,200

                              (Yield 25%)

                              (Capital/income ratio 4:1)

C. Provision of additional capital for 3.75 persons outside agriculture

    Cost: at $800 per person = $3,000   Benefit: $750

                                            (Yield 25%)

                                          (Capital/income ratio 4:1)

Financing

Total cost (A + B + C)　$21,800　　　Total benefit (A + B + C)

  "Naturally available"　　6,000　　　$4,283 per annum of which $3,033 is in-

Deficit　　　　　　　$15,800　　　crease per capita

(Cost increases by 1¼% per annum)

	Disposition of per capita increase:		Development becomes
	New development	Increase in consumption	self-supporting in
Case I	$1,500 (50%)	$1,500	13 [or 11] years
Case II	$ 600 (20%)	$2,400	50 [or 27] years
Case III	$ 180 (6%)	$2,820	never [or 67 years]

The Model Scheme shows in its top part the typical structure of an underdeveloped economy.

The Model Scheme assumes that 70 per cent of the population is in the agricultural sector, that the share of agriculture in the total "national" income is 40 per cent, and that the ratio of agricultural per capita income to average per capita income is 57 per cent. It is of considerable interest to note that in the period 1799–1860, when the United States national per capita income was $216 of 1926 purchasing power, 72.8 per cent of the population was in agriculture, agriculture accounted for 39.3 per cent of the total national income, and the ratio of per capita income in agriculture to the average was 54 per cent.[1] These figures come remarkably close to those assumed in the Model Scheme.

We consider a group of 1,000 persons in an underdeveloped community and assign to this community a per capita income of $100 at current prices. As far as national income figures can be relied upon, this would represent a community which could be considered as about average for the underdeveloped parts of the world. The total "national" income of the group would then be $100,000. We are not concerned here with the difficulties of accurate measurement of national income with its meaning in underdeveloped communities. We shall merely assume that a satisfactory way has been found of measuring incomes. We shall leave it open whether the figure represents a measurement of economic welfare, of material resources, or only of resources entering into the market economy. Any one of these definitions will do as long as it is consistently kept in mind.

We next divide our group into an agricultural sector and a non-agricultural sector. It is one of the characteristics of underdeveloped communities that 60 to 80 per cent of the population is engaged in agriculture. We assume 70 per cent in agriculture and 30 per cent outside. This is a proportion which seems to be pretty closely correlated with the income levels assumed.

Next, the Model Scheme assigns a per capita income of $57 to the 700 persons in the agricultural sector, of $200 to the 300 persons in the nonagricultural sector. The available statistics, for what they are worth, seem to be remarkably unanimous in determining per capita income in the agricultural sector of underdeveloped economies as around 55 to 60 per cent of the average per capita income.[2]

In view of the small size of the nonagricultural sector, the assignment of 57 per cent of the average per capita figure to the agricultural sector carries with it the corollary that per capita income in the nonagricultural sector is twice the national average.[3]

---

[1] Robert F. Martin, "National Income in the U.S., 1799–1938," National Industrial Conference Board, Inc., New York, 1939; quoted in Simon Kuznets, "National Income Estimates for the U.S. prior to 1870," *Journal of Economic History*, Spring, 1952.

[2] It is remarkable that this relation also applies to more developed countries. In the United States, income per head in agriculture in 1930 was 59 per cent of the average national income, in the United Kingdom, 63 per cent. In Sweden, it was 58 per cent in 1920, but this seemed to have dropped to 40 per cent in 1930. Figures taken from E. M. Ojala, *Agriculture and Economic Progress*, Oxford, Fair Lawn, N.J., 1952, table LI.

[3] This latter figure is, of course, higher than the corresponding figures for the

A high ratio of average income in the nonagricultural sector to the national average is in accordance with observed facts and general impressions.

In considering the assumed per capita income levels in the agricultural sector and the nonagricultural sector, it may be useful to recall again that income is not necessarily used here as a measure of relative welfare in the two sectors.

It follows for our model—and for reality if our assumptions are realistic—that "national" income originating in agriculture accounts for only 40 per cent of the total "national" income, even though the bulk of the population is engaged in the agricultural sector. Thus, it is only with reference to employment and not with reference to national income that agriculture can, in strict truth, be described as the "basic" activity in underdeveloped countries. This point is worth making, since reports of missions and similar documents abound with statements that improvements in agriculture are in some sense "more important" than nonagricultural improvements because agriculture is the "basic activity."

So much for the present structure of our underdeveloped group. Economic development for this group will mean a structural change. The proportion of population in agriculture will have to fall, and the nonagricultural sector will have to expand. It may be noted that for our present purpose it is *entirely irrelevant* whether this structural change is considered as the "purpose" or "objective" of economic development or as its consequence. Whether we start off with "industrialization," with agricultural development, or in any other way, rising income levels will have to be accompanied by a corresponding change in structure, i.e., a relative shrinkage of the agricultural sector. If a 70:30 ratio of agriculture is typical of underdeveloped countries, something like a 20:80 or 15:85 ratio is typical of countries at a high state of economic development, which are assumed to be closed systems (i.e., after allowance has been made for surpluses of exports or imports of agricultural products).

The speed, or rate, of economic development may then be described by the rate at which the 70:30 ratio in economic structure is approximated to the 20:80 ratio which represents ultimate equilibrium at a high level of development.

A convenient assumption for an economy in a fairly rapid process of economic development is the assumption that the agricultural population will remain constant in absolute numbers and that the change in structure is brought about by a concentration of the natural increase in population

---

United States, the United Kingdom, and Sweden, since the nonagricultural sector is much larger there. In none of these three countries did nonagricultural income approach twice the national average, although Sweden in 1870 came fairly close to that ratio. *ibid.*

in the nonagricultural sector. This assumption has been satisfied with a fair degree of approximation in a number of countries going through a process of development in an area of settled population.[4]

Thus, over long periods of British, Swedish, Russian, and Japanese development, the agricultural population remained approximately constant in absolute size. This assumption of constant absolute size of the agricultural population has been incorporated in our model. It should be emphasized, however, that this represents fairly rapid economic development.[5]

The Model Scheme could be adjusted to any other slower rate of development. Thus, it could be assumed that one-third or one-half of the natural increase in population goes into agriculture or that the rate of increase in the nonagricultural sector is twice or three times or five times that in the agricultural sector, etc.

In our model, we assume an increase in population of 1.25 per cent per annum. This is the estimated actual figure in the underdeveloped world as a whole. Contrary to a general impression, there is no clear-cut evidence that the population in the underdeveloped world as a whole increases significantly faster than in the more developed parts.[6] The model population of 1,000 will thus increase by 12.5 persons in the first year.

In accordance with our assumption, the agricultural population remains at 700, and the total increase of 12.5 persons is added to the 300 persons in the nonagricultural sector, resulting in a rate of growth of about 4 per cent per annum in the nonagricultural sector. The structural ratio on this assumption is changed from 70:30 to 69.1:30.9, approximately. If the rate of population increase should slacken in the course of economic development, the resulting degree of structural change each year would be correspondingly less.

The increase of 12.5 persons in the nonagricultural sector may be divided up into 3.75 persons representing the natural increase of population in the nonagricultural sector[7] and 8.75 persons representing the transfer of the natural increase of population in the agricultural sector from that sector to the nonagricultural sector. This distinction between the two increments in the nonagricultural sector may or may not be considered

[4] Excluding such countries as the United States, Canada, Australia, etc., where development was associated with new settlement, and agriculture and nonagriculture expanded together.

[5] Although it would take 108 years on this assumption for a 70:30 ratio to be converted into a 20:80 ratio, assuming a rate of population increase over the whole period of 1.25 per cent per annum.

[6] The contrary impression may be due largely to a fixation on a few areas of rapid population growth, such as Puerto Rico, Ceylon, and others. (These areas are often islands.) It may also partly be due to comparison with the low birth rate of industrialized countries in the 1930s. See, however, the introductory note of this chapter.

[7] Assuming that the natural rate of increase in population is the same in the agricultural and nonagricultural sectors.

relevant in a numerical-model approach. One can either assume that the increase from whatever source has to be provided with new capital on standards identical to both groups or assume different standards. For instance, in our model we consider the two increments separately. We assume that the natural increase of population in the nonagricultural sector (the 3.75 persons) is fitted into the nonagricultural sector at prevailing standards of productivity and capital equipment, whereas the 8.75 persons, representing transfer from agriculture, are the labor spearhead of a more advanced technology amounting to some "capital deepening" in the nonagricultural sector.

THE DEVELOPMENT OUTLINE

We are now in a position to consider a development outline for our underdeveloped community. The community is faced with three tasks:

A. To equip the 8.75 persons transferred from the agricultural to the nonagricultural sector in such a manner that they can become the spearhead of an improved technology. This transfer may be called "industrialization" if we remain conscious of the fact that it includes transfer to commercial, financial, and personal services, etc.

B. To increase agricultural production, with the constant number of persons employed in agriculture, sufficiently to provide food for the increased population in the nonagricultural sector and also to provide for such increases in consumption as are part of the development program.

C. To provide for the natural increase of population in the nonagricultural sector at prevailing standards.

We shall consider these three steps in turn.

A. The cost and results of "industrialization" will depend on the specific circumstances of the individual country. The cost may best be estimated as a dollar investment per person transferred or per worker. Cost per worker will be high where the proportion of public utilities and heavy industries included in the development program is high and also where large-scale units of production at advanced standards of technology are provided. Some years ago, the cost of providing additional employment of a nonagricultural type was frequently estimated to be $2,500 per worker transferred, or $1,000 per person transferred.[8] For our present purposes, this figure would have to be somewhat increased, partly because of the rise in prices since then, partly because a community at a standard of $100 national income per capita would have to include in a long-range development program a high proportion of capital-intensive basic services and utilities. The standard of technologies will partly depend on what technologies are available; and since technological research is centered in capital-rich

---

[8] Allowing one and one-half dependents for each worker.

countries and capital goods will have to be largely imported, it follows that the standard of technology will have to be more advanced than the standard that would naturally correspond to the circumstances of the underdeveloped group. It may be noted that overpopulation, while it makes "industrialization" more necessary, also tends to make it cheaper, provided that the right kind of labor-intensive technologies are at the disposal of the underdeveloped countries. Hence, it is true only in a restricted sense that overpopulation is an obstacle to economic development.

We shall assume a cost of $4,000 per worker transferred, or $1,600 per person transferred. This would provide at present prices for a reasonable proportion of such capital-intensive installations as large-scale irrigation, power, and railways, while at the same time assuming a modest standard of technology and leaning toward smaller-scale and light industries as well as toward commercial and personal services. It makes some slight allowance for housing provision and urban community services, but would still involve considerable strain in that respect.

On the basis of this assumption, the transfer of 8.75 persons would cost our underdeveloped community $14,000 per annum, or 14 per cent of the "national" income of $100,000.

What yield can be expected from this investment of $14,000 on "industrialization?" At this point, we shall have to discard the economist's bias in favor of assuming a high marginal productivity in underdeveloped countries. In underdeveloped countries, it is rarely possible simply to add a piece of directly productive equipment and at the same time observe the *ceteris paribus* of marginal productivity. Basic services, such as power, transport, etc., are already overstrained, and it is not possible to add to the load without also including in the investment an extension of basic services themselves (or else taking away services from other enterprises, thus again diminishing true social marginal productivity). Thus, although marginal productivity in underdeveloped countries is often assumed to be high, in view of the universal shortage of capital it is, in fact an irrelevant concept. The relevant concept is the productivity of the complete "package" of directly productive capital equipment *plus* that required to produce components or complementary goods *plus* the provision of basic services required for the new investment. If it is related to this whole package, productivity may come out quite low, as has been the experience (often unanticipated) of many investments in underdeveloped countries. On the other hand, as investment proceeds and becomes cumulative, the productivity of investment begins to increase again as economies of linkage and scale come into operation.

In our model, since we assume a poor community in its early stages of development and undertaking an all-round investment program, we will have to assume fairly low productivity (with its converse, a high capital/

income ratio). We shall assume a productivity of 17 per cent, giving us a capital/income ratio of 6:1.[9]

On this assumption, the investment of $14,000 will yield an annual net income of $2,333, or 2.3 per cent of the initial "national" income.

B. The agricultural investment target can be derived from the rate of structural change. Since the total population increases by 1¼ per cent per annum while the agricultural population remains constant, it follows that agricultural productivity (output per person) must increase by at least 1¼ per cent per annum if food supplies are to be maintained.[10]

This 1¼ per cent increase in productivity is, however, in the nature of a minimum. In practice, agricultural productivity will have to be increased by more. In the first place, it is not enough to *produce* 1¼ per cent more food; it is also necessary to *transfer* it to the nonagricultural sector. In fact, transfer of food must increase by at least 4 per cent per annum if food supplies per person outside agriculture are to be maintained. In practice, in order to increase the transfer of food by 4 per cent, it will be necessary to increase the productivity by more than 1¼ per cent, since farmers will not normally transfer their total increase in food production but will want to consume some of it themselves. The supply curve of farmers in underdeveloped countries is notoriously inelastic or even backward rising. Furthermore, in the process of economic development, it will be necessary to provide for at least a moderate increase in consumption in the nonagricultural sector. Short of strong-arm methods, some kind of incentive will have to be given to farmers themselves and to the population in the nonagricultural sector. Assuming that consumption per capita is to be increased by at least 1 per cent per annum—a small improvement—and assuming that farmers will transfer one-half of their increased production, it follows that the increase in agricultural productivity must be at least 3 per cent. Since present agricultural output is $40,000 in our model community, an increase of $1,200 must be achieved. This is the agricultural target, consistent with the general development outline.

How much will it cost to achieve this increase of $1,200 per annum in agricultural production? Again, circumstances differ. In this case, overpopulated countries may find it more expensive to increase agricultural output than countries with a plentiful supply of land. In nearly all underdeveloped countries, opportunities exist for raising agricultural output by comparatively cheap methods, such as improved seeds, local irrigation,

---

[9] In view of some of the subsequent arguments, it may be useful to add that this capital/income ratio is based on the assumption of orthodox forms of investment, i.e., special utilization of unemployed and underemployed labor for direct capital formation, and other unorthodox forms of investment are excluded. See, however, the introductory note to this chapter.

[10] In underdeveloped countries, food supplies may often be considered as representative, for practical purposes, of consumption in general.

better rotation, better tools, etc. Assuming that such opportunities exist and are systematically used, it has been estimated that a yield of 25 per cent (or a capital/income ratio of 4:1) would be possible in agricultural investment.[11]

If we accept this estimate, it would be possible to achieve the required increase of $1,200 per annum in the agricultural sector by a capital investment of $4,800. It should be understood, however, that this is based on optimistic assumptions; in some countries at all stages and in most countries at some stages, it may be more expensive to achieve this agricultural target.

C. We have next to consider the cost of providing for the natural increase of population in the nonagricultural sector. We shall assume that no attempt is made to provide the natural increase of population with a more advanced technology than that corresponding to the present level of the group under review. This means that 3.75 persons representing the natural increase in the nonagricultural sectors should be equipped with sufficient capital to produce $200 per capita per annum. The capital/income ratio presently obtaining in the nonagricultural sector is assumed to be 4:1. This corresponds to a net yield of 25 per cent per annum. This assumption seems to fit in with the scattered data available as to net yield outside agriculture in underdeveloped countries. It assumes a lower capital/income ratio than in the case of a more advanced technology because of a higher proportion of personal services, commercial activities, and very small-scale enterprise—all of them containing, in underdeveloped countries, an element of underemployment or disguised unemployment. On the other hand, the yield is assumed to be somewhat lower (or the capital/income ratio somewhat higher) than in more developed countries. The reasons for this are the strain on public services, lack of external economies, lower managerial standards, less reliable flows of raw materials, and difficulties in skilled-labor supply. The absence of a technology suitable to the abundance of labor and shortage of capital also makes the capital/income ratio higher than it otherwise would be.

If the above assumption of a yield of 25 per cent is correct, it would take an investment of $800 for each of the 3.75 persons representing the increase in population to be fitted into the nonagricultural sector. This results in a total investment of $3,000 and an increase in annual net income by $750.

FINANCING OUR DEVELOPMENT PROGRAM

We are now in a position to consider the aggregate cost and benefits of the outlined development program and assess its feasibility in relation

---

[11] *Measures for the Economic Development of Under-developed Countries,* a report by a group of experts appointed by the Secretary-General of the United Nations, UN Publication Sales No. 1951 II.B.2, table p. 76.

to the available resources. The total cost of the development program is $21,800. Of this, $14,000 represents the cost of "industrialization," $4,800 represents the cost of agricultural development, and $3,000 represents the cost of providing for the natural increase of population in the nonagricultural sector.

The benefits from this investment add up to a $4,283 increase in net income per annun. This represents an increase in the total "national" income of 4.3 per cent. When allowance is made for the increase in population, the increase in per capita income is 3 per cent. This is a fairly rapid rate of increase, partly because of the assumed rapid rate of structural change and partly because of the assumed increase in the rate of consumption as a necessary accompaniment of the structural change assumed. The figure of 3 per cent increase in "national" per capita income could be reduced if milder assumptions were made in both these respects.

The total cost of $21,800 represents 22 per cent of the assumed national income. This is a rate of investment which, at low income levels, has been occasionally achieved under special conditions,[12] but clearly cannot be financed by voluntary savings, even if supplemented by the moderate budget surpluses possible by fiscal techniques practicable in underdeveloped countries. Nor can it be expected that the mild degree of inflation which would still be compatible with the execution of a rational development program could result in "forced savings" of anything like this degree.

If we assume that net savings available for new investment at a per capita income level of $100 are no more than 6 per cent, it follows that only $6,000 out of the $21,800 required would be available for the financing of this development outline. (Net savings of 6 per cent at this income level represents the present state of affairs in underdeveloped countries; the assumption that all these net savings are available for the financing of a development program represents a considerable improvement over what is now actually achieved.) Our underdeveloped group is therefore faced with a deficit of $15,800 in the financing of its development program.

The conclusion at which we have thus arrived is that a community of the type considered in the Model Scheme cannot finance a program of rapid economic development through capital investment from its presently available domestic resources. Unless we admit defeat at this point, there are four possible approaches:

1. To reduce the cost of the development program by lowering the capital/income ratio (or increasing the yield per unit of capital employed). This would require adoption of labor-intensive technology and possibly unorthodox forms of investment based on utilization of the unemployed and underemployed labor of our underdeveloped group.

[12] Thus, rates of investment exceeding 20 per cent have been estimated for early stages of Japanese, Russian, and perhaps also British economic development.

2. To increase net savings through attempts at reducing consumption below the initial level of $94 per capita assumed to be voluntarily accepted with the existing distribution of income.

3. To reduce the rate of population increase. This would, in our model, reduce capital requirements in three ways: (*a*) less people would have to be transferred out of agriculture in order to keep agricultural population constant in size; (*b*) accordingly, the increase in food production would have to be less, and thus the agricultural investment program could be cut; and (*c*) natural increase of population in the nonagricultural sector would be smaller. Thus, in our model, total expenditure on the development program and the rate of increase in population would decline exactly in proportion.

4. Finally, it would be possible to carry out the development program if the domestic resources of the group were supplemented from outside.

The first three cases are perhaps more conveniently summarized in the general form of a "dynamic equation" of the Domar-Harrod type rather than in a numerical model. This is done in the last section of this chapter. Before this, however, the fourth case may be illustrated with the help of the lower section of the Model Scheme on page 118.

If we assume that the total deficit of $15,800 in the initial year and the deficits in subsequent years are covered by an influx of foreign capital, the following questions—all of them related—arise: "How long must the influx of foreign capital continue before development can be financed from domestic resources?" "What will be the resulting final capital debt?" "What balance-of-payments surplus must our receiving community have to repay the debt initially incurred?"

Obviously, the answers to these questions depend largely on the disposition of the increments in output achieved in the course of economic development. In the limiting case, if the whole increase is consumed and net savings remain at $6,000 annually, the problem is clearly insoluble. Since requirements will gradually increase with the increase in aggregate population, the deficit will increase, the period over which foreign capital is required will be infinite,[13] and the final debt burden will be infinite.

The Model Scheme on page 118 incorporates three different assumptions about the disposition of the per capita increase in income. In Case I, a high marginal rate of savings of 50 per cent has been assumed; in Case II, a still high marginal rate of savings of 20 per cent has been assumed; in Case III, it has been assumed that the marginal rate of savings is no higher than the average rate of savings, i.e., 6 per cent. The Model Scheme shows that in the first instance, development becomes self-

---

[13] Or at least it will last until the structure of the economy has been changed to the 20:80 ratio between agriculture and nonagriculture which has been defined as the structure of a mature economy.

supporting in thirteen years; in the second instance, in fifty years; in the third instance, never at all. The last conclusion is rather interesting: since the total cost of the development program increases by 1¼ per cent each year, i.e., by $197 in the first year and cumulatively more in subsequent years, it follows that a constant increase in savings of $180 each year will be as useless for achieving self-promoting development as no savings at all.

It may also be noted that a reduction in the marginal rate of savings by a little over one-half, i.e., from 50 to 20 per cent, will increase the period over which the influx of foreign capital is required (and thus the ultimate capital debt) not twice but fourfold. This shows that the final debt burden is highly elastic in respect of marginal rates of savings. A little austerity now will save a lot of austerity later.

The Model Scheme thus illustrates the strategic role of marginal rates of savings. Present incomes of underdeveloped countries are so low that there are fairly strict limits to the volume of savings out of *present* incomes. The main hope for increased savings rates lies in saving a high proportion of the *increments* in income arising in the course of economic development. This also indicates the importance of giving priority in development programs to projects in which a high proportion of the benefits can be recaptured for new investment. Simple benefit/cost calculations are only part of the story.

A simple calculation from the Model Scheme will show that if the marginal rate of savings is as high as 50 per cent—i.e., if consumption per capita increases at the rate of 1½ per cent, while income per capita increases at the rate of 3 per cent—the total influx of foreign capital required over a period of thirteen years will be approximately $100,000. Assuming that this debt carries an average interest and dividend burden of 8 per cent but that no amortization is required, the repayment burden will be $8,000 per annum. This will represent approximately 5 per cent of the "national" income at the moment when development has become self-supporting and a falling proportion after that as the "national" income continues to increase. Over the average of the thirty years after development has become self-supporting, the repayment burden will amount to 3 per cent of the "national" income. Since the underdeveloped countries as a whole export about 20 per cent of their estimated national income, the initial repayment burden will require additional exports amounting to about one-quarter of present "normal" exports, falling to an export surplus of around 15 per cent over the average of the first thirty years of self-supporting development. These figures would, of course, be increased if the initial capital debt had to be repaid as well as serviced, but the initial burden of repayment would be compensated by the subsequent reduction in interest charges.

These figures in proportion do not look unfeasible, but it should be remembered that they are based on an extraordinarily high rate of marginal savings, viz., 50 per cent.

If the marginal rate of savings is 20 per cent (Case II), the required total influx of capital will amount to $400,000, and the repayment burden after fifty years, when development becomes self-supporting, will be over 8 per cent of the national income, even without amortization. In view of the large capital debt, amortization would add heavily to the annual burden. Thus, in Case II the influx of foreign capital would not only have to be long sustained, but it would also either presuppose a heavily export-oriented economic development or create balance-of-payment troubles (unless, of course, the repayment burden were lightened through waivers, grants-in-aid, or defaults).

In Case III, with the marginal rate of savings no higher than the average rate of savings, since the deficit increases each year by more than the assumed increment to savings of $180 per annum, development obviously will never become self-supporting.

The above calculations are made on the assumption of a constant absolute increment to net savings, equal to 50, 20, and 6 per cent respectively, of the initial increase in per capita incomes. This may be a somewhat pessimistic assumption. in view of the fact that "national" income per capita increases over the period contemplated by 3 per cent per annum. Despite the fact that recent research seems to have shown that the assumption of a rising propensity to save does not seem to hold over periods beyond trade cycles, it may be hopefully assumed that the annual increment to savings will also rise by 3 per cent per annum. In that case, of course, the period when development becomes self-supporting will be shortened and the ultimate repayment burden correspondingly less. The respective periods required for development to become self-supporting, on this assumption, are also shown in the Model Scheme on page 118, in brackets.

It will be noted that if the increment in savings is assumed to rise by 3 per cent per annum, development becomes self-supporting even in Case III, in which marginal savings are assumed to be only 6 per cent. In that case, even though additional savings fail to meet additional costs of development in the first years, they ultimately make self-supporting development possible, since they rise at the rate of 3 per cent per annum, whereas the cost of development only increases at the rate of $1\frac{1}{4}$ per cent per annum. Even so, sixty-seven years are required for development to become self-supporting, and the ultimate capital debt will be very high. However, since national income doubles every fifteen years, the total national income in sixty-seven years will be around 2 million dollars (instead of the present $100,000), and the resulting repayment burden will not necessarily be impossibly high. It is not so much a high repayment burden, but rather the very long period of time over which the capital influx would have to be steadily maintained, which makes this approach to economic development seem unfeasible.

A DYNAMIC EQUATION

We may now try to look at this problem in a more general fashion. A very simple, almost tautological equation can be constructed which links the rate of economic development D (defined as growth of per capita income and assumed to be proportionate to growth of per capita capital) with the rate of net savings s, the productivity of new investment per unit of capital p,[14] and the rate of annual increase of population r. The equation reads as follows:

$$D = sp - r$$

This equation can be used to answer four different questions, and it provides a surprising amount of insight into the mechanics of development.

1. Given the rate of net savings, productivity, and population increase, what is the possible rate of development?

2. Given the target rate of economic development and the productivity of capital and rate of population increase, what net savings are necessary to support the stipulated rate of development?

3. Given the stipulated rate of economic development and the rate of savings and of productivity, what rate of population increase can be supported?

4. Given the stipulated rate of economic development and the rate of savings and population increase, what must be the productivity of new investment per unit of capital employed? (The answer to this question is of particular interest.)

The answer to all these questions can be obtained by substituting parameters in the equation.

In illustrating the answers to be obtained, we shall stipulate a rate of economic development of 2 per cent annual increase in per capita income, a rate of net savings of 6 per cent of net national income, a rate of population increase of 1¼ per cent, and a capital/income ratio for normal investment of 5:1.[15]

The answer to Question 1 is as follows: *With 6 per cent net savings, a capital/income ratio of 5:1, and a rate of population increase of 1¼ per cent, no improvement in the national per capita income and no*

[14] The previously mentioned inverted capital/income ratio is also represented by p.

[15] The assumptions correspond fairly closely to those underlying the United Nations expert group's report *Measures for the Economic Development of Underdeveloped Countries."*

economic development by means of investment are possible. The economy is a stationary economy. Since the estimated parameters for savings, population increase, and capital/income ratio are believed to be fairly realistic, this would seem to explain the absence of spontaneous development in so many underdeveloped countries at very low income levels.

The answer to Question 2: *With a stipulated rate of development of 2 per cent per annum, a capital/income ratio of 5:1, and a rate of population increase of 1¼ per cent, a rate of net savings of 16¼ per cent is necessary to make possible the stipulated rate of development.* This rate of savings is about three times the rate often observed in underdeveloped countries.

The answer to Question 3: *With a stipulated rate of development of 2 per cent, a rate of net savings of 6 per cent and a capital/income ratio of 5:1, no increase in population can be supported.* Development at the stipulated rate would only be possible in a society of stationary—indeed, declining—population.

The answer to Question 4: *With a stipulated rate of economic development of 2 per cent per annum, a rate of net savings at 6 per cent, and population increasing at the rate of 1¼ per cent per annum, the productivity of investment per unit of capital would have to be 54 per cent (or a capital/income ratio of less than 2:1).* If the normal productivity of investment is 20 per cent (the capital/income ratio being 5:1), this means that the stipulated rate of economic development can only be sustained if technologies can be found which use a little over one-third the amount of capital per unit of output used in orthodox capital investment.

The last result gives us the crux of the problem. Assuming that the yield of capital is only 20 per cent and that the technology is fixed at a capital/income ratio of 5:1, no economic progress by investment is possible unless output can be increased by direct utilization of unemployed and underemployed manpower and natural resources with no, or practically no, further application of capital. Alternatively, the whole technology of all new investment must be diluted in the direction of labor intensity; the equation indicates the degree to which such dilution will be necessary.

There is yet another approach. If the required yield per unit of capital is 54 per cent but the actual yield is only 20 per cent, it might still be possible to sustain the stipulated rate of economic development, provided that an increase in output 1.7 times that achieved by *new* investment can be achieved by increasing the productivity of *existing* capital. Since the required increase in output is 3¼ per cent (2 per cent per capita and 1¼ per cent increase in population), and since the new investment is assumed to be associated with a corresponding increase only to the extent of population increase, i.e., 1¼ per cent per annum, it follows that to further increase output by 2 per cent, the productivity of existing capital must be increased by 2 per cent. *The stipulated rate of development can be sustained if, in addition to normal investment, the productivity of existing capital is increased by a further 2 per cent per annum.* A study of the cotton-textile industries in Latin American countries, among other studies, has shown the scope for improvement in the productivity of existing capital.[16]

A last word may be indicated about the *r* (rate of population increase) in the equation. It will be noted that in the equation *r* appears as a negative factor, with a minus sign. This must not be interpreted as "proof" of the view that "population is an obstacle to economic development." If *r* appears as a negative factor, this by no means excludes the possibility that a high *r* may have such an effect on *s* or *p* that the net effect of an increased *r* may not be as negative as the formula seems to show, and may even be positive. The effect on *s* is not likely to be especially helpful, but the relation between *r* and *p* is different. A state of overpopulation—the result of a high previous *r*—as well as a high current rate of increase in population—a high current *r*—provides not only a challenge but also an opportunity. An opportunity, that is, so to adjust the technology of new investment that *p*—increased output per unit of capital—rises; and also so to increase the productivity of existing capital by the application of additional labor that *p* is again increased.   .

[16] *Labour Productivity of the Cotton Textile Industry in Five Latin-American Countries,* UN Publication Sales No. 1951 II.G.2.

11

Deficit Financing of
Public Capital Formation

The purpose of this article is extremely modest. It merely attempts to list some of the general interrelation swhich determine the effects of financing government capital formation by deficit and then to mention some of the considerations that have special validity in underdeveloped countries. In this way, it is hoped to clarify some concepts and to provide a basis for discussion. It should be made clear that the article is limited to a discussion of deficit financing for productive public investment only.

GENERAL INTERRELATIONS AND EFFECTS

The problems of definition and measurement of deficit financing are many and confusing. Apart from the obvious need of first defining the scope of "government" and of "capital expenditure," there are different justifiable measures of the public deficit, each of them of specific significance and specific application to different purposes. Definitions can be adjudged bad only where they are inappropriate—or not the most useful ones—in relation to the specific purpose of a particular discussion or analysis.

For the purposes of an introductory discussion here, it may be best to fix attention firmly on the allocation of real resources. We may start out with "unborrowed" private domestic savings, i.e., the excess of private domestic incomes, personal and corporate, over private consumption of goods and services. It should be noted that we have excluded from available private savings any part which may have been placed at the disposal of the government by loan prior to the public capital formation here considered. These unborrowed private savings are available to be used for three purposes: (1) financing private capital formation, (2) financing an

This article, in which special reference is made to the inflationary process in underdeveloped countries, originally appeared in *Social and Economic Studies*, vol. 7, no. 3, Jamaica, September, 1958. It formed a contribution to a Study Conference on Economic Development in Underdeveloped Countries held at the Institute of Social and export surplus,[1] and (3) deficit financing of public capital formation. The concept of deficit financing most suitable to this particular approach must be the excess of public capital formation over and above any surplus[2] of "genuine" government revenue left after covering other (noncapital) government expenditure, due adjustment being made for transfer items and cash balances. Genuine government revenue is defined as government revenue which represents a real transfer of a claim to resources prior to, and independently from, the process of public investment. Revenue does not cease to be genuine because its real incidence is on savings rather than consumption or because it involves a future commitment to repay the provider of the revenue.

The purpose of this definition is to throw light on the disposition of the real resources not claimed by the owners of the "available," i.e., unborrowed, private savings. Thus defined, an increase in the government deficit—whether due to an increase in public capital formation or a reduction in genuine government revenue or an increase in other public consumption of goods and services—forms an additional claim against the available private savings. This additional claim will be accommodated by *making room for it* through separate (autonomous) adjustments, whether a reduction of other claims or an increase of available private savings, or else it will have to be *squeezed in* and cause (induce) adjustments in the other claims or in the available savings. Prominent among the mechanisms which induce such adjustments when the claims are squeezed in are inflationary pressures exercised by the increased deficit.

We can now say that an increased government deficit will be inflationary to the extent that no room is made for it by one or the other of the following changes (or, of course, a combination of these):

1. A voluntary reduction of private consumption (increased propensity to save) without increase in private capital formation or in export surplus.

2. A voluntary reduction of private capital formation without an increase in private consumption.

3. An increase in private incomes without an increase in private consumption or private capital formation.

4. A foreseen or prearranged reduction in the export surplus or increase in the import surplus, e.g., if foreign exchange reserves can be drawn down, if increased foreign grants, loans, or credits are known or assumed to be available, or if income from foreign investments is expected to increase.

Economic Research, University College of the West Indies, Jamaica. I gratefully acknowledge Mrs. O. B. Forrest's valuable comments on an earlier draft.

[1] Which may, of course, be negative; if so, it is the import surplus which finances, and the sentence should be turned around.

[2] This may also be a negative figure.

While the absence of such adjustments produces inflationary pressures, the presence of such adjustments is not sufficient to ensure the absence of inflationary pressures. It is clear that problems may arise concerning the mobility of resources released by the reduction in private consumption and their transformation into the resources required for the increase in public capital formation. Resource immobility may be a separate cause of inflationary pressure even if room is made and the deficit is matched in the aggregate analysis. This is further discussed in the latter part of this article.

An increase in public capital formation will not be inflationary—at least in the aggregative sense—if it is accompanied by a corresponding reduction in other government consumption of goods and services or a corresponding increase in genuine government revenue, or a suitable combination of the two. In this case, there is in fact no deficit financing on the definition used here, i.e., no additional claims on available savings and no reduction of available savings, if other things are assumed to remain equal. Discussion on the inflationary impact of an increased government budget, even when balanced, has served to emphasize, however, that other things are not likely to remain equal. One can hardly neglect the incidence of increased taxation and genuine borrowing on private savings.

But this complication applies also to the adjustments listed above, which imply an assumption of other things remaining equal. In the actual economic process, the aggregates mentioned here—private consumption, private savings, private capital formation, import surplus, foreign investment, public capital formation, other public consumption of goods and services, and public revenue—form an interdependent system. Changes in any one item are highly likely to produce changes in the others. There are obviously numerous possible situations and chains of events following upon a change in any one of these interdependent quantities, and their analysis could become extremely complex. The great range of possible situations also offers scope to a great variety of policies capable of influencing the events flowing from a change in one of these quantities, such as public capital formation, and hence bearing upon the nature and extent of inflationary pressure.

What happens if these adjustments to make room are not made or if their effect is canceled out by their impact on the interdependent system? It is clear that in an *ex post* sense, a deficit-financed attempt to increase public capital formation *must always* be financed by consequential changes in the other aggregates, or else the attempted increase in capital formation cannot in fact take place. Where the government increases public capital formation and other things remain equal, in the end there *must* be a reduction of private consumption or of private investment or a deficit on the current balance of payments or a reduction in current government expenditure or an increase in government revenue. And in the end the sum total of these changes must be equal to the increased public capital formation.

The important difference is that where room is made for the additional claims on available savings by the prior or simultaneous autonomous adjustments described, the increased deficit will not have an inflationary impact. Where adjustments are induced by squeezing in the additional claims, these adjustments are almost certainly[3] the result of an inflationary impact of the government deficit, even though this impact may be repressed or concealed, and even though the final, as distinct from the immediate, impact need not necessarily be inflationary.

But there are three facts which rob these propositions derived from elementary static interrelations of much of their usefulness: (1) The inflationary impact of a deficit incurred for public capital formation is not just a mechanism of adjustment, of squeezing in the additional claims on available resources. It has other repercussions of its own which may affect the immediate situation as well as the long-range objectives of public policy. (2) The changes in the other aggregates—autonomous or induced—which will "finance" the deficit one way or another are changes *in the relative sense only.* (3) The increased public capital formation is, in fact, intended to change the other national income items and their relations, so that it is hardly consistent to assume constancy of these other factors. Something more should be said about these three complicating factors.

First, the inflationary impact has a life of its own. The nature of the interdependence of public capital formation and of the deficit incurred to finance it with the other economic aggregates is such that the extent of the inflationary expansion required to complete the process of squeezing in and produce the final *ex post* "finance" of the government deficit may be large; or it may not be easily predictable; or it may contain in itself strong cumulative elements, particularly when different social groups attempt to shift the incidence of the required adjustments; or it may itself have strong repercussions on the aggregates involved, e.g., affect the productivity of the economy or the productivity of the capital formation which takes place. The adjustment mechanism will affect the distribution of incomes and thus affect the underlying aggregates and propensities. In fact, it is in the redistribution of income toward profits and the consequent increase in savings (or perhaps in the built-in high marginal rate

---

[3] The exception is where we can attribute an immediate, i.e., simultaneous, increase in total output directly to the increased public capital formation; in that case, even the immediate impact need not be inflationary. The exception is obviously more important for the long-term than for the immediate impact, although even during the period of capital formation it is conceivable that the anticipated effects of public investment formation will increase the total available supplies of consumption goods.

of taxation which results from progressive tax rates combined with fixed monetary income ranges) that most analysts see the main way in which the inflationary mechanism brings itself to an end and results in a new equilibrium of available savings and total demand for savings. But these self-adjusting forces may be weakened in their operation (especially in inflation-alert economies), or they may even be overwhelmed by opposite, cumulative forces. At any rate, the inflationary process created by government deficits—quite apart from its function of providing finance for the increased deficit—may have most important effects of its own which may nullify, or more than nullify, any hoped-for benefits from increased public capital formation. We can not disregard these other effects of the mechanism by which an increase in the deficit "finances itself." Inflationary pressure is a mechanism of providing "induced backing" for public investment, but it is also a great deal more than that.

Second, a government deficit is only one of many elements which determine the total of inflationary or deflationary pressures. The preceding analysis tells us only whether increased public capital formation financed by deficits will have inflationary effects or not, compared with the situation *as it would be otherwise.* It is quite possible that in the absence of increased deficit-financed public capital formation the general economic situation would have been deflationary, e.g., because of a decline of private investment or an increase in private savings, a drop in export incomes not compensated by a reduction in imports, abundant crops or an increase in the productivity of labor, or an increased demand for money perhaps due to a shrinkage in the subsistence sector and an expansion of the monetary sector of the economy. Or, indeed, for many other possible reasons. In this case the above analysis remains formally correct. But deficit-financed public capital formation will then be inflationary only in a relative sense, namely in that it compensates for a deflationary trend. It will be reflationary rather than inflationary.[4]

On the other hand, the trend, even without the increased deficit-financed public capital formation, may already be inflationary, perhaps as a result of similar previous deficits. Since we are interested in the absolute impact of government deficits, we must take into account the prevalence of inflationary or deflationary trends in the economy apart from public capital formation financed by deficits. It is at this point that the existence of unemployed resources becomes important. It also follows that once a government deficit has created an inflationary situation, the question of whether or not to continue an original deficit becomes entirely

---

[4] This is especially so, if deficit financing occurs after the collapse of a previous export boom, within the framework of a compensatory budget policy under which surpluses built up during the export boom are gradually used up. Such surpluses can include both budgetary reserve funds and foreign exchange reserve funds.

different from the question of the original justification for the deficit. Hence the analysis, in any case complex because of the mutual inter-dependence of all the factors involved and because of the nonneutral effects of the adjustment mechanism itself, will become even more complex when the situation in the absence of a deficit, or increased deficit, cannot be as-sumed to be stable.

Third, there is the effect of the public investment itself. As has been pointed out in a different context, if, during the period of deficit-financed public capital formation, output shows an increase so large that additional private savings out of increased incomes equal the additional public capital formation, the effect of the deficit will be reflationary rather than in-flationary. If this increase in output can be directly connected with the public capital formation, then the impact of the latter could be justly described as noninflationary. Such a connection is natural to assume in the longer run. Public investment may directly produce output, or, more likely, it may induce additional output by making private capital more productive or by raising the productivity of labor generally. But all these effects will normally follow only with a time lag upon the period of actual capital formation. Furthermore, quite apart from this time lag, the observed marginal output/capital ratio, except in periods of recovery from depression, is not normally more than 40 to 50 per cent; and this includes the increases in output not causally associated with increased capital formation. If we assume that half the actually observed increase in output can be attributed to investment as such, the "causative" output/capital ratio would be, say, 25 per cent. This means that it would take four years for the increased output to equal the deficit incurred; and even if all additional income arising from the additional output were immediately saved or taxed away in the first round, it would take four years for the supply of savings to catch up with the increased demand for them. In the meantime, of course, the adjustment mechanism set in motion by the deficit as well as expenditure out of increased incomes (since in practice not all the increased income will be saved or taxed) would have transformed the original situa-tion, and other determinants of the economic situation would also be changed beyond recognition.

Where there are unemployed resources to begin with, the causative output/capital ratio may of course be higher than 25 per cent, and the increase in output required to provide the additional savings necessary for restoring equilibrium could be achieved correspondingly more quickly. But even under the most favorable assumptions, it is unlikely that the increased savings out of additional output per se will come along in sufficient time to overtake the effects of the inflationary mechanism. Instead, we must put our hopes either in deflationary policies during the period of capital formation or in self-equilibrating tendencies of the inflationary mechanism itself.

The special justification of deficit financing for public capital formation where there are unemployed resources would normally have to be on different grounds. The opportunity cost of the additional public investment will be less, and hence its social productivity higher, if the resources used would otherwise be unemployed. The restoration of equilibrium will then be at a higher level of production—and probably a lower level of prices— than otherwise. With unemployed resources present, one buys more additional output with each unit of deficit finance; hence the price is more likely to be worth paying, and the resulting inflationary pressure is more likely to be amenable to compensatory action or to remain within the safety limits beyond which cumulative forces are released.

SOME SPECIAL FACTORS IN UNDERDEVELOPED COUNTRIES

Within the context of the general analysis presented above, some special factors may now be briefly listed which determine the effects of deficit-financed public capital formation in underdeveloped countries.

The situation is superficially similar to that of developed countries in a depression, in that in many underdeveloped countries a supply of un-utilized labor can be assumed to exist at the going wage rates in the "modernized" sector of the economy. It is admitted that unemployment of labor may take different forms—it may be disguised rather than open, or it may be concealed by the economic and social structure of agriculture and handicrafts—but one may assume an oversupply of labor, in the sense that a potential working force for expanded production is in existence and that its present marginal productivity is nil or very close to nil. There may indeed also be unutilized reserves of raw materials and even of fixed capital equipment, although certainly not to the same extent as in an industrial economy in underemployment equilibrium or in depression. But as against this superficial similarity, there is the important difference that the more productive employment of this unemployed or underemployed labor force is obstructed by something more than a shortage of effective demand.

The difficulty of transforming latent resources into actual output in underdeveloped countries is more deeply rooted. Different analysts have differed about what these other root difficulties are, and indeed they may be different as between different underdeveloped countries. Lack of entrepreneurship or technical knowledge, lack of an adequate framework of public services, lack of incentives for increased effort, ignorance, lack of a market or credit organization, lack of communications, immobility of resources, and absence of adequate economic institutions have all been cited with different degrees of emphasis. A common factor of all these cited obstacles is that they relate to deficiencies of effective supply rather than of effective demand.

Insofar as a lack of essential public services and of communications is among these obstacles, public capital formation assumes particular importance in creating the preconditions for an expansion of output, and this may add to the importance of public investment, financed, if necessary, by deficits. Again, however, the analogy with the case for public investment and compensatory public finance in more developed countries during periods of depression is more superficial than real. The purpose of the public expenditure is different in the two cases. In the depression case, it is to increase incomes and create the demand and price incentives for resumed production; the greater the multiplier, the greater the effect. The public capital formation is justified by its monetary and secondary effects. That is why it might even consist of building pyramids or burying gold or bank notes in disused coal mines. In underdeveloped countries, public investment could be economically justified only for its impact on productivity, for lowering cost curves and increasing the elasticity of supply curves, not for raising demand curves. Hence, the monetary income effects of deficits incurred to finance public investment are not the main purpose but an unintended by-product. If output cannot be expanded under the impact of rising demand, the case for deficit-financed public investment is obviously greatly weakened. It is, in fact, reduced to an argument of *pis aller* or of political or administrative expediency. The expansion of public services is essential, and better ways of doing this may be barred for political or administrative reasons. The income effects of a deficit will normally be at best a helpful accessory. The redistribution of income in favor of profits, as well as the broadening of demand, may possibly serve to assist in the movement toward the main objective, e.g., by adding a further inducement to private investors to take advantage of the opportunities presented by lower cost as a result of the provision of better public services. But the lowering of real cost curves remains the chief objective.

Marginal rates of savings and taxation in underdeveloped countries are often—but not necessarily or universally—very low. This can be attributed to the low level of incomes, the nature of tax systems, the difficulties of effective tax administration, the lack of savings institutions and facilities, a high propensity to consume even in the face of a redistribution of incomes toward profits, etc. Whatever the reasons, the multiplier must often be assumed to be quite high in underdeveloped countries. To this should be added that often there are no surplus foreign exchange reserves, so that the capacity to run an import surplus is small, while the marginal propensity to import may be high. Where foreign exchange, especially accretions of foreign exchange, is largely reserved for producers' goods and there is little or no home production of these producers' goods— both being the case in many underdeveloped countries—the availability of imports becomes a determinant of investment. Thus an increase in the import surplus may be in fact associated with inflationary pressures.[5]

The marginal rate of savings or taxation may be particularly low where the increase in incomes associated with the act of deficit-financed public investment will accrue partly in kind. For instance, where previously unemployed or underemployed farmers are drawn from the countryside as a result of deficit-financed public works or construction of urban public utilities, the real per capita income of those remaining on the land is increased. But this increase may take the form, not of higher money incomes through additional sales, but of increased consumption in kind. Since the persons drawn from the countryside will in their turn also have a high propensity to consume, specifically to consume food, the multiplier may become *pro tanto* very high, and the inflationary gap may express itself sharply in terms of food shortages.

Thus, while the multiplier is likely to be high in underdeveloped countries, the response of supplies to price increases and pressure of demand is likely to be small. Where the factors reducing productivity or lowering elasticity of supply are simultaneously tackled, there may, of course, be an expansion of supplies hand in hand with the deficit-financed public investment; alternatively, the public investment may itself be specifically directed toward removing some of the obstacles.[6] In the first case, the combined result need not be inflationary; in the second case, while the immediate effects would be inflationary, the longer-term effects would be beneficial, and the inflation would be self-correcting after a time if it were not allowed to become cumulative in the earlier stages. Productive public investment directed toward reducing obstacles to increasing supply in the more immediate future, or simultaneously with an attack on these obstacles by other means, provides the classical case in defense of deficit financing.

Added to low productivity and low elasticity of supply when confronted with increased demand, there is a third related yet distinct characteristic. This is resource immobility, i.e., a low capacity of shifting resources from

---

[5] This does not invalidate the general analysis presented in the first part of this article. If the increased level of investment word carried out without the larger import surplus, the situation would be even more inflationary than it actually is. But the point here is that the attempt to step up investment would not and could not have been made without the availability of more imported capital goods. In this sense we can say that an increased import surplus will *de facto* increase rather than diminish inflationary pressures, since the increased investment based on it requires also domestic resources and raises domestic incomes.

[6] This latter possibility is limited by the fact that not all the obstacles holding back supply can be affected by public investment.

one use to another or from one sector to another. While resource immobility obviously contributes to inelasticity of supply, the distinction is of analytic and practical value. Superimposed upon the difficulty of increasing supplies of a given sector from the resources already committed to it, there is the further difficulty of augmenting the resources committed to one sector by reducing the resources committed to another. In a developed economy, especially an industrial economy with a large stock of capital, resource mobility is to some extent provided by the depreciation of capital. This continuously sets free resources in one branch which are then available for use elsewhere. In a growing economy, resource mobility is facilitated by the fact that it is easier to change the allocation of new resources than to change the distribution of resources already committed; it is easier to have differential rates of growth in different sectors of the economy than to have some absolutely declining. An underdeveloped country has neither much capital to depreciate nor a large volume of fresh resources from growth. Fundamentally, however, the greater ability to shift resources observed in more developed economies must be treated as a concomitant of technical progress, technical ability, and a high level of skill and training in the population. That is to say, the same forces which are fundamental to a high level of income are also fundamental to resource mobility. The two tend to go hand in hand.

Resource immobility has an important implication. To set free resources to the extent of, say, 5 per cent of national income in order to augment investment by that amount, it is not sufficient that the same amount of resources should be taken away from consumption or private investment or current public expenditure. This is a necessary but not sufficient condition. If the resources set free by the reduction in consumption or other expenditure cannot be transformed into the resources required for additional investment, the sacrifice will *pro tanto* have been made in vain. It is not difficult to conceive of situations where an increase in investment by 5 per cent of national income may involve curtailments in other directions of perhaps 8 or 10 per cent of national income. This situation has some resemblance to the multiplier effect involved in curtailing domestic incomes in order to achieve certain required reductions in total import demand.

The comparative immobility of resources between sectors in underdeveloped countries, combined with a greater inelasticity of supply within each sector, has consequences which can be expressed in various ways. First, in underdeveloped countries global pressure of demand on resources is more dangerous and more liable to lead to inflation; hence, to maintain stability, underdeveloped countries may have to forego, at least partially, the use of one of the instruments which might otherwise be conducive to economic growth. Second, in underdeveloped countries measures to increase the mobility of resources as between sectors are a precondition for raising the degree of pressure of total demand on resources, since a pressure of total demand will inevitably require adjustments in the allocation of resources between sectors. Third, in the underdeveloped countries the burden of adjustment which will be thrown on imports will tend to be correspondingly greater; the difficulties of achieving an expanded balance of supplies from domestic production lead to an increased need to add to supplies, especially in the bottleneck sectors, through imports from outside.

This last point perhaps deserves special emphasis. One of the means of overcoming the difficulties created by resource immobility and inelasticities of supply is by utilizing export proceeds, foreign exchange reserves or foreign credits. Such foreign exchange resources are normally freely available for supplementing supplies wherever they are particularly short, and offer an escape from the limitations of resource immobility. This alone would give export promotion a high priority in many actual situations in under-developed countries. Added to this there is the fact that export promotion also offers an escape from the limitations set by the narrowness of domestic markets. For these reasons export promotion, where possible, appears to be the natural answer to some of the fundamental dilemmas of economic development.

Within limits, the effects of export promotion can also be achieved by import substitution. But only within limits: import substitution will itself require investment with an import content; hence it may add to the im-mediate problems even where it holds prospects of a long-run solution. Second, import substitution may adversely affect exports. Third, it may result in uneconomic industries. On the other hand, import substitution avoids the marketing difficulties and some of the risks of export promotion. And the resources set free by import substitution would also normally be freely available as between different uses. Export promotion and import substitution will often offer the only immediately possible solutions to some of the problems posed by resource immobility.

As has been indicated above, in underdeveloped countries, with their fluctuating export proceeds, foreign exchange reserves may be accumulated during export booms for use in subsequent periods of export slumps, in which deficit-financed public capital formation could then be nonin-flationary. This procedure, however, presupposes a capacity for self-denial and restraint during periods of export booms. It also presupposes political stability and a government which resists the temptation to snatch quick advantages during its own term of office. Where impatience, popular or governmental, is great and where the need for progress is pressing, such self-denial is not easy. Furthermore, in any given export boom it is not easy to be sure that it is only a temporary situation. Nevertheless, the policies of governments and statutory marketing boards, as well as the existence of currency linkages which introduce an element of automatic stabilization, have in fact opened up opportunities for compensatory policies of this kind. There remains the problem of making certain that such temporary or compensatory phases of deficit financing are in fact kept on a temporary or compensatory basis, i.e., terminated at the proper time. (This difficulty is akin to the difficulty of terminating protection given to infant industries.) In both cases, there is the ever-present danger that "nothing is so lasting as the provisional."

While underdeveloped countries are at a disadvantage, generally speaking, in respect of adjustment of supplies to intensified demand, they are perhaps at an advantage as regards the danger of a cost inflation, or wage-price spiral. It is difficult to be dogmatic about this. The bargaining position of nonagricultural labor, especially of skilled labor, in underdeveloped countries is sometimes very strong. But by and large, especially where unemployment and underemployment prevail and where there is pressure of population on land and on developed resources, the general picture is that temporary inflationary pressures are less likely to set off wage-price spirals. This must not be confused with the possibility that industrial wage rates in underdeveloped countries may be higher than would be best in the light of the resource endowment of these countries and of the low marginal productivity of labor in alternative occupations, especially agriculture and handicrafts. Wage rates can be structurally too high without being very sensitive to moderate increases in prices induced by deficit-financed capital formation. To the extent that this is true, cuts in real wages induced by rising prices may in fact help *pro tanto* to correct the structural "excess" of industrial wages, judged in relation to economic growth requirements. But this would be a dangerous approach unless the policy makers can be certain of the point at which the wage-price spiral begins to operate.

If a combination of high multipliers, low elasticities of supply, and resource immobility is typical of underdeveloped countries, it follows that deficit financing of public investment is particularly dangerous, at least unless these three characteristics are modified prior to, or simultaneously with, the deficit-financed expenditure. These warnings could be fortified by reference to other characteristics of underdeveloped countries. Where habits of monetary exchange and use of monetary institutions are still in their infancy and have to be carefully nursed, it may be especially dangerous to let the value of money depreciate. Where the discipline of reconciling ambitions with limited resources has to be developed, the requirement of a balanced budget should not be easily abandoned. Where shifts to profits may easily result in increased speculation, high-level consumption, or capital flight, the mechanism of inflation loses much of its purpose. Where administrative controls are particularly difficult, inflation may more easily get out of hand. This is indeed a formidable array of warning signals to those thinking of applying the technique of deficit financing in underdeveloped countries, even as the counterpart of productive public investment. The warnings look serious enough to cause acute apprehension in regard to deficit-finance proposals in most, or nearly all, actual combinations of circumstances that are likely to be encountered in underdeveloped countries.

But there remains the exceptional combination of circumstances. There remains the case where perhaps there is a special opportunity to increase production of food and other consumer goods conspicuously and rapidly with the aid of public works and to bridge the interval by drawing on a previously accumulated surplus of foreign exchange. There is perhaps the case of the underdeveloped country with very high marginal rates of savings or taxation. There is the case of underlying deflationary tendencies offering scope for public deficits.

There is, finally, the case where better alternatives to deficit financing, such as increased taxation, are politically or administratively impossible or where their broader economic effects are especially harmful, and where yet some forms of productive public investment are an absolute precondition of economic progress, and where economic progress in turn is an absolute precondition for political and social stability. But even where deficit financing leads to increased capital formation, the dangers of deficit financing must still be weighed against the dangers of economic stagnation or deterioration; and it is often far from clear that the nonexistence of better alternatives should be accepted as a genuine premise of debate. Where the need for public investment over and above what present revenues permit is so crucial and imperative, it is difficult to see why the effort to overcome the obstacles obstructing the use of less dangerous methods of financing could not also be made. A determination to achieve the end would seem to presuppose a determination to make possible the best means. So that even if the discussion is restricted, as it is in this paper, to the financing of productive investment, it would appear that the circumstances justifying deficit financing as a deliberate choice would be rather special and the justified doses closely circumscribed.

12

The Role
of the Public Sector in
Economic Development

THE TASKS OF THE GOVERNMENT

One way of realizing the crucial importance of the public sector, or government, in economic development is to have in mind a list of the various tasks which it is called upon to fulfill in an underdeveloped country during the process of development. It should be emphasized that the listing of these tasks is not in order of priority or importance, as will be explained later.

These tasks may be listed under nine headings:

1. The public sector is directly responsible for about 50 per cent of total investments in an underdeveloped country even where commodity production in agriculture and industry is left entirely to the private sector as a matter of policy or pragmatic fact. This figure of 50 per cent is, of course, a rough-and-ready indicator. In countries where commodity production is particularly vigorous and where a development boom is going on, the figure may be below 50 per cent; in other cases it may be above 50 per cent. But roughly speaking, the capital formation in the public sector will be found to be around 50 per cent. This includes those types of capital formation which are now almost invariably considered to be in the public sector—the infrastructure investments in transport, major power, public buildings, urban utilities, local works, construction of schools, hospitals, etc.

2. Beyond this minimum of investments, in itself amounting to around half the total, the public sector may also be engaged in direct commodity production. Sometimes some of the basic industries are considered to be the public sector, either because of their strategic importance or because of their large capital requirements. Sometimes the public sector also engages in commodity production in nonbasic industries—sugar fac-

This article has been prepared for a volume on "Public Finance and Policy in Under-developed Countries," due to be published under the auspices of the Institute of Fiscal Studies (Instituto de Estudios Fiscales), Madrid. At the time of preparing this manuscript, the volume in which this article was to appear had not yet been published.

tories, cement factories, etc. In economies of this kind, where the public sector penetrates to some extent into commodity production, the share of the public sector in total investments may typically be 60 to 70 per cent of the total. India provides an example of this kind of ratio. The public sector also may assume major or total responsibility for industry or agriculture, as in the U.S.S.R. and countries with a similar system; in such countries the share of the public sector in total investment may approximate 100 per cent. We are not, however, here concerned with the special problems of such economic systems.

3. The public sector also determines the pattern and volume of private investment. Where public investments are largely of an infrastructure character, e.g., transport, power, and urban utilities, they are an essential precondition for private investments which require transport, power, etc. Education and training can also be considered as a vital infrastructure investment by the public sector which is a precondition for private activities. A discussion has been raging among economists over how far it is good development policy to lay down the infrastructure pattern of public-sector investment first and thus facilitate private activities. In practice, underdeveloped countries do not limit themselves to a passive policy of "following the market" in their infrastructure investment, since this creates the danger of a vicious circle: private enterprise may fail to develop for lack of facilities, and the facilities may fail to be provided for a lack of demand for them, in the form of private activities. Where there are actually serious bottlenecks in transport, power, training, etc., as a result of an already existing demand, it is obvious sense to give this type of investment priority over other infrastructure investment. But beyond this, the government can hardly fail to act as a pacesetter in providing infrastructure facilities in advance of actual demand. However, the critics of this policy are rendering a useful service in pointing out that such provision, being purely permissive, offers no guarantee that the private activities will actually follow, and may have to be reinforced by other policy measures or possibly may have to be followed by public sector production of commodities.

4. The governments are also making current expenditures which amount to a minimum of 10 per cent of the national income and may amount to 20 per cent of the national income or more. If governmental expenditures at the regional or local level are included, 20 per cent of the national income in current expenditures should be a normal level for under-developed countries. It is vitally important that these current expenditures should be as efficiently planned and allocated as a public investment pro-gram, perhaps even more so. Many current expenditures are truly develop-mental. This is most clearly the case with expenditures on health and educa-tion, but efficient general administration and the maintenance of law and order are no less vital to economic development than are transport, power,

and steel factories. Other current expenditures are not developmental, and it is important to reduce them to a minimum, to the extent compatible with the other objectives of the government, so that they do not clash too much with the needs of development. It is also important to organize them in such a way that they claim no vital specific resources away from development and even, if possible, make an incidental contribution to development. Defense expenditure is an important category of a basically nondevelopmental expenditure to which the above considerations should be applied. The line of division that is drawn between capital expenditure and current expenditure for purposes of development planning or in selecting projects for foreign aid, etc., is often economically quite artificial, although the former category may be labeled as "development," while the latter category is not. Thoughts in this respect are rapidly changing, particularly as the importance of "human investment" in the process of economic development is realized. The practice of aid-giving institutions or those presenting plans or budgets, however, is not yet fully adjusted to the progress of thinking.

Prof. Arthur Lewis has produced a formula according to which the governments of underdeveloped countries should collect in revenue 20 per cent of the national income and should spend in current expenditures 12 per cent of the national income (i.e., 60 per cent of the total revenue) ; they should save the rest for public investment or support of private investment. But few governments live up to this prescription, which is in any case sufficient only if all branches of public expenditures, capital as well as current, are efficiently organized and if revenue is collected without serious disincentive effects. But these proportions are nevertheless useful for general guidance and as a checklist for governments of underdeveloped countries, as long as it is remembered that their individual circumstances and requirements differ, so that no uniformity can be expected.

5. An essential element in the economic development of a country is in the field of institution building. From trade unions to cooperatives, from an agricultural extension service to a banking system, from a national planning organization to savings clubs—economic development is based on a network of institutions and associations of people of many different kinds. It is an essential job of the government to establish the right kind of institutions or to provide the setting in which the right kind of institutions can be encouraged and can flourish. The creation of institutions is not as glamorous as public investment projects are, and therefore it is often neglected in development planning; but it is essential all the same.

6. The government must adopt and pursue policies that are conducive to economic development. To mention only a few examples: Monetary policy is necessary to prevent inflation, which distorts development and lowers its efficiency, and also to prevent deflation, which can have the same effect. Monetary policy must also see to it that credit is available on the

right terms at the right time to the right people for the right purposes, and that such credit is withheld from people and activities which are not conducive to, or are incompatible with, the development of the country. Fiscal policy is essential to collect revenue in such a way that private savings and investments are discouraged to the least possible degree. Tax exemption and other fiscal incentives can be a powerful stimulus to economic development, as has been shown by the experience of a number of developing countries; but they can also be quite dangerous and costly to the government if not properly handled. Government policy regarding tariffs, import duties as well as export duties, and domestic excise taxes can be powerful factors in shaping the pattern of investment and development. Trade policies and conclusion of trade agreements comprise another field in which good development policies are essential. Fiscal policy can also be of decisive importance in creating or destroying, as the case may be, popular support for the development plan of a country—support that can be vital for its success or failure; this refers particularly to the equity and incidence of taxation on different classes and different social groups. It is often not easy to combine the consideration of equity and popular support with the incentive for investment and savings. Where considerations pull in opposite directions, reasonable compromises and combinations have to be found and hammered out. Many other policies of the government are important— policies in respect to patents, treatment of foreign investors, trade associations and monopolies, industrial arbitration, wage controls, etc. In fact, there is hardly any governmental policy measure which does not have developmental repercussions and so does not have to be fitted into a system of governmental policies. Among development policies, land reform can be of particular importance in many developing countries. The raising of agricultural productivity is bound to be one of the priority problems of any underdeveloped country and is actively tied up with the possibilities of financing industrialization. The increase in agricultural productivity, in turn, will often depend on legal clarification, property rights, security of tenure, and other elements of land reform, particularly better distribution and utilization of the land.

7. The government must also render a large number of preliminary services without which productive activities are greatly handicapped. Investment can only proceed on the basis of a certain degree of knowledge; this requires statistics, other economic information, surveys of natural resources, measurements of river flows, geological and soil-classification surveys, industrial feasibility studies, transport and power surveys, research laboratories, testing of raw materials, quality control, etc. Young enterprises in underdeveloped countries need help with training of their workers, management-advisory services, credit lines, etc. In many cases, it has been found advantageous to build industrial or trading estates

where new enterprises can reduce their risks by renting their factories instead of buying them and by having transport facilities as well as other managerial aids provided. If they fail, the loss is minimized and another young plant can be tried out; if they succeed, they can stand on their own feet and they also should make room for another pilot project.

All these manifold facilities, from statistics to trading estates, have to be almost wholly provided by the government, since the private incentive to do so is not sufficient even where this is possible. Experience in developing countries has served more and more to point out the critical importance of such preinvestment facilities in the economic growth of a country. Earlier economists may have assumed that investment opportunities would automatically be good where capital was scarce. It is now more clearly realized that investment opportunities do not just exist, but can and must be created; and that they are certainly not automatically created by a mere shortage of capital. This growing emphasis on the creation of investment opportunities has added yet another function to the tasks of the public sector in economic development.

8. Another task of the public sector is the setting of goals. Economic development implies an expanding economy, the various constituent elements of which must stand in a considerable and consistent relationship to each other. To minimize bottlenecks and waste, the growth of agriculture, industry, exports, services, etc., must proceed in a balanced pattern. All this requires some kind of overall view of (1) the rate and direction of expansion of the economy as a whole and (2) the derived impact on the different sectors, regions, and types of activity. It is only the government, or public sector, which can establish such an overall view and set up the framework of targets which describe a path of balanced expansion of the economy. The private inducement to invest and produce will be greatly strengthened if the individual, planning his investment or activities, can see a picture of what is likely to happen in the rest of the economy. Uncertainty in regard to this picture will in itself reduce investment and thus contribute to stagnation. If the picture formed is one of balanced expansion and if the government's record inspires confidence that it has the intention and the means of seeing that the projected picture of balanced expansion is actually carried out, this may release powerful incentives to invest and also bring to life sources of finance for the additional investment thus motivated. If reasonably set and consistently related and if combined with an intention and ability to implement them, such goals can be to a certain degree self-justifying, in that their achievement is more likely than if they had never been set.

9. And so, finally, we come to planning. Most developing countries now draw up development plans which they try to make as comprehensive as possible. Experience has shown that such general development plans can

be of very great value. Development planning is nothing more than performing all the functions previously listed, seeing them as a related and consistent whole, and putting them forward as a public document for the information of the citizens of the country itself, including its officials, and also for the information of foreign governments or individuals who are interested in extending aid or in developing activities in the country publishing the plan. The exercise of drawing up the plan enforces upon the government the necessity of studying the interrelationships and consistency of all its various goals and objectives, its development policies, etc. It helps to set the annual budget and other measures of the government within a background which can make them at the same time more intelligible and acceptable to parliaments, taxpayers, and public opinion generally. The necessity to report on the progress and implementation of the plan will keep the government on its toes. Successful implementation of the plan can inspire confidence. A good plan, by indicating priorities, can make foreign aid more effective, attract additional foreign aid which might not be forthcoming otherwise, and indicate priorities for technical support and assistance. A good plan also provides the necessary guidance for activities which require a clear long-term picture, such as the making of decisions regarding the educational system, training institutions, road systems, and national power grids.

The technique of preparing and presenting plans has been much discussed and much developed in recent years. In many ways, the Indian planning procedure and planning techniques have served as models in this field, and it is in India that the value of planning procedures has been clearly demonstrated. Among Western countries, there was at one time considerable suspicion of the idea of development planning because of a confusion between planning, on the one hand, and public ownership and public control, on the other hand. However, this confusion has now largely been cleared up. On the one hand, the underdeveloped countries have learned to think of development planning as much more than public investment only, as including the encouragement and development of private activities and the development of good policies; on the other hand, the industrial countries have learned to avoid the confusion between planning and control and have learned to see that their aid will be more effectively used within the framework of a plan. We can therefore list the preparation of a general development plan and its execution as among the new generally recognized tasks of the public sector in newly developing countries.

The Relative Importance of Public-sector Functions. It should be emphasized again that the above tasks and functions of the public sector have not been put down in any order of priority. All too often, it is assumed that public investment projects are the most important contribution of the public sector to economic development. Nothing could be more mistaken than this view; it is an example of the "fallacy of misplaced concreteness." We always tend to attribute more importance to the physically tangible than to the physically intangible. For the same reason, we always tend to underrate the importance of "human capital"—skills, training, scientific knowledge, cooperative habits—as compared to physical investments. It is not really sensible to establish any order of priority among these different tasks of the public sector. But to the extent that this is possible at all, one may say that development policies are fundamentally more important than the public investment program. Naturally, a good investment program is also important. If the scarce resources of an underdeveloped country are scattered on prestige projects or wasted on technically unsound projects, the best development policy will not prevail. Yet there is some sense in saying that development policies are more fundamental than specific public development projects. Good development policies can create a setting for the unfolding of human activities and resourcefulness which will keep creating a capacity for growth, and this will find its expression in development in due course. Moreover, growth thus brought about is likely to be more enduring and self-sustaining than growth merely brought about by some piece of individual investment. The latter may well create isolated enclaves in an otherwise backward economy and fail to have multiplying effects. This is the problem of the "dual economy" which has preoccupied many students of underdeveloped countries.

A Concrete Example of the Government's Role. So far, we have tried to visualize the importance of the public sector by describing its various tasks and functions. This is necessarily a somewhat abstract and general procedure. A more concrete and perhaps more impressive way would be to select specific development problems and demonstrate how in under-developed countries the solution of such problems is not possible without energetic action by governments and the public sector.

Take, for instance, the case of an underdeveloped country, perhaps in Africa, which has possibilities of cattle raising as a promising avenue of economic development. At first sight, this does not seem to have much to do with the public sector. Nobody proposes state farms or state owner-ship of herds of cattle; nobody proposes state factories for meat canning; nobody proposes state trading in cattle or meat.

However, even an elementary examination of the problem shows the essential role of the public sector. The cattle are diseased and must be inoculated to eliminate this disease. Who is going to train the veterinarians and send them out to the villages? Who is going to provide the serum? Who is going to persuade the villagers that the veterinarian assistants with their needles are not agents of the devil scheming to kill their cattle off? Who is going to persuade the farmers that cattle can be an economic asset and that fewer but healthy cattle are better than a large herd of diseased cattle? At present, cattle in this country are a symbol of social status and a form of investment of accumulated wealth. Who is going to provide alternative symbols of social status or better forms of investment, such as savings banks?

Improvements in cattle raising will mean new grazing grounds, which will require land reform. Who can undertake the necessary land-reform measures? Who can tell the farmers about proper grazing methods or proper feeding techniques? Cattle without control will lead to soil erosion and thus do more harm than good. Who is to be responsible for necessary measures against soil erosion? Cattle raising will be useless without transport facilities to take the cattle or the cattle products to markets, whether internal markets or ports for exports. Who is to be responsible for the transport facilities—roads, railways, port facilities, perhaps refrigeration and storage facilities? The exportation of meat or dairy products or live cattle may depend on trade agreements with neighboring countries. Who is to conclude these agreements? The production of meat may require foreign capital in the form of investment in meat-packing plants. Who will give the foreign investors the necessary securities, guarantees, or conditions under which they are willing and able to operate? Similar questions arise if the investors are nationals and not foreigners.

The above list of questions is by no means exhaustive, but it is already long enough to indicate the crucial role of the public sector at each and every stage of this project. All the questions are rhetorical only. There can only be one answer to them, and that is the government—the public sector.

So, by following through individual problems we arrive at the same results we arrived at earlier in the chapter: the role of the public sector in economic development is all-pervading even where it is not immediately visible.

MAKING THE PUBLIC AND PRIVATE SECTORS WORK TOGETHER

The discussion so far has not thrown much light on what many people might instinctively feel should be the first question which comes to mind. I refer to the question of public ownership, of the line of demarcation between the public and private sectors. This omission has been deliberate. Although the question of public ownership occupies a good part of the discussion concerning the role of the public sector in economic development, it is by no means as important as it seemed to be until recently. Like development planning, the question of public ownership has been often treated as a question of economic dogma, and as such has aroused all the proper religious passions. Again, as in the case of economic planning and for related reasons, there is now a much greater tendency to discuss this question as pragmatic rather than dogmatic and, accordingly, with less heat.

Once the question is approached pragmatically, it becomes more difficult to lay down general rules concerning the proper size of the public and private sectors respectively. However, a few general remarks can be safely made. The first general rule is that the public sector in under-developed countries normally has its hands so full with the manifold tasks described in the first part of this chapter that it will be well advised to leave alone any tasks which can be done just as well or better by the private sector. The overriding exceptions to this general rule exist (1) where the private sector would be foreign rather than national, and there seem political reasons against letting foreign interests dominate, or even partici-pate in, a particular sector or particular enterprises; (2) where the govern-ment decides that a particular sector or particular enterprises are of such strategic or social importance that even national private enterprise should not be given such positions of power and influence.

The second general rule is that the question of public and private ownership should be considered separately from the question of public or private finance. Even where economic development is financed from public savings—such as a surplus of public revenue over expenditures, or the receipt of aid from foreign governments—it does not follow that the develop-ment must be publicly owned or managed; it can be financed or subsidized by the government and yet be owned and managed by private enterprises. The public development corporation can channel finance into the private sector. Admittedly this may call for special methods of controlling the use or preventing the abuse of public money. Conversely, if the source of savings is private, this need not preclude government operation and management if the government has the appropriate techniques for borrowing and using private savings.

The third general rule is that underdeveloped countries are usually dismally short of persons capable of running and managing enterprises. This shortage exists in both public and private sectors. It is therefore of desperate urgency for underdeveloped countries to utilize and foster such talents wherever they may be found, whether in public or private sectors. It is not easy to generalize as to whether the shortage of suitable people is greater on the one side or the other. The normal civil service methods, based more on routine and allocation of responsibility than on initiative and alertness, are not the most suitable for the management of economic enter-prises. It is therefore very important for countries with publicly owned enterprises to try to find methods of organization which lead away from normal civil service rules or to find people from outside the normal civil service for this purpose. The device of special boards or government corporations which are not subject to ordinary civil service rules has often been found successful in this. The country must, of course, be careful, in attempting to get the best of both worlds, not to end up getting the worst of both. A good deal of experience with such special boards and corpora-tions exists, and underdeveloped countries can learn much from this experience.

Another way to make the best use of existing situations and existing talents is to develop mixed forms of organization. There is an infinite variety of possibilities of mixing the different elements of ownership, control, and management as between the private and public domain. The dogmatic approach to the question of public and private ownership leads to a dis-regard of these mixed forms, but with a more pragmatic approach they are coming strongly to the foreground. Mixed forms of ownership of this kind have been particularly prominent in development banking and develop-ment corporations.

The dogmatic approach has also tended to obscure the fact that the relationship between the public and private sectors is essentially comple-mentary, not competitive. The real problem is not one of demarcation but one of mutual interaction. The complementary relationship between the public and private sectors has been clearly demonstrated in the case of India. In India, public ownership and public-sector activities are strongly stressed in the plan. About two-thirds of all planned investment is public investment. At first it was wrongly feared that this situation might lead to an atrophy of the private sector—that it would wither away in the shadow of the powerful public sector. But nothing of the sort happened. Quite on the contrary, when the conviction spread that the government was willing and able to implement the targets of the five-year plan, people began to think in terms of an expanding economy and expanding markets. The result was a burst of private investment in all directions. Coming on top of the public-sector investment, this private investment explosion led to strong balance-of-payments difficulties (and inflationary pressures). These troubles, however, were healthy troubles of growth, and were in fact largely alleviated by concerted aid from abroad, also based upon the evidence of a realistic de-velopment plan with the will to carry it out. At any rate, the situation was not one of an atrophy of the private sector as a result of an energetic action of the public sector, but exactly the opposite. Such relationships tend to be obscured by concentrating attention on "demarcation."

The example we have just given also illustrates a further function of government policy in a developing economy, i.e., to prevent inflationary pressure and adjust the economy to balance-of-payments difficulties. Any strong pressure of demand on existing resources tends to create inflationary pressure, but it is wise to counteract inflationary pressure by financing investment from genuine public or private savings. The relationship between inflation and economic development is not entirely clear-cut. Inflation can be the result of strong economic development not properly counteracted, and in that case it can statistically go together with growth. But growth financed by inflation is likely to be less soundly based and less enduring than noninflationary growth. On the other hand, growth itself is a cure for inflation; it is easier to keep prices stable when the volume of goods and services is constantly increasing and when wage increases can be granted without raising prices as a result of rising productivity. As a result, a controversy has arisen among those who emphasize the need for stability as a platform for sound economic growth (the "monetarists") and those who feel that the inflationary danger is inherent in the structure of underdeveloped countries and can only be cured by growth (the "structuralists"). Both approaches contain an element of truth, and in practice it is perhaps one of the most difficult jobs for a government to decide what kind of inflationary pressure signifies self-terminating growing pains, and what kind of inflationary pressure is unhealthy and to be eliminated. The combination of maximum growth and maximum stability calls for public statesmanship of a high order. But this issue, although closely related to the role of the public sector in developing countries, cannot be pursued here in any more detail.

The really important question is not the one of demarcation of the public sector and the private sector but rather the question whether the essential tasks of the public sector in economic development are effectively carried out or not. If the public sector extends itself too much beyond its administrative and personal resources, then its tasks presumably cannot be well done—and in this case the public sector is too large. On the other hand, if the public sector fails to take the necessary energetic action required and permits a vacuum to arise which the private sector does not or cannot fill, even with inducements by the public sector, then again the tasks falling to the public sector are not well done—and in this case the public sector can be considered to be too small.

In every case, the key problem is not a line of demarcation but the energetic action which is required. This action includes not only public-sector activity as usually defined but also the development of good policies and proper encouragement and assistance to the private sector. Development can be disharmonious because the public sector is overexpanded; it can also be disharmonious because there is not enough energetic public action. The best line of demarcation must be determined in each country in accordance with its own objectives and circumstances.

Both the public sector and the private sector are faced, in the process of economic development, with new, unaccustomed tasks. Adaptation and adjustment in ingrained habits of thinking and operation are required from the civil servant. the private businessman, and others. Whether the civil servants in the public sector or individuals in the private sector are in a better position to make the right kind of adjustment and develop the right attitudes is again a question of fact, not of dogma. All that can safely be said is that, in both cases, traditional methods in underdeveloped countries are, almost by definition, not the ones most suitable for economic development. If economic development is really wanted, even at the price of breaking traditional habits, this poses a problem to be solved. This does not mean, however, that a violent break with tradition is necessarily required or the best method. To the extent that it is possible, to build upon existing traditions and evolve them in the desired directions may lead to better results and produce a type of development more in accordance with the wishes of the people.

PART 4

Some Issues
of Trade and Aid

13

The Distribution
of Gains between Investing and
Borrowing Countries

How the Importance of Foreign Trade to Underdeveloped Countries Has Been Obscured. International trade is of very considerable importance to underdeveloped countries, and the benefits which they derive from trade and any variations in their trade affect their national incomes very deeply. The opposite view, which is frequent among economists, namely that trade is less important to the underdevelopd countries than it is to industrialized countries, may be said to derive from a logical confusion —very easy to slip into—between the absolute amount of foreign trade, which is known to be an increasing function of national income, and the ratio of foreign trade to national income. Foreign trade tends to be proportionately most important when incomes are lowest. Second, fluctuations in the volume and value of foreign trade tend to be proportionately more violent in trade of underdeveloped countries and therefore *a fortiori* also more important in relation to national income. Third, and *a fortissimo,* fluctuations in foreign trade tend to be immensely more important for underdeveloped countries in relation to that small margin of income over subsistence needs which forms the source of capital formation, for which they often depend on export surpluses over consumption goods required from abroad.

In addition to the logical confusion mentioned above, the great importance of foreign trade to underdeveloped countries may also have been obscured by the great discrepancy in the productivity of labor in the underdeveloped countries as between the industries and occupations catering for export and those catering for domestic production. The export industries in underdeveloped countries—metal mines, plantations, etc.—are often highly capital-intensive industries supported by a great deal of im-

This paper was originally presented at the December, 1949, meeting of the American Economic Association. It was printed in *American Economic Review, Papers and Proceedings,* vol. 11, no. 2, May, 1950. The author wishes to acknowledge help and advice received from many friends and colleagues—in particular, Mr. Henry G. Aubrey,

ported foreign technology. By contrast, production for domestic use, especially of food and clothing, is often of a very primitive subsistence nature. Thus the economy of the underdeveloped countries often presents the spectacle of a dualistic economic structure: a high-productivity sector producing for export coexisting with a low-productivity sector producing for the domestic market. Employment statistics in underdeveloped countries do not adequately reflect the importance of foreign trade, since the productivity of each person employed in the export sector tends to be a multiple of that of each person employed in the domestic sector. Since, however, employment statistics for underdeveloped countries are notoriously easier to compile than national income statistics, it is again easy to slip from the fact that the proportion of persons employed in export trade is often lower in underdeveloped countries than in industrialized countries to the conclusion that foreign trade is less important to them. This conclusion is fallacious, since it implicitly assumes rough equivalence of productivity in the export and domestic sectors. This equivalence may be safely assumed in the industrialized countries but not in the underdeveloped countries.

A third factor which has contributed to the view that foreign trade is unimportant in underdeveloped countries is the indisputable fact that in many underdeveloped countries there are large self-contained groups which are outside the monetary economy altogether and are therefore not affected by any changes in foreign trade. In industrialized countries, by contrast, it is true that repercussions from changes in foreign trade are more widely spread; but they are also more thinly spread.[1]

The Drain on the Benefits of Investment. The previously mentioned higher productivity of the foreign trade sector in underdeveloped countries might, at first sight, be considered as a cogent argument in favor of the view that foreign trade has been particularly beneficial to underdeveloped countries in raising their general standards of productivity, changing their economies in the direction of a monetary economy, and spreading knowledge of more capital-intensive methods of production and modern technol-

---

Dr. Harold Barger of the National Bureau of Economic Research, Dr. Roberto de Oliveira Campos of the Brazilian delegation to the United Nations, Dr. A. G. B. Fisher of the International Monetary Fund, Prof. W. Arthur Lewis of the University of Manchester (England), and Mr. James Kenny. He also had the inestimable advantage of a discussion of the subject matter of this paper in the graduate seminar at Harvard University, with Professors Haberler, Harris, and others participating.

[1] A more statistical factor might be mentioned. Some underdeveloped countries—Iran would be an illustration—exclude important parts of their exports and imports from their foreign trade statistics insofar as the transactions of foreign companies operating in the underdeveloped country are concerned. This is a tangible recognition of the fact that these pieces of foreign investments and their doings are not an integral part of the underdeveloped economy.

ogy. That, however, is much less clearly established than might be thought. The question of ownership as well as of opportunity costs enters at this point. The facilities for producing export goods in underdeveloped countries are often foreign-owned as a result of previous investment in these countries. Again we must beware of hasty conclusions. Our first reaction would be to argue that this fact further enhances the importance and benefits of trade to underdeveloped countries, since trade has also led to foreign investment in those countries and has promoted capital formation with its cumulative and multiplier effects. This is also how the matter is looked at in the economic textbooks—certainly those written by nonsocialist economists of the industrialized countries. That view, however, has never been really accepted by the more articulate economists in the underdeveloped countries themselves, not to mention popular opinion in those countries; and it seems to the present writer that there is much more in their view than is allowed for by the economic textbooks.

Can it be possible that we economists have become slaves to the geographers? Could it not be that in many cases the productive facilities for export from underdeveloped countries, which were so largely a result of foreign investment, never became a part of the internal economic structure of those underdeveloped countries themselves except in the purely geographical and physical sense? Economically speaking, they were really an outpost of the economics of the more developed investing countries. The main secondary multiplier effects, which the textbooks tell us to expect from investment, took place not where the investment was physically or geographically located but (to the extent that the results of these investments returned directly home) where the investment came from.[2] I would suggest that if the proper economic test of investment is the multiplier effect in the form of cumulative additions to income, employment, capital, technical knowledge, and growth of external economies, then a good deal of the investment in underdeveloped countries which we used to consider as "foreign'" should in fact be considered as domestic investment on the part of the industrialized countries.

Where the purpose and effect of the investments were to open up new sources of food for the people and for the machines of industrialized countries, we have strictly domestic investment in the relevant economic sense, although for reasons of physical geography, climate, etc., it had to be made overseas. Thus the fact that the opening up of underdeveloped countries for trade has led to or been made possible by foreign investment in those countries does not seem a generally valid proof that this combination has been of particular benefit to those countries. The very differential

---

[2] Often underdeveloped countries had the chance to use royalties or other income from foreign investment judiciously for the transformation of their internal economic structure—a chance more often missed than caught by the forelock!

in productivity between the export sectors and the domestic sectors of the underdeveloped countries, previously mentioned as an indication of the importance of foreign trade to underdeveloped countries, is also itself an indication that the more productive export sectors—often foreign-owned—have not become a real part of the economies of underdeveloped countries.

The Nonprogressive Nature of Traditional Investment. We may go even further. If we apply the principle of opportunity costs to the development of nations, the import of capital into underdeveloped countries for the purpose of making them into providers of food and raw materials for the industrialized countries may have been not only rather ineffective in giving them the normal benefits of investment and trade but positively harmful. The tea plantations of Ceylon, the oil wells of Iran, the copper mines of Chile, and the cocoa industry of the Gold Coast may all be more productive than domestic agriculture in these countries; but they may well be less productive than domestic industries in those countries which might have developed if those countries had not become as specialized as they now are in the export of food and raw materials, thus providing the means of producing manufactured goods elsewhere with superior efficiency. Admittedly, it is a matter of speculation whether, in the absence of such highly specialized "export" development, any other kind of development would have taken its place. But the possibility cannot be assumed away. Could it be that the export development has absorbed what little entrepreneurial initiative and domestic investment there was, and even tempted domestic savings abroad? We must compare, not what is with what was, but what is with what would have been otherwise—a tantalizingly inconclusive business. All we can say is that the process of traditional investment taken by itself seems to have been insufficient to initiate domestic development unless it appeared in the form of migration of persons.

The principle of specialization along the lines of static comparative advantages has never been generally accepted in the underdeveloped countries, and it has not even been generally intellectually accepted in the industrialized countries themselves. Again it is difficult not to feel that there is more to be said on the subject than most of the textbooks will admit. In the economic life of a country and in its economic history, a most important element is the mechanism by which "one thing leads to another," and the most important contribution of an industry is not its immediate product (as is perforce assumed by economists and statisticians) and not even its effect on other industries and immediate social benefits (thus far economists have been led to go by Marshall and Pigot) but perhaps beyond this its effect on the general level of education, skill, way of life, inventiveness, habits, store of technology, creation of new demand, etc. And this is perhaps precisely the reason why manufacturing industries are so universally desired by underdeveloped countries: they provide the growing points for increased technical knowledge, urban education, and the dynamism and resilience that goes with urban civilization, as well as the direct Marshallian external economies. No doubt under different circumstances commerce, farming, and plantation agriculture have proved capable of being such growing points, but manufacturing industry is unmatched in our present age.

By specializing on exports of food and raw materials and thus making the underdeveloped countries further contribute to the concentration of industry in the already industrialized countries, foreign trade and the foreign investment which went with it may have spread present static benefits fairly over both. They may have had very different effects if we think from the point of view, not of static comparative advantages, but of the flow of history of a country. Of this latter school of thought the "infant" argument for protection is but a sickly and often illegitimate offspring.

To summarize, then, the position reached thus far, the specialization of underdeveloped countries on export of food and raw materials to industrialized countries, largely as a result of investment by the latter, has been unfortunate for the underdeveloped countries for two reasons: (1) it removed most of the secondary and cumulative effects of investment from the country in which the investment took place to the investing country; and (2) it diverted the underdeveloped countries into types of activity offering less scope for technical progress, internal and external economies taken by themselves, and withheld from the course of their economic history a central factor of dynamic radiation which has revolutionized society in the industrialized countries. But there is a third factor of perhaps even greater importance which has reduced the benefits to underdeveloped countries of foreign trade-*cum*-investment based on export specialization in food and raw materials. This third factor relates to terms of trade.

It is a matter of historical fact that ever since the seventies the trend of prices has been heavily against sellers of food and raw materials and in favor of the sellers of manufactured articles. The statistics are open to doubt and to objection in detail, but the general story which they tell is unmistakable.[3] What is the meaning of these changing price relations?

The Meaning of Unfavorable Price Relations. The possibility that these changing price relations simply reflect changes in the real costs of the manufactured exports of the industrialized countries relative to those of the food and primary materials of the underdeveloped countries can be dismissed. All the evidence is that productivity has increased if anything less fast in the production of food and raw materials, even in the industrialized countries[4] but most certainly in the underdeveloped countries, than has

---

[3] See *Relative Prices of Exports and Imports of Under-developed Countries,* United Nations, Department of Economic Affairs, Sales No. 1949 II.B.3.

[4] According to data of the WPA research project, output per wage earner in a sample of fifty-four manufacturing industries increased by 57 per cent during the

productivity in the manufacturing industries of the industrialized countries. The possibility that changing price relations could merely reflect relative trends in productivity may be considered as disposed of by the very fact that standards of living in industrialized countries (largely governed by productivity in manufacturing industries) have risen demonstrably faster than standards of living in underdeveloped countries (generally governed by productivity in agriculture and primary production) over the last sixty or seventy years. However important foreign trade may be to underdeveloped countries, had deteriorated terms of trade (from the point of view of the underdeveloped countries) reflected relative trends of productivity, this could most assuredly not have failed to show in relative levels of internal real incomes as well.

Dismissing, then, changes in productivity as a governing factor in changing terms of trade, the following explanation presents itself: The fruits of technical progress may be distributed either to producers (in the form of rising incomes) or to consumers (in the form of lower prices). In the case of manufactured commodities produced in more developed countries, the former method, i.e., distribution to producers through higher incomes, was much more important than the second method, while the second method prevailed more in the case of food and raw-material production in the underdeveloped countries. Generalizing, we may say that technical progress in manufacturing industries showed in a rise in incomes, while technical progress in the production of food and raw materials in underdeveloped countries showed in a fall in prices. Now, in the general case, there is no reason why one or the other method should be generally preferable. There may, indeed, be different employment, monetary, or distributive effects of the two methods; but this is not a matter which concerns us in the present argument where we are not concerned with internal income distribution. In a closed economy the general body of producers and the general body of consumers can be considered as identical, and the two methods of distributing the fruits of technical progress appear merely as two formally different ways of increasing real incomes.

When we consider foreign trade, however, the picture is fundamentally changed. The producers and the consumers can no longer be considered as the same body of people. The producers are at home; the consumers are abroad. Rising incomes of home producers to the extent that they are

---

twenty years 1919–1939; over the same period, agriculture increased only by 23 per cent, anthracite coal mining by 15 per cent, and bituminous coal mining by 35 per cent. In the various fields of mineral mining, however, progress was as fast as in manufacturing. According to data of the National Bureau of Economic Research, the rate of increase in output per worker was 1.8 per cent per annum in manufacturing industries (1899–1939) but only 1.6 per cent in agriculture (1890–1940) and in mining, excluding petroleum (1902–1939). In petroleum production, however, it was faster than in manufacturing.

in excess of increased productivity are an absolute burden on the foreign consumer. Even if the rise in the income of home producers is offset by increases in productivity so that prices remain constant or even fall by less than the gain in productivity, this is still a relative burden on foreign consumers, in the sense that they lose part or all of the potential fruits of technical progress in the form of lower prices. On the other hand, where the fruits of technical progress are passed on by reduced prices, the foreign consumer benefits along with the home consumer. Nor can it be said, in view of the notorious inelasticity of demand for primary commodities, that the fall in their relative prices has been compensated by total revenue effects.

Other factors have also contributed to the falling long-term trend of prices of primary products in terms of manufactures, apart from the absence of pressure of producers for higher incomes. Technical progress, while it operates unequivocally in favor of manufactures—since the rise in real incomes generates a more than proportionate increase in the demand for manufactures—has not the same effect on the demand for food and raw materials. In the case of food, demand is not very sensitive to rises in real income, and in the case of raw materials, technical progress in manufacturing actually largely consists of a reduction in the amount of raw materials used per unit of output, which may compensate or even overcompensate the increase in the volume of manufacturing output. This lack of an automatic multiplication in demand, coupled with the low price elasticity of demand for both raw materials and food, results in large price falls, not only cyclical but also structural.

The End Result: Maldistribution of Gains. Thus it may be said that foreign investment of the traditional type which sought its repayment in the direct stimulation of exports of primary commodities, either to the investing country directly or indirectly through multilateral relations, had its beneficial cumulative effects in the investing country; and the people of the latter, in their capacity as consumers, also enjoyed the fruits of technical progress in the manufacture of primary commodities thus stimulated and at the same time, in their capacity as producers, enjoyed the fruits of technical progress in the production of manufactured commodities. The industrialized countries have had the best of both worlds, both as consumers of primary commodities and as producers of manufactured articles; the underdeveloped countries have had the worst of both worlds, as consumers of manufacturers and as producers of raw materials. This perhaps is the legitimate germ of truth in the charge that foreign investment of the traditional type formed part of a system of "economic imperialism" and of "exploitation."

Even if we disregard the theory of deliberately sinister machinations, there may be legitimate grounds in the arguments set out above for maintaining that the benefits of foreign trade and investment have not been equally shared between the two groups of countries. The capital-exporting countries have received their repayment many times over in the following five forms: (1) possibility of building up exports of manufactures and thus transferring their population from low-productivity occupations to high-productivity occupations; (2) enjoyment of the internal economies of expanded manufacturing industries; (3) enjoyment of the general dynamic impulse radiating from industries in a progressive society; (4) enjoyment of the fruits of technical progress in primary production as main consumers of primary commodities; (5) enjoyment of a contribution from foreign consumers of manufactured articles, representing as it were their contribution to the rising incomes of the producers of manufactured articles.

By contrast, what the underdeveloped countries have to show cannot compare with this formidable list of benefits derived by the industrialized countries from the traditional trade-*cum*-investment system. Perhaps the widespread though inarticulate feeling in the underdeveloped countries that the dice have been loaded against them is not so devoid of foundation after all as the pure theory of exchange might have led one to believe.

It is, of course, true that there are transfer difficulties on the part of the underdeveloped countries which are avoided by production for export directly to the investing countries, but the above analysis may perhaps make a contribution to understanding why this traditional investment system broke down so rapidly and so irreparably in 1929 and 1930. The industrialized countries had already received real repayment from their foreign investments in the five forms described above, and in these ways they may have collected a pretty good return on their investments. When, on top of the returns received in those five forms, they also tried to "get their money back," they may perhaps have been asking (in the economic though not in the legal sense) for double payment; they may have been trying to get a quart out of a pint bottle.

The False Impression of Recent Change in Terms of Trade. There is a fairly widespread impression that this traditional trend toward deteriorating price relations for primary producers has been sharply reversed since prewar days, although this impression is not as strong now as it was in the middle of 1948. Even if we take that point of time, which represents the peak of postwar primary-commodity prices up till now, a detailed analysis does not bear out the impression that terms of trade have significantly improved in favor of the underdeveloped countries since prewar days.[5]

It may be suggested that the impression that price relations have sharply improved for primary producers can be attributed partly to the abnormal composition of primary-commodity imports into the United States,

[5] For details see the UN study, *Relative Prices of Exports and Imports of Under-developed Countries.*

where coffee plays a predominating part (coffee prices have increased particularly heavily in the immediate postwar period), but specially to the widespread idea that foreign trade between underdeveloped countries and industrialized countries is an exchange of the primary commodities of the former for the capital goods of the latter. In fact, among the imports of the underdeveloped countries capital goods do not generally form the largest category, mainly because the import of capital goods from abroad requires a great deal of complementary domestic investment in those countries for which the domestic finance does not exist or is not mobilized.

The major proportion of the imports of the underdeveloped countries is in fact made up of manufactured food (especially in overpopulated underdeveloped countries), textile manufactures, and manufactured consumer goods. The prices of the type of food imported by the underdeveloped countries and, particularly, the prices of textile manufactures have risen so heavily in the immediate postwar period that any advantage which the underdeveloped countries might have enjoyed in the postwar period from favorable prices realized on primary commodities and low prices of capital goods has been wiped out.

A further factor which has contributed to the impression that relative price trends have turned sharply in favor of primary producers since the war is the deterioration in British terms of trade and the publicity which this deterioration has received because of the strategic importance of the British balance of payments in the network of world trade. It should not be forgotten, however, that the changes in British postwar terms of trade do not merely represent *ceteris paribus* price changes but reflect considerable quantum changes; namely an increase in the quantity exported and a decrease in the quantity imported. It may be suggested, perhaps, that these quantum changes rather than underlying price changes account for the adverse trend before devaluation of British terms of trade. Unless it is to be assumed that the elasticity of demand for British exports is infinite, it is obvious that an expansion in the volume of total exports of manufactured goods by almost 100 per cent will be reflected in lower unit prices for British exports; conversely, the reduction in the quantity of British imports is also reflected in higher prices paid than would otherwise have been the case, partly as a reflection of the diminishing bargaining strength of Britain in consequence of lower imports and partly as a necessary political concession to primary producers to enable them to maintain their incomes in the face of lower quantities sold. The supposition that the changed quantity relations in British trade (as well as deliberate colonial development policies) rather than price changes in world markets are largely responsible for the adverse trend in British terms of trade is greatly strengthened by the fact that other Western European exporters of manufactured goods did not seem to experience any deterioration in their terms of trade but, on the contrary, showed improved terms of trade.[6] The effect of quantum changes on British terms of trade is of course difficult to disentangle statistically. It is more in the nature of a gain missed through inability to exploit the postwar sellers' market price-wise to the full. It is surely a remarkable fact that in a world hungry for capital goods and with its two most important direct industrial competitors eliminated, England should have experienced adverse terms of trade in the years 1945 to 1948.

At this point it may be worth noting the curious ambivalent role which price relations in foreign trade play for the underdeveloped countries. Good prices for their primary commodities, especially if coupled with such a rise in quantities sold as occurs in a boom, give to the underdeveloped countries the necessary means for importing capital goods and financing their own industrial development; yet at the same time they take away the incentive to do so, and investment, both foreign and domestic, is directed into an expansion of primary-commodity production, thus leaving no room for the domestic investment which is the required complement of any import of capital goods. Conversely, when the prices and sales of primary commodities fall off, the desire for industrialization is suddenly sharpened; yet at the same time the means for carrying it out are sharply reduced. Here again it seems that the underdeveloped countries are in danger of falling between two stools: failing to industrialize in a boom because things are as good as they are, and failing to industrialize in a slump because things are as bad as they are.[7] It is no doubt true that failure to utilize high boom export proceeds more determinedly for capital formation because of purely temporary price relations shows a deplorable lack of foresight, but this is hardly very apposite criticism of those underdeveloped countries which rely mainly on private development. All private activity tends to be governed by the price relations of the day.

North America: A Strategic Case. If our view is accepted (namely that the traditional type of foreign investment as it was known prior to 1929 was "foreign" only in the geographical sense and not in the relevant economic sense), does it then follow that foreign investment has failed to fulfill one of the functions traditionally ascribed to it (and hoped for from it for the future), i.e., to spread industrialization more widely and more evenly throughout the world? It would be premature to jump to this conclusion. What has been maintained in the preceding part of this argument is that past foreign investment and the type of foreign trade which went with it failed to spread industrialization to the countries in which the investment took place. It may be, however, that for a full understanding of the

[6] *Economic Survey of Europe in 1948,* United Nations, Department of Economic Affairs, pp. 93–106, especially 97–99, sales No. 1949, II, E.1.

[7] This ambivalence of changing terms of trade has also been stressed in a different context by Lloyd Metzler in his important article "Tariffs, Terms of Trade and Distribution of National Income," *Journal of Political Economy,* February, 1949.

process we have to consider not merely the investing and the invested countries but a third group of countries as well.

It is an interesting speculation that European investment overseas was the instrument by which industrialization was brought to North America. Roughly speaking, the supplies of food and raw materials pouring into Europe as the result of the investment-*cum*-trade system and the favorable terms of trade engendered by this system enabled Europe to feed, clothe, educate, train, and equip large numbers of emigrants sent overseas, principally to the United States and Canada. Thus the benefits to the investing countries of Europe arising out of the system described above were in turn passed on to the United States—the converse of the Marshall Plan—and were the main foundation of the enormous capital formation the result of which is now to be observed in North America. This "macroeconomic" analysis is, of course, in no way contradicted by the fact that the individual migrant was motivated by the prospect of raising his standards of living by the transfer.

Attention may be drawn to the interesting statistical computation of Corrado Gini that even the enormous capital stock characteristic of the United States economy is not more than the equivalent of the burden in consumption goods and in such services as health, education, and other provision for the immigrants—a burden which the United States was enabled to save by shifting it to the European mother countries of the immigrants. Perhaps in the final analysis it may be said that the ultimate benefits of the traditional investment-*cum*-trade system were not with the investing countries of Europe but with the new industrial countries of North America.[8]

If this analysis is correct, the industrialization of North America was made possible by the combination of migration and the opening up of underdeveloped overseas countries through European investment and trade. To that extent, Point Four and technical assistance on the part of the United States would be a gesture of historical justice and return of benefits received in the past.

Potential Consequences of This Analysis. Rather than end on a wild historical speculation, it may be useful to summarize the type of economic measures and economic policies which would result from the analysis presented in this paper. The first conclusion would be that in the interest of the underdeveloped countries, of world national income, and perhaps ultimately of the industrialized countries themselves, the purposes of foreign investment and foreign trade ought perhaps to be redefined as producing

[8] In more recent years, specially since 1924, United States capital accumulation had of course become quite independent from the original stimulus supplied by immigration, and proceeded without any visible check in spite of a heavy reduction in immigration. The argument put forward here is meant as a historical explanation rather than an analysis of the present sources of capital investment.

gradual changes in the structure of comparative advantages and of the comparative endowment of the different countries rather than developing a world trading system based on existing comparative advantages and existing distribution of endowments. This, perhaps, is the real significance of the present movement toward giving technical assistance to underdeveloped countries not necessarily linked with actual trade or investment. The emphasis on technical assistance may be interpreted as a recognition that the present structure of comparative advantages and endowments is not such that it should be considered as a permanent basis for a future international division of labor.

Insofar as the underdeveloped countries continue to be the source of food and primary materials and insofar as trade, investment, and technical assistance are working in that direction by expanding primary production, the main requirement of underdeveloped countries would seem to be to provide for some method of income absorption to ensure that the results of technical progress are retained in the underdeveloped countries in a manner analogous to what occurs in the industrialized countries. Perhaps the most important measure required in this field is the reinvestment of profits in the underdeveloped countries themselves, or else the absorption of profits by fiscal measures and their utilization for the finance of economic development, and the absorption of rising productivity in primary production in rising real wages and other real incomes, provided that the increment is utilized for an increase in domestic savings and the growth of markets of a kind suitable for the development of domestic industries. Perhaps this last argument, namely the necessity of some form of domestic absorption of the fruits of technical progress in primary production, provides the rationale for the concern which the underdeveloped countries show for the introduction of progressive social legislation. Higher standards of wages and social welfare, however, are not a highly commendable cure for bad terms of trade except where the increment leads to domestic savings and investment. Where higher wages and social services are prematurely introduced and indiscriminately applied to export and domestic industries, they may in the end turn out to be a retarding factor in economic development and undermine the international bargaining strength of the primary producers. Absorption of the fruits of technical progress in primary production is not enough; what is wanted is absorption for reinvestment.

Finally, the argument put forward in this paper would point the lesson that a flow of international investment into the underdeveloped countries will contribute to their economic development only if it is absorbed into their economic system, i.e., if a good deal of complementary domestic investment is generated and the requisite domestic resources are found.

14

Stabilization and Development of Primary Producing Countries

The origins of this article require a few words of explanation. In 1958 *Kyklos* published a symposium, "The Quest for a Stabilization Policy in Primary Producing Countries," consisting of an article by Ragnar Nurkse and comments on it by a number of other economists. The symposium aroused widespread interest, and in view of the topical nature of the subject at that time and since—as well as its intrinsic importance—the editor decided to produce a further symposium the following year. I was invited to contribute an introduction to the second symposium, commenting on some of the problems raised in the first symposium, and this is the article reprinted here.

Nurkse's paper dealt with the effects of cyclical fluctuations in commodity prices on incomes, output, and investment in the export sector in primary producing countries, and discussed the uses of buffer stocks and various forms of variable export taxation, including buffer funds, commodity marketing boards, and exchange control, in counteracting the more undesirable of these effects. His own suggestion, to which I refer in the first paragraph of my article, was that the incomes of producers should be stabilized through changes in the general level of taxation rather than by direct levies on their export earnings, with the object of interfering as little as possible with the incentive given to producers by high prices to expand output and investment. The commentators, with a few exceptions of which the most notable was Prof. Maurice Byé, confined themselves to discussing some of the specific points raised and did not touch on the wider issue of the relationship between a stabilization policy for primary products and policies for development and growth. For the second symposium, however, the scope of the inquiry was broadened—as indicated by its title, "Stabilization and Development of Primary Producing Countries"—to include discussion of these dynamic problems.

INCENTIVES AND THE DYNAMICS OF TRADE

Since my contribution takes as its point of departure the views expressed by Nurkse in the original article which stimulated the symposium,[1] it should be said at once that I find myself in considerable sym-

[1] "Trade Fluctuations and Buffer Policies of Low Income Countries," *Kyklos*, vol. 11, fasc. 2 pp. 141–154, 1958. All the following references to *Kyklos* are to the same volume: "The Quest for a Stabilization Policy in Primary Countries."

174 SOME ISSUES OF TRADE AND AID

pathy with Nurkse's general position; it is indeed difficult not to be. That those in charge of fiscal and financial policies of underdeveloped countries should pay considerable attention to the incentives which are so vital for the whole process of economic development; that it is a deplorable state of affairs for the general machinery for revenue collection and assessment to be so inefficient that export proceeds should have to be singled out for imposts as a matter of administrative convenience; that stabilization of incomes is a worthier overall economic objective than stabilization of export proceeds or of exporters' incomes alone—all these elements of Nurkse's approach will be widely shared. He also draws empirical support for his case from the 1952 United Nations study *Instability in Export Markets of Underdeveloped Countries.*

On this latter point, however, a word of caution may be indicated. The United Nations report was a strictly behavioristic study which took as its model the pioneer work of F. C. Mills, *The Behavior of Prices.* It was not intended to throw light on the elasticity of supply or its components; in so far as it does so, it can only be on the short-run elasticity which can be but loosely related to production incentives. The results of the United Nations study seem to show some connection between price fluctuations and volume fluctuations, in the sense that total proceeds fluctuate more than prices alone. But this is not in itself full proof of a responsiveness of supply— and even less so of production[2]—to changing prices. The United Nations study seems to suggest that a great deal of the larger fluctuations of total proceeds, as compared with the fluctuations in prices alone, may be attributable to the fact that volumes are also extremely volatile—indeed, so volatile that in a significant number of observations the change in volume is more than double the fluctuations in prices. It stands to reason that wherever that happens, export proceeds may fluctuate more than prices alone even if the source of change should be on the supply side rather than on the demand side. A more direct attempt to trace correlations between price and volume movements in the United Nations study, by computing correlation coefficients, did not yield very clear-cut results in establishing evidence of an elastic supply of exports. It would perhaps be best to interpret the United Nations study—as far as it went—as suggesting that fluctuations in volume are of greater importance in causing changes in export proceeds than is commonly realized in a discussion which concentrates attention strongly on price fluctuations. This, however, is not the same thing as saying that it establishes responsiveness of supply to prices even though it *does* strengthen the case for paying close attention to supply factors and the causes which determine the changes in volumes supplied.

Insofar as the increased volumes supplied come out of stock rather than production—the United Nations study provided no evidence on this one

[2] This important distinction has been underlined by Kafka. *Kyklos,* p. 215.

way or the other—the effect of such a stock movement would support Nurkse's argument that buffer stocks do not necessarily add to the total stocks carried and that to some extent they merely rationalize and formalize what is happening anyway. Moreover, before one can deduce what group or country benefits or is hurt by the fact that larger quantities are bought at higher prices and vice versa, one would want to know about the ownership of such stocks as are released in response to higher prices. On all these matters empirical knowledge is lacking, and possibly there is a fruitful field for further research here. Moreover, a discussion of the likely incentive effects of price changes would require not only data concerning stock changes and production changes and on the components of export supply mentioned by Kafka but also some knowledge of the "vertical" relations between the actual producer, landlord, merchants, and the marketing and land-tenure system generally.

> "Systems of land tenure, the cultivator's indebtedness and dependence on landlords or merchants for credit, and the inadequacies of the marketing systems all make it difficult to ensure that the cultivator does, in fact, receive the price intended. The non-commercial nature of much of agriculture in the region also blunts the effects of prices on production. Probably for these reasons, incentive prices, in the relatively few instances when they have been tried, have not always had the result hoped for."[3]

Nurkse rightly points out that a positive correlation between price and quantity actually points to an interest on the part of the importing countries in price stabilization at the average recorded price. If there were no correlation between price and quantity, the average *paid* price per unit of the commodity bought over a cycle would be identical with the average *recorded* price quotation, averaged by the number of time units observed. The positive correlation observed means that the average paid price per unit of commodity traded over a period is higher than the average recorded price over the same period. The gap between the two would measure the direct interest of the importing countries in price stabilization and would indicate how much they could actually concede agreements by which the average quoted price would be increased without necessarily having to pay more for their imports. No calculations of this kind have yet been made as far as I am aware, but they should not be difficult and they might be of interest.

But in relating such statistical exercises to the question of incentives, it should perhaps be more clearly brought out than is often done that the only elasticity relevant here is the short-run elasticity of supply, meaning

[3] "Problems of Agricultural Support and Stabilization in Asia and the Far East," *Monthly Bulletin of Agricultural Economics and Statistics*, vol. 7, combined nos. 7 and 8, p. 1. Food and Agriculture Organization of the United Nations, Rome, July–August, 1958.

(1) the increase or decrease of supply by release from, or additions to, stocks, or the release from other uses such as home consumption; and (2) the short-run adjustments to production that can be made from existing capacity (e.g., more intensive tapping of existing rubber trees or more careful harvesting). The long-run elasticity of supply, i.e., adjustments involving changes in total capacity (acreage, etc.), cannot, with any degree of confidence, be said to be in the interests of the exporters: in view of the instability of prices, even from year to year, there seems to be no more than an even chance that the output resulting from the increased capacity will be sold at higher than average prices. This last limitation is clearly seen by Bauer and Paish,[4] who in general are so thoroughly aware of the importance of incentives.

PROBLEMS OF TAXATION AND PRICE STABILIZATION

Harrod emphasizes, as an argument against Nurkse's proposal to shift taxation from exporters to the economy as a whole, that increases in exporters' incomes due to sudden price increases are a particularly suitable object for taxation, since they represent "windfalls."[5] In considering whether or not Nurkse's case is damaged by Harrod's argument, the whole question seems to turn on incentives. The reason why it is a canon of taxation to tax windfalls is precisely that such windfalls, being undeserved and unexpected, will not lead to any beneficial adjustment on the part of the recipients.[6] The typical textbook case of windfalls is the "unearned increment" from urban land. Here, there can be no question of direct incentives, since the supply of urban land in a given location is limited. Since, however, Nurkse's case was entirely based on the assumption that exporters *do* adjust quantities to changing prices, Harrod's objection seems to assume away the basis of Nurkse's proposal. If Nurkse is wrong on incentives, his case collapses anyway, without Harrod's point. If Nurkse is right on incentives, Harrod's point does not damage him.

Nor is Nurkse's proposal damaged by the objection raised by Bauer and Paish that general taxation may " . . . slow down the switch from subsistence production to production for exchange upon which the growth of real national income so greatly depends."[7] This particular objection does not seem convincing to me, since exporters' incomes are also in the exchange sector almost by definition, and it seems difficult to see how a switch from taxing exporters to taxing incomes in general—as distinct from a general increase in taxation—could possibly produce such an undesirable effect.

Professor Nurkse argues that the instability of export prices " . . . dis-

---

[4] *Kyklos,* pp. 174–175.
[5] *Ibid.,* p. 211.
[6] See, for example, Hugh Dalton, *Principles of Public Finance,* London, 1922.
[7] *Kyklos,* p. 176

courages investment in primary production itself." But he produces no evidence in support of this obiter dictum,[8] and the argument is not convincing. In the first place, it is equally plausible to argue that the encouragement to expand production due to temporarily high prices outweighs or more than outweighs the deterrent effect of abnormally low prices. Moreover, if it is remembered that price fluctuations combined with supply elasticity mean increased actual average receipts per unit traded for the exporting country, other things being equal, the probability would seem to be that instability encourages investment in primary production. Perhaps Nurkse has identified the discouragement to the savings and investment process generally, arising from the instability of economic life in underdeveloped countries, with the effect of instability on the *distribution* of investment over different sectors. These problems seem to be different and should not be confused.

If the effect of unstable prices on investment is in doubt, so also is the effect of more investment on the terms of trade of exporters. Against the possible increase in factor efficiency—lower real cost—must be set the possible fall in prices. These doubts are raised but hardly resolved in J. H. Adler's contribution.[9] Adler seems to agree with Nurkse that more stable prices will stimulate investment. But he avoids the inherent paradox, i.e., that stabilization could be to the disadvantage of exporters, by also assuming that stabilization will lead to lower real costs of production and improved efficiency. In making this assumption, he enters into an important and tricky new field of discussion. In the first place a great deal would depend on the *nature* of the new investment; some might not be more efficient than the old; we are dealing with primary production, the classic area of diminishing returns. In the second place, even assuming that, as a result of lower real costs of production, the factoral terms of trade—as distinct from the commodity terms of trade—do not turn against the exporting countries when larger investment is induced by more stable prices, it is still by no means certain that the increased output made available by the possible alternative use of resources set free in the export sector would compensate for the loss of foreign exchange involved in lower average export prices. I think that Adler takes such a compensation too much for granted when he writes, " . . . thus, on reflection, the answer to the question posed above is that price stabilization is in fact to the advantage of primary producing countries even if it entails a long-run decline in earnings from primary production."[10] My own reflection does not make me so confident on this. Considering that the development of underdeveloped countries, which is a precondition for the productive use of the resources set free in the export sector, depends on

---

[8] In fact, Sydney Caine mentions some evidence to the contrary. *Ibid.*, p. 188.
[9] *Ibid.*, pp. 155–168.
[10] *Ibid.*, p. 161.

investment, that investment in turn depends on imports of capital goods, and that such imports in turn depend on foreign exchange earnings, and further considering the dominant role of exports in the money sector of the economies of many underdeveloped countries—I cannot help feeling considerable residual doubt about Adler's conclusion.

Accepting Nurkse's demonstration that (assuming some supply elasticity) stabilization at the actual average recorded price will be to the advantage of importers and *pro tanto* to the disadvantage of exporters, and adding to this the possibility – *pace* Professor Nurkse – that investment in primary production may be discouraged by stabilization and thus real cost presumably raised (following the implications of Adler's reasoning), one might be forgiven for thinking that there is quite a lot to be said for price instability from the exporters' point of view.

Yet one feels—indeed one knows—that there must be something wrong with this conclusion. In order to make clear what is wrong, one must perhaps paint on a larger canvas than Nurkse does in his article. To illustrate: Instability almost certainly has, in fact, a discouraging effect on investment in primary production but in a way which is at the same time more fundamental and more roundabout, deriving from the feedback on supply from the impact of fluctuating prices on demand. When prices of primary products increase beyond a certain normal level, strong pressure is created to develop synthetic materials in place of natural materials or to increase the technological possibilities for substitution or to change over to different methods of production which economize the primary commodity in question. And such is the technological ingenuity of the industrial countries that once synthetic production is started or substitution processes or new methods of production are developed, they come to stay and extend even if the price of the natural primary product subsequently falls again. This is so for three reasons: In the first place, the cost of newly established synthetic production or new processes of production will itself fall as they become better established, on lines familiar from the "infant industries" discussion. In the second place, the new synthetic industries or new processes of production economizing in materials will often be capital-intensive, and once established they will not disappear again unless prices fall below their prime cost, which may be only a fraction of their full cost. Third, technological progress has a way of proceeding and becoming "autonomous" as well as cumulative once it has reached a certain point. In this way, the stimulation to substitution given by high prices of primary products is *not* offset by subsequent low prices, and instability hurts the long-run position of primary producers (but may speed up technological progress and benefit importers or conceivably even the world as a whole).

The above illustration obviously applies more to industrial materials than food, but similar irreversible processes may be at work in that field also wherever domestic production in the importing countries can be sub-stituted for imported food. Once domestic expansion has taken place, justified by temporarily high prices of imported food, such domestic expansion is not easily reversed, but will be henceforth protected by subsidies, import quotas, tariffs, and so on.

SOME LONG-RANGE CONSIDERATIONS

Let us return for a moment to Nurkse's point, already mentioned, that buffer stocks would not necessarily involve larger stocks than are actually already being carried now, but—in his own words—"would seek mainly to impose a steadying pattern on the movements of stocks of primary products."[11] Rightly, Nurkse does not carry this argument very far, since he must assume a need for additional stocks when he subsequently states that "buffer stocks can only be started in times of recession, not in boom periods"[12] and that "a state of inflationary pressure and full employment is obviously not suitable for the initial setting up of buffer stocks."[13] The fact seems to be that international commodity agreements require, if not larger commodity stocks, at least more firmly held stocks, and this would *pro tanto* raise the average price per unit of time. But one could go further than Nurkse does in arguing that the accumulation of "idle" commodity stocks need not be a wasteful use of capital. Nurkse points out that such stocks are not necessarily wasteful if the indirect benefits of stability are taken into account, particularly the promotion of long-term development in primary producing countries and its beneficial repercussions upon the importing countries. One might perhaps add the slightly more tangible point that in-creased commodity stocks, contributing as they do to "international liquidity," should make possible more forward policies of domestic expansion and reduce the concern for balance-of-payments troubles that might arise as a result. Here, however, we are approaching the touchy subject of the commodity exchange standard, and we must turn away from this glimpse of the skeleton in our economic cupboard. But since Nurkse does point out that buffer funds and buffer stocks are to some extent alternative means of *national* stabilization, we should perhaps not altogether flinch from realizing that this may be true *internationally* as well. Goudriaan was well entitled to remind us of this.[14] Several variations of the "international buffer fund" type have been proposed and are waiting for a reexamination.

---

[11] *Ibid.*, p. 145.

[12] *Ibid.*, p. 146. As a matter of fact, as Kafka points out, the one postwar inter-national buffer stock, i.e., tin, was started during a boom period (July, 1956), but Nurkse could plausibly reply that this fact has contributed to the subsequent serious difficulties; in the light of hindsight this experience may be said to confirm Nurkse's statement rather than contradict it.

[13] *Ibid.*

[14] *Ibid.*, p. 206.

A serious limitation of Nurkse's approach is still to be mentioned. Stabilizing policies in underdeveloped countries are not easily disentangled from development policies. In times of rising export proceeds, there is a desire, intermingled with the desire of stabilizing incomes, to use this particular windfall for investment rather than consumption.[15]

If this is not always clearly distinguished from stabilization, that is not entirely a result of muddled thinking, but it is also because increased investment should lead to development and development should lead to diversification and to more stability. Even more directly, high investment in good years can yield income in bad years, and thus truly stabilize.[16] That is why I consider Sydney Caine's judgment about governments being "less far sighted than individuals" rather harsh in this context. The underdeveloped countries may be forgiven if in their thinking and their policies, stabilization and development are not always kept tidily apart.

It helps to clarify ideas to separate the two things in discussion, as Nurkse does, by keeping a "fundamental remedy" in a somewhat shadowy background; but it may easily mislead when it comes to policy suggestions: the shadow in the background has a disturbing way of merging with the central area under scrutiny. There is no doubt that Bauer and Paish are perfectly right logically in arguing that stabilization and taxation " . . . are entirely different aims, requiring entirely different policies, and failure to observe the distinction between them has vitiated much of the recent discussion of the subject."[17] Perfectly correct—logically. Yet the failure to make the distinction clearly is more in the policies of the underdeveloped countries than in the approach of economists. Nurkse has the right feeling for this when he indicates at the beginning of his article[18] that he sets his whole discussion in the context of the "fundamental remedy" of diversified growth and industrialization (Gudin's "structural solution"). And Byé hits the nail on the head when he says, "Indeed the stabilisation demands of poor countries can be justified only by reference to the aim of growth which these countries for the most part have in view."[19] The economist finds himself in a dilemma here. Should he accept the "confusion" of objectives in

[15] Sydney Caine points out that an inflationary environment which penalizes the holding of buffer funds also creates a desire for investment rather than saving in good times. *Ibid.*, pp. 192–193. This point is well taken, but the point made above seems to me more fundamental. Moreover, an inflationary environment should encourage the alternative method of stabilization, involving buffer stocks.

[16] This presupposes the availability of quick-yielding investment opportunities and justifies a higher priority for such quick-yielding projects—an aspect neglected in the current discussion on "investment criteria" in underdeveloped countries. This "dynamic" approach to stability is not the same thing as Kafka's "semi-dynamic" argument that buffer stocks of capital goods may be preferable to buffer stocks of either cash or primary commodities. *Kyklos,* pp. 222–223.

[17] *Ibid.*, p. 169.

[18] *Ibid.*, p. 143.

[19] *Ibid.*, p. 181.

real life at the price of logical muddle in his argument, or should he hew to the line of logical purity at the price of creating a gap between his analysis and application? It is interesting to note that Adler,[20] with his experience of underdeveloped countries, takes it for granted that the proceeds of export taxes will in fact be spent for development purposes, since he argues that where the benefits of public expenditure accrue to the export sector, this may outweigh the tax burden and the disincentive effects associated with it. Similarly, Bauer and Paish go on, after emphasizing the distinction, to discuss a case where the proceeds of these cyclical export taxes are "used to finance increased domestic government expenditure on either income or capital account" and to analyze the resulting expansion of money supplies.[21] And Sydney Caine really makes the same point when he suspects that governments are "more apt to spend income as it comes in."[22] This unanimity within a group with practical experience is surely significant.

Obviously, if the desire is to stabilize in the long-run sense via development, Nurkse's problem is transformed: the question is no longer whether export taxes or general taxes are preferable for general incentives, but which is the most efficient way of transforming the additional income into additional investment. And once the question is put in that form, there seems to be a lot to be said for a policy of catching the increment as early as possible, before it has become "generalized" through the economy, i.e., at the exporter stage, at the price of maintaining consumption in the bad years. This policy is perfectly rational on the assumption that if once you let consumption increase in the good years of high export proceeds, it may be difficult subsequently to reduce consumption again in the bad years, so that on the average consumption would be higher and investment would be lower.[23] This view of the matter should appeal to Nurkse, who has familiarized us with the international demonstration effect in the consumption function.

How important is price instability as a future policy problem? Knorr—and he is not alone—is mildly cheerful and has given us a description of "the changing scene" in which he pronounced the problem of instability in primary-commodity prices to be one of "diminishing calamity."[24] I wonder. The scene certainly changes, but it changes in many ways. Some of these changes diminish the calamity, but others may augment it. Even assuming that the major employment cycles of prewar vintage are a thing of the past and will be greatly dampened in the future, there seems every indica-

---

[20] *Ibid.*, p. 163.

[21] *Ibid.*, p. 174.

[22] *Ibid.*, p. 189.

[23] Byé, by a different line of reasoning, also arrives at the conclusion " . . . that stabilization may mean overall reduction of investment." *Ibid.*, p. 182.

[24] *Ibid.*, p. 230.

tion that they will be replaced by equally strong cycles of alternation between brimful employment with strong inflationary pressure, on the one hand, and return to more normal employment during periods of strong concern about inflation accompanied by disinflationary policies, on the other. It is not immediately obvious that the change-over from the old cycle of boom-depression-boom to the new cycle of ripping inflation–disinflation–ripping inflation will involve any less instability for the exporters of primary products. Furthermore, the specific methods chosen to disinflate, particularly those that go under the general label of "revival of monetary policy," are of such a kind as to bear with particular force upon the willingness of traders and producers to hold stocks of primary commodities.

Furthermore, one important aspect of the changing scene is presumably the spreading "revolution of rising expectations." No end to that revolution seems to be in sight. A revolution of rising expectations means chronic balance-of-payments pressure and a chronic scarcity of foreign exchange, as Knorr would certainly agree. From this I would draw the conclusion that as the revolution of rising expectations spreads and as the techniques of forward development planning spread with it, the plans and activities of underdeveloped countries will for a considerable time depend increasingly on foreign exchange, and their sensitivity to sudden fluctuation in foreign exchange receipts will increase rather than decrease. I think it must remain a matter of opinion whether the calamity under review is diminishing or increasing.

15

Use and Abuse of
Local Counterpart Funds

Local currency counterpart funds are of different kinds and have different origins. Some of them are the result of surplus-food sales, and these are in the legal ownership of the United States government, broadly speaking. Others, arising from aid transactions under the Mutual Security Act, are in the legal ownership of the receiving country, broadly speaking. Different accounts are open to different uses and different procedures depending on their origin and the nature of agreements that govern their use.

These distinctions, however, are of more interest to lawyers than economists. Local counterpart funds all have in common the following economic characteristics: They are the counterpart of some preceding aid transaction, in the form either of money or of goods; their use or disposal can take place only by agreement between the two partners to the original aid transaction; and they are supposed to be either wholly or in major part for the benefit and economic development of the receiving country.

In what follows, attention will be concentrated on the funds that have arisen as a result of transfer of surplus food under United States Public Law 480. These are about half of the total funds and have had a definite tendency to increase in recent years. *Mutatis mutandis,* however, the argument would also apply to any other kind of counterpart funds.

Again broadly speaking, as a result of the rising volume of counterpart funds there is a problem of their use, or "disposal." The question arises whether this is a real or an imaginary problem. Even an imaginary problem can, of course, have real effects if it is considered to be a real problem.

The Multiplier Fallacy. There is a widespread belief that counterpart funds offer a real opportunity for constructive action. The very legislative concept that these local funds are to be "used for the benefit of the receiving country" implies that here is something that *can* be used and can give real benefits. In its crudest form the belief is that the use of

This article originally appeared in *International Development Review,* vol. 3, no. 3, pp. 14–16, October, 1961.

counterpart funds provides a means of repeating, or doubling, the value of aid given. First you give aid by transferring money or surplus food; then you give further aid by using the arising local counterpart funds wisely. If you lend the counterpart funds rather than grant them to the receiving country, the process may go on more or less indefinitely as you relend the original funds. In this way, so it is believed, you can introduce a sort of multiplier into your foreign aid and make $1 worth of aid do the work of $2, $3, or $4.

In this crude form, such a belief would not be shared by persons with a degree of economic sophistication, but it is sufficiently plausible to the unsophisticated to make it worthwhile pointing out that it can cut both ways. By the unsophisticated supporters of foreign aid it can be used as an argument in favor of aid because of the imagined multiplier effects. By the unsophisticated opponents of foreign aid it can be used as an argument for cutting aid, since the local funds are imagined to be there to take the place of further aid appropriations.

Contributions and Worthy Causes. In a somewhat less crude form, the belief in the "reality" of these local counterpart funds takes the form of using them as contributions by the owning governments—for instance, as contributions to international organizations or as the local cost contributions of governments to further aid programs or technical-assistance operations. It should be noted at this point that such suggestions may be made either by those who believe in the reality of these funds or by those who, while not believing in the reality of the funds, propose to use their existence as a handle for promoting worthy causes.

A demonstration of the essentially unreal nature of these local funds should not, however, be taken as an argument against the worthy causes proposed; nor is the use of local funds as a handle to promote such causes necessarily to be considered unworthy. It seems justified to try to get worthy causes promoted by methods that rouse least resistance and give the greatest chance of success; beyond this, it can often legitimately be argued that unless used for the promotion of worthy causes, the accumulation of local currency funds would give rise to continuous irritation and, by troubling relations between the aid-giving and the aid-receiving country, defeat one of the chief purposes of such aid.

Even so, it is important that the proponents of worthy causes should not deceive themselves. It is one thing to use the existence of counterpart funds for getting things done that for rational or irrational reasons would not otherwise get done. It is quite another thing to imagine, for instance, that the acceptance of local counterpart funds as local cost payment of aid or technical-assistance programs is genuine evidence of a matching local effort. The purpose of insisting on local contributions from aid-receiving governments is precisely to provide evidence that the receiving government is attaching priority to the project and is willing to put in its own resources as evidence of such priority, but the acceptance of the funds as a local cost equivalent does not clearly satisfy this basic purpose of a local cost contribution.

Crucial Importance of the Original Aid Transaction. The belief that local currency funds represent real resources and that their subsequent use and possibly repeated reuse could multiply the effects of foreign aid is easily confused with similar statements about the multiple benefits of foreign aid. There certainly is a possible multiplying effect of foreign aid. Foreign aid worth $1 can conceivably do $2 or $4 worth of good in the receiving country. If, for example, the supply of surplus food makes it possible to mobilize otherwise unemployed manpower and other resources or to break a vital bottleneck in the development of the country, it might legitimately be said that the availability of $1 worth of aid at the right time and used in the right way can increase the national income of the receiving country by a high multiple of this sum. But this has nothing to do with the establishment and subsequent use of local currency funds; it has to do entirely with the nature and effectiveness of the original aid transaction.

Similarly, aid can certainly have multiple functions. It can add to available investment funds; it can help to mobilize domestic resources; it offsets inflationary pressure; it may secure continuity when export proceeds drop; it may be an instrument for adding socially desirable objectives to the development program of the receiving country. But again, these multiple benefits have nothing to do with the establishment and use of counterpart funds. They are entirely inherent in the original aid transaction and in the way in which it is incorporated in the general development plans and policies of the receiving country.

It is also true that there is perhaps need for a halfway house between straight grants and straight loans. The grant relationship is usually not ideal between two sovereign countries, while the loan relationship is perhaps not ideal between developed and underdeveloped countries. Hence soft loans may often be imagined to satisfy the recognized need for such a halfway house between grants and loans. But in fact, the establishment of local currency accounts is again irrelevant. Terms and conditions of soft loans may be arranged beforehand without involving local currency funds at all.

Likewise it is true that if the original injection of surplus food has been effectively used as the basis for an enlargement of development programs and an increase in capital formation, this will provide additional resources flowing from the newly formed capital, and these resources can be ploughed back into new development on a rising scale (since savings out of increments to income may easily be higher than savings out of low present incomes). Indeed, it is one of the prime purposes of aid to lead to such "self-sustaining" growth. But here again, although there seems a superficial similarity, the accumulation and use of local counterpart funds is not relevant to this process. The process may happen without any local counterpart funds being accumulated; vice versa, the accumulation and use of counterpart funds provides no evidence whatsoever that this process is actually taking place.

The effectiveness of the aid originally given, say, through a supply of surplus food, is determined by the quality of the planning and use of aid at the time the surplus food is injected into the economy of the receiving country. If the aid is effectively used *at that stage,* it helps to mobilize the domestic resources of the receiving country. The subsequent use of counterpart funds cannot add to the effectiveness of the use of the aid or remedy any failures in such use at the time the aid is given. Hence the belief that the use of aid is determined, not at the time of the original transaction, but at the subsequent time when the counterpart funds are assigned may result in a situation where the boat is missed at the crucial moment and the aid becomes ineffective.

The local counterpart funds may be used subsequent to the aid either for a project that is part of the development plans for the assisted country or for an additional project that the receiving country would not otherwise have undertaken. In the former case, the use of counterpart funds is an unnecessary formality, since the government could have printed the money. In the second case, the use of the funds is harmful, since it leads to inflation and causes submarginal projects to be executed at the expense of better ones.

This is the purist position, and a proviso should be added in both cases. In the former case, there may be legal or administrative reasons why the government cannot print money or otherwise obtain authority to pay for the local cost, even of a proper noninflationary program. In such circumstances, the use of counterpart funds can avoid the legal difficulty. In the second case, it is of course possible that the additional project squeezed in by the use of counterpart funds is better than the project it displaces. It is also possible that the inflationary pressure generated by the additional project helps to add to the total volume of investment. But these are clearly secondary possibilities. Essentially, the use of counterpart funds for these purposes is either unnecessary or harmful.

One particular case where the use of counterpart funds in new development projects becomes more meaningful must be mentioned. If the original food aid has not been effectively used to enlarge investment and promote development in the receiving country, the arrival of the surplus food will depress agricultural prices and may discourage the local farmers. In that case the intended aid would have done more harm than good.

The subsequent use of local counterpart funds for additional investment may then serve to reemploy the local resources that have been put out of action by the unintended harmful effect of the original aid, and it may serve to raise domestic food prices back to the level where they would have been if the aid had not arrived and had not backfired in the first place. This is a rather faint justification for the use of counterpart funds, since it applies only where the original aid was not properly organized and had harmful effects. Even in this case, of course, the compensating benefits of counterpart-fund expenditures could also have been achieved by printing the money.

Future Contacts. Provided the real (or rather unreal) nature of counterpart funds is clearly understood, they may be a useful device for keeping the aid-giving country and the aid-receiving country in contact with each other. Strictly speaking, of course, between two friendly and rational countries there should be no need to set up counterpart funds so that their subsequent disposal might provide an opportunity or pretext for continued contacts and discussions. Such discussions may be helpful, particularly if they lay the foundation for continued cooperation and possibly renewed acts of aid and generally maintain that atmosphere of friendly cooperation which the aid relation is presumably intended to promote. But all this does not in any way substitute for the necessary contacts and cooperation at the time the aid is provided, since the effectiveness of the aid is determined at that earlier point and not when counterpart funds are used.

Moreover, if the function of counterpart funds is understood as merely to provide an occasion for subsequent contacts, this again may cut both ways. If the subsequent contacts are of an unfriendly nature and lead to mutual irritation, the benefits of the original aid act may be undone rather than followed up. There is nothing more irritating to sovereign governments than having to discuss with others the use of "our own money." These dangers can be avoided only when both sides are sophisticated enough to know what they are talking about when they discuss the "use" of counterpart funds.

Illusions of the Project Approach. Insofar as the counterpart funds are used for specific projects, as is often the case, rather than for general budgetary support, the illusions of the project approach may in fact be added to illusions about the real nature of counterpart funds. The project approach is itself basically illusionary, since whatever the project label may be, aid really finances, not the project that provides the label, but the marginal project in the total investment picture of the country, that is, the project that would be cut out if the foreign aid should not materialize. Like the use of counterpart funds, the project approach may be a useful device in spite of its basically fallacious nature, provided both sides are aware of the underlying illusion. When the "use" of counterpart funds for a specific development "project" is under discussion, the problems of escaping the double illusion involved become very difficult.

The preceding discussion has dealt with the use of local counterpart funds only insofar as these funds are used for the benefit, real or at any rate intended, of the aid-receiving country. That part of the counterpart funds that is used for local expenditures for which dollars would otherwise have to be used—such as expenses of United States embassies abroad—has not been considered in this article. Insofar as local counterpart funds are used for such purposes, that part of the food aid of which they are the counterpart obviously should not be treated as aid but rather as trade.

In conclusion, if local counterparts are to be used at all, the important thing seems to be to have no illusions about their nature and to try to give them a decent burial while using the occasion for such incidental advantages as the counterpart-funds technique may offer.

PART 5

Problems and Experience: Africa

16

Demographic Factors in African Economic Development

SIZE AND DENSITY OF POPULATION:
UNDERPOPULATION AND OVERPOPULATION

Africa south of the Sahara presents a demographic patchwork which defies all generalization. There are islands of very high population density; Zanzibar and Ruanda Urundi are examples which come readily to mind. Similarly, there are areas of very low density of population; examples are South-West Africa, Somalia, and parts of what used to be called French West Africa, such as the Central African Republic, Chad, the Republic of the Congo, and Gabon. In many cases, such as Somalia, Mauritania, and South-West Africa, the low population density clearly corresponds to the low population-carrying capacity of the country under present conditions, e.g., desert country without natural resources. The example of Libya should warn us, however, not to assume that such a static picture will not change. Libya used to be quoted as a country where a poor resource endowment would make economic development very difficult, but recent oil discoveries have changed the picture there quite dramatically. Obviously the population-carrying capacity of Libya is greater now than it was assumed to be before the oil discoveries.

Taken as a whole, the area is clearly not overpopulated in the same sense as China or India. Broadly speaking, the picture is more like that of Latin America, where we also find islands of overpopulation in a continent which as a whole is clearly not overpopulated.

The mobility of African populations is great. Areas in which employment opportunities are particularly good, such as the Union of South Africa, the mining areas of Northern Rhodesia and Katanga,

This paper was presented to the Conference on Indigenous and Induced Elements in the Economics of Sub-Saharan Africa held at Northwestern University in November, 1961. In preparing the paper I had the benefit of being able to revise earlier notes in the light of the discussions at the Regional Conference on Economic Development

Ghana, Senegal, and certain parts of Southern Rhodesia, tend to attract migrants from considerable distances. These population movements afford a relief to areas which are overpopulated in relation to their present employment opportunities, such as Ruanda Urundi and Nyasaland. The demographic picture in tropical Africa, therefore, presents one aspect if we can assume free migration and opportunities for redistribution of population but quite a different one if this assumption cannot be made. If the movement toward independence of African countries should lead to an interference with migration across the national frontiers, demographic pressure in certain countries could become quite acute.

The economic value of migration has been reduced to some extent by the fact that much of this migration has been only temporary. Temporary migration reduces the productivity of labor, prevents the establishment of a permanent industrial labor force, pevents the acquisition of skill and labor organization, and leads to grave social problems in the rising towns or mining areas where male migrants from different ethnic groups, often without their families, are thrown together in an unfamiliar environment. On the other hand, temporary migration can also be well adjusted to social and economic conditions and requirements. It has been pointed out that where women do most of the field work on farms, the men return often enough to take care of the periodic need for such work as is done by men—building, fencing, etc.—and to make improvements to farms with the help of the money earned during their absence.

Great care must be taken with statements as to whether tropical Africa is underpopulated or not. Such terms as "underpopulation," "overpopulation," and "optimum population" make sense only in relation to a given or assumed economic structure and a given state of opportunities. In this respect, the situation in tropical Africa is certainly fluid and largely unknown, as can be seen from the above example of Libya. Although the soil and mineral resources of tropical Africa are generally listed as poor, this judgment must be considered as premature or not proved. The immediate future may see a great intensification of resources survey and resources research work. In a decade, we may be in a better position to make a judgment. The rate of industrialization is very low at present throughout tropical Africa. If the productivity of agriculture can be increased so that population can be released for industrial and other nonagricultural work and if the necessary resources and skills can be found to lead to

---

in Africa South of the Sahara held by the International Economic Association in July, 1961, at Addis Ababa. In particular, I refer to the paper prepared by J. J. Spengler, "Population and Population Trends," although no specific reference could be made to this paper. Since my paper was prepared while traveling in Africa, it was not possible to cite the usual statistical or documentary evidence for the points made.

economic growth and industrialization, the population-carrying capacity of tropical Africa could well be a multiple of what it is now. But the obstacles to such development are formidable. What then shall we assume? The safest assumption seems to be that some parts of Africa will develop quite rapidly, as they have done in the recent past, while others will more or less stagnate, also as they have done in the recent past. Superimposed on this will be the unpredictable effects of resource discoveries and developments as a result of the above-mentioned expected intensification of surveys.

Very few systematic surveys of natural resources have yet been made. In the absence of such surveys, it is difficult to say with any degree of meaningfulness whether such countries as Ethiopia and Kenya are under-populated or not. Moreover, in many countries even now the actual population is almost as unknown as the resources. In Ethiopia, for instance, although a figure of 20 million people is often quoted, there is a reasonable possibility that the population may be as low as 12 to 13 million or as high as 25 million. We simply do not know. Even in areas where it was believed that the size of the population was fairly accurately known, recent censuses and sample surveys have often resulted in showing much larger populations than had previously been assumed; Uganda is a case in point. All quoted figures of population in tropical Africa should be taken as very uncertain indeed. It does not follow that countries with sparse population per acre or even per acre of arable land are underpopulated in the economic sense, or vice versa.

In one sense, it is often said with assurance that Africa is underpopulated. Quite often the population, particularly in the hinterland away from the islands of urban developments, is very sparse. This has the consequence of making the provision of transport facilities uneconomic because the low density of population and the resulting low demand for transport services make the construction of railway lines and major roads or investments in making waterways navigable uneconomic. Such improvements in transport are considered vital in creating a market economy to replace the present subsistence economy, which in turn is an essential first step in economic development. Here we seem to have a clear case of underpopulation in the economic sense. But it should be noted that the real obstacle which makes railway lines or roads uneconomic is not so much the sparsity of population per se as the small market. The small market, however, is due not only to the sparsity of population but also to its low per capita purchasing power and the fact that many of its transactions are of a subsistence nature and therefore do not represent any demand for transport services. Given the existing structure of production and low incomes, it is certainly correct to say that the sparsity of population represents an obstacle to economic development. But it is equally true to say that the raising of per capita incomes and the development of cash crops can remove or soften this obstacle. It has frequently been observed that the building of a railway or road, by opening up new markets and leading to additional production of cash crops and by thus raising agricultural incomes in the area opened up by the railway or road, has economically repaid the cost of building the railway or road, perhaps many times over, even though the construction seemed originally uneconomic in view of the sparse population.

In general, many observers of the African rural scene have concluded that, in the given stage of agricultural knowledge and within the given tribal or village organization and given the strong elements of subsistence production, African populations have achieved an ecological low-level equilibrium between population and resources. This would represent a sort of Malthusian equilibrium at a comparatively low density of population. This, however, seems to neglect the fact that the population-carrying capacity can be sharply increased even within the existing production structure by comparatively minor or at any rate inexpensive improvements. Particularly important among these are health controls (particularly control of malaria), pest controls (for instance, control of the tsetse fly and the desert locust), better crop rotation (reducing the needs for shifting cultivation and burning of soil cover), and the regrouping of villages. In the latter respect, for instance, it has been observed that where villagers live close together, perhaps for reasons of mutual protection and security, the total amount of land which they can cultivate is sharply limited by the requirement that all fields must be within daily walking distance from the village; this leaves much good land uncultivated. If the agricultural population could be loosened up and placed in individual holdings or smaller settlements, the amount of land cultivated could be greatly increased even without any new investment or change in methods of cultivation. A good deal of soil erosion by rain, excessive numbers of unproductive cattle, wind, or bad agricultural methods takes place in parts of tropical Africa. In the past, the population has often been decimated by slave trading, tribal wars, epidemics, etc. In these circumstances it seems difficult to attach any precise meaning to the term "ecological equilibrium." To the present writer, it would appear a somewhat romantic and not very helpful concept.

The sparsity of population in large parts of tropical Africa and the lack of transport (which is largely the result of it) has a number of important economic consequences, some of which may be mentioned here. There often is no unified market and price system in African countries but only localized markets and local prices which may differ very sharply from prices in other localities. Conditions of food shortages and high prices may exist in one part of a country while there are surpluses and low prices in other parts. The small markets make the development of large-scale industries very difficult; in many cases, the development of efficient small-scale industries including rural industries would seem to be one of the most urgent requirements.[1] The high transport costs also put a premium on sub-sistence production and afford powerful protection against external com-petition to such local activities as already exist, thus removing an incentive to economic efficiency. The lack of transport and the lack of power—simi-larly connected with the sparsity of population—makes many local deposits of mineral and other resources uneconomic to exploit. In spite of the sparsity of population, improvements of transport and power, perhaps as a result of new techniques, could therefore have multiple economic effects.

RATE OF INCREASE OF POPULATION

The two statements made above concerning the size and density of population are also true of the rate of increase of population, namely (1) we do not know the facts; and (2) tropical Africa presents a patchwork pattern, and it is not possible to generalize.

As regards the first point, it has already been mentioned that recent censuses and enumerations have often resulted in much higher figures than had been previously enumerated or assumed. From this it is sometimes con-cluded that the rate of population increase must be higher than was pre-viously believed or that it must have speeded up considerably in the recent past. However, we simply do not know to what extent the higher figures are due to better statistical coverage or to what extent they reflect a speed-ing up in the rate of population increase. A general guess—it is no more—might be that while most of the apparent discrepancy is due to improved statistical coverage, there also has been some acceleration in the rate of population increase as a result of lower death rates reflecting more effective disease control, higher standards of living in some parts of Africa south of the Sahara, better education, and urbanization.

The last cause of (probably) accelerated population increase is some-what doubtful, since the unsanitary conditions, bad housing, and widespread unemployment in a number of African towns may offset the better health services. The abandonment of birth-reducing tribal and rural customs and taboos may, however, prevent birth rates from falling. The statistics are again somewhat inconclusive, and we cannot be certain to what extent the recorded deaths and births in the towns reflect the people from the sur-rounding countryside utilizing hospitals in the towns or, on the contrary, to what extent town people, when ill, go back to their villages to die there. As so often, all we can say is, "Ignoramus."

As regards the second point, the available figures present a true patch-work impression. Some of these show very rapid recent population growth (for instance in the Ivory Coast, the Upper Volta, Uganda, and Ruanda Urundi), while other areas show a practically stationary population or

[1] For a further discussion of this point, see the following chapter, "Small-scale Industry in African Economic Development."

even a decline (for instance Gabon, the Portuguese territories, Somalia, and Gambia). These statistical differences may be assumed to correspond broadly to real differences, but only broadly. Qualified observers estimate the current rate of population increase to be around 2 per cent per annum, and the UN estimates broadly result in this figure. This, if true, must mean an acceleration in the rate of population growth compared with the period between European colonization and the Second World War, during which the population cannot have increased by more than, say, ½ per cent per annum. In view of the fairly well-established differences between different countries, a current overall rate of 2 per cent per annum would also mean that there must be some areas in which population growth—much of it by migration—is very rapid even by present world standards, while in others population increase must be quite slow.

In Ethiopia, conclusions drawn from national history, village structure, the absence of major conurbations, and general observations, as well as such sample data as exist, all seem to suggest that the rate of population increase over the last generation must have been quite modest, probably 1 per cent per annum. The present writer would venture a guess that the current overall rate of population increase in tropical Africa may be below rather than above 2 per cent per annum. The naïve idea sometimes encountered in the advanced countries that virtually all African women have the physiological maximum of children is certainly far from the truth. It must not be forgotten that over wide parts of the area effective birth control is exercised in the form of long nursing periods for babies and religious taboos of many kinds against sexual intercourse during such nursing and other periods, that fertility-reducing diseases are still widespread, that customary marriage ages are sometimes high, that death rates are still very high in many areas, and that the average expectation of life is so low that many women die before reaching, or at any rate before completing, their childbearing period. Furthermore, the prevalence of migratory labor means that men and women of reproductive ages are often separated for considerable periods of time. However, this list also shows that the acceleration potential of population increase is very great: nursing periods for babies may be reduced under the impact of the European "demonstration effect"; religious taboos may vanish with urbanization and dissolution of the tribal society and the spread of education; fertility-reducing diseases may be controlled, etc. So even if the guess is correct that the present rate may be below the figure of 2 per cent per annum which is now often implied or postulated, it is quite possible that this rate may be exceeded in a few years time.

In any case, it is not so much the rate of population increase which matters economically as the way in which it is brought about. The rate of population increase is the combined result of birth rates and death rates, and for the economic effects it is the components rather than the aggregate which should be considered.[2] A rate of population increase of 2 per cent per annum can be brought about either by a birth rate of 3 per cent and a death rate of 1 per cent or by a birth rate of 5 per cent and a death rate of 3 per cent. While the statistical net result is the same, the economic implications are quite different in the two cases. A combination of high birth rates and high death rates is economically highly unfavorable.

Broadly speaking, this combination is economically very unfavorable for three reasons:

1. It results in an age composition of the population with a very high rate of dependency, namely that of children below producing age. Resources which might otherwise go into capital formation have to be diverted to the feeding and clothing of a high proportion of dependents. The resulting differences in the proportion of producers to the total population may themselves be sufficient to account for considerable differences in rates of capital formation and economic growth, and over a long period could in fact explain the present disparity between rich and poor countries almost by themselves.[3]

2. The vast expenditure on the feeding, clothing, etc., of children, which normally should be considered as a productive investment of the community in raising the next generation of producers, remains unproductive consumption expenditure because in consequence of high death rates a high proportion of the children die before they complete or even reach their productive period. This is clearly implied in the average expectation of life of forty years or even less—down to thirty years estimated to prevail in a number of African countries.

3. It does not pay to give to children and to productive workers the same amount of education and training as would be the case if death rates were lower and the expenditure made on education and training would therefore be repaid over the full productive period. At the same time as the incentive for education and training is diminished, so are the resources available for this purpose, since the large extent of dependency preempts the scarce existing resources for the sheer feeding, etc., of children for survival instead of raising their quality. Thus the combination of high birth rates and high death rates tends both ways to result in a lower level of quality of "human capital." Recent thinking on problems of economic growth has tended increasingly to emphasize the importance of the human factor and of expenditures on education, training, and research as fundamental. This further highlights the importance of the obstacle presented by

[2] Chap. 8, "Population and Economic Development."
[3] In addition to Chap. 8, reference may be made to similar models in the well-known book by Coale and Hoover, *The Economic Consequences of an Increasing Population*, Princeton, N.J., 1958.

I find that Spengler, in the paper mentioned in the introductory footnote of this chapter, also provides quantitative data bearing upon this point.

the demographic combination of high birth rates and high death rates. The tremendous educational and training deficiencies in Africa and the high cost of their removal are strikingly discussed in the report of the Conference of African States on the Development of Education in Africa, held in Addis Ababa in May, 1961.[4]

Whatever the uncertainties concerning the actual rate of population increase in Africa south of the Sahara, there can be little doubt that both birth rates and death rates are comparatively high. Thus, the statement in the preceding paragraph concerning the unfavorable effect of the combination of high birth rates and high death rates applies with full force to the area.

At a meeting of economists held under the auspices of the International Economic Association in Addis Ababa in July, 1961, to consider the general development problems of Africa south of the Sahara, the following consensus seemed to prevail: While obviously the area ultimately (i.e., after economic growth and a certain measure of industrialization) could carry a population much larger than now exists, it would be of economic advantage if the rate of population increase could be held down at a lower level of, say, 1 to 1½ per cent per annum, and this in such a way that while death rates should be lowered as rapidly as possible, birth rates should adjust themselves to the falling death rates with a minimum time lag so as to reduce the rate of growth to 1 to 1½ per cent per annum. This formula, would, I believe, be supported by practically all those familiar with the area and certainly by the present writer; but the formula is more easily prescribed than realized. Obviously, a multitude of historical, social, and medical factors are at work which may make the realization of this ideal formula virtually impossible. An accelerating rate of population increase above the economic ideal seems certain.

To some extent, the acceleration will finance itself. Disease control will show not only in falling death rates (and hence more rapid population growth) but also in better health (and hence higher productivity). High birth rates and low average age of the population favor economic mobility and increase the chances of modernization and perhaps receptiveness to new methods of production. But we cannot rely on such built-in compensations to solve by themselves the economic problems raised by population increase. This must be done by the successful execution of development programs which raise the productivity of agriculture, lead toward industrialization, and lay the necessary physical and, above all, human infrastructure for self-sustaining economic growth. This is a formidable task, and it is social, technical, and political as well as economic.

[4] Report published by the United Nations Economic Commission for Africa and the United Nations Educational, Scientific and Cultural Organization, UNESCO Document ED-181.

17

Small-scale Industry in African Economic Development

This question can be considered at two levels, the general and the particular. At the general level, one can discuss the pros and cons of emphasis on small-scale industries in development plans and investment patterns, perhaps with some special emphasis on societies at very early stages of economic development, as African countries usually are (in Rostow's terminology, "traditional societies" or societies in the early phases of the "pre-condition" stage). At the particular level, one should pay special attention to special features peculiar to African economies which would not necessarily be displayed by Asian, Middle Eastern, or Latin American economies at the same income level and would not be found in earlier European history.

The particular approach is more meritorious, but suffers from the difficulty that it may not be possible to generalize too much. The matter had really best be discussed for individual countries, and for this, the present author lacks time, space, and competence. All the same, an attempt will be made along the lines of the particular approach, since it seems to me that in the special African circumstances, a specially strong case can be made in favor of small-scale industries. Let me briefly try to list what I consider to be the main points in this specific case.

THE PARTICULAR CASE FOR SMALL-SCALE INDUSTRY

Autonomous Technology. In Africa more than anywhere else, the map of development is still *tabula rasa*. This means that there is still a greater chance than elsewhere to develop an element of autonomous technology, i.e., technology adjusted to the resource endowment of the African countries. In general, underdeveloped countries have to rely on the technology of more advanced countries which naturally reflect their own resource

This paper was presented to the International Economic Association's Regional Conference on Economic Development in Africa South of the Sahara, held in Addis Ababa in July, 1961.

199

endowment, i.e., a relative abundance of capital and skills and a relative scarcity of labor. In spite of the best efforts made to adapt subsequently this alien technology to the different circumstances of underdeveloped countries, the result is not ideal. To cope with this situation, it has been suggested that technology should be based, not on market prices, but on "shadow prices" or "accounting prices" of capital and labor and other factors of production. This however, introduces an element of arbitrariness and in any case does not solve the fundamental dilemma that the best-adapted technology simply may not be there (or not known to those preparing investment projects). The adaptation of the mechanized technology in the direction of the smaller scale and demechanization is as difficult as it is to unscramble scrambled eggs.

There is no doubt that an autonomous technology for African countries would result in typically smaller-scale units of production than in Europe or North America. If, therefore, the development of small-scale industry could be based also on the development of an autonomous technology for Africa—admittedly this is a very big if—the resulting smaller-scale industries could also be high-productivity industries in the African context. In this way, something new in economic development could still happen in Africa. Admittedly the chances seem to be against it, since the development of an autonomous technology for Africa is a difficult and revolutionary undertaking. The line of least resistance is to transfer technology and adapt it rather than to create it. However, in the present context, the chance of a new departure at least exists and deserves to be mentioned.

Industry Run by Africans. One of the great problems in African development will be to make it as fully African as possible from the very beginning. The more we can avoid the creation of enclave economies, the more we can avoid transferring to the economic field the frictions arising from "colonialism" (I am using this unhappy shorthand expression with all due apology), the happier we shall all be. The efficient management of large-scale industries, both in the sense of business management and in the sense of technical responsibility for large machinery complexes, is not at present accessible to large enough numbers of Africans. On the other hand, Africans have already shown and had the opportunity to develop skill in the running of small-scale business and the types of mechanical skills that are applied to individual pieces of machinery and personal forms of organization rather than to big complexes and corporate organizations. Therefore, the choice is not an entirely economic choice between small-scale industries and large-scale industries; rather, the choice is between African or largely African small-scale industries and foreign or largely foreign large-scale industries. I think this situation should tip the balance, in many cases, toward the small-scale developments.

The Learning Process. The development of small-scale enterprises of all kinds can be a stepping-stone to larger-scale enterprises, a part of the learning process. I realize that economists differ on this point. I am particularly sorry to disagree on this point with Hirschman, to whose insight we owe so much. I suppose Hirschman would argue that the best way to learn is to plunge into large-scale organization and learn by trial and error. I must disagree with this prescription. I do believe that in these matters there is such a thing as an organic link between small-scale, medium-scale, and large-scale forms of organization. On the whole, it is more productive to move, wherever one can, from the lower end of the range to the upper end rather than jump directly to the top. For one thing, with small-scale organization the learning process can be spread over much larger numbers. In the second place, the number of different arrangements and situations in which learning can take place with small-scale organization is a multiple of what it is with large-scale organization. Third, (coming back to the preceding point), with small-scale units the learning would be done largely by Africans, but with large-scale units it would be done largely by outside enterprise.

Findings or presumptions that small-scale industries are "inefficient" by comparison with large-scale industries are often based on the economist's narrow concept of "output," or "capital formation." Part of the "output" of small-scale industries consists of the creation of skills—"human capital formation"—which, although it does not enter the economist's figures, is of extreme importance in the development of underdeveloped countries. But even in terms of physical productivity, small industries (less than one hundred employees) produce about 90 per cent of the average industrial output per person in the United States and Puerto Rico and about 85 per cent in the United Kingdom (but only about 65 per cent in Japan).

Spreading Development. The development of Africa has so far largely proceeded by forming a large number of "islands." Broadly speaking, there seems a choice of either multiplying the islands or deepening the islands. By this I mean that development might either create more and more islands of development until ultimately they link up with each other or it might push forward industrial development inside the islands which have already been created. I would venture the proposition that insofar as there is a policy choice in these matters, it would be better to multiply the islands than to deepen them. This proposition is based on a number of reasons, particularly on the desirability of avoiding excessive migration with its resultant social friction and economic difficulties, and also on the experience (so striking in contemporary Brazil, Italy, and elsewhere) of how difficult it is to revive a region after it is once allowed to become "backward." The creation of new islands of development will naturally shift emphasis to smaller-scale forms of organization, because of the greater scattering of investment that is involved and also because islands typically start with smaller-scale units unless they are based upon a big mining complex. Outside the islands, in any case, population is often sparse, and transport is so poorly developed that only local markets exist. This is true both for products and factors of production, and creates a setting for small-scale and mainly rural enterprise.

Savings Potential. The African savings potential is typically localized or tribalized and in any case highly specific. Small-scale industries can make good use of specific forms of saving, which it would not be easy to mobilize on an institutional basis. The most tangible expressions of unutilized local savings potential are in the available spare time of people—in many parts of Africa particularly among men rather than women—and in the present building up of economically useless assets, such as unproductive cattle and other status symbols. The conversion of this unutilized potential into small-scale industries seems feasible; its conversion into large-scale units does not. The importance of status symbols also points in the same direction. It is conceivable to translate the attitude to cattle—counting heads as a status symbol—to the running of a small firm or business. This would mean that the owner of such a firm would plough back any profits actively into the firm to see it grow as a tangible expression of his social worth and success; thus a high marginal rate of savings and reinvestment would be achieved. True enough, as experience in Northeast Brazil shows, for instance, this attitude may become an obstacle to development at later stages, since it sets limits to the growth of the firm; owners who are willing to plough back their own earnings up to the hilt are unwilling to adopt nonpersonal forms of organization, accept partners (at least outside the family), or even utilize bank credit. Thus, while firms grow surprisingly rapidly up to a certain point, the difficulties of growing beyond that point are quite formidable. But in Africa, this kind of problem lies more in the future, to be dealt with when it arises. For the moment, the problem is not how to remove such an obstacle but to promote growth up to the point where the obstacle arises. At this stage, the advantages of personal ownership and the smaller scale which it implies seem quite strong.

Human Groupings. It is also relevant to point out that in the case of Africa the homogeneous ethnic and linguistic units are often quite small; they may be limited to the village or tribal level. This means that any large-scale unit of production will have to assemble its labor forces from different ethnic, linguistic, and religious groups, which may produce labor friction, difficulties of communications, and lower labor efficiency. For the same reason, in large-scale units management and workers may be drawn from different groups, which adds a further complication. It may be argued that the linguistic and tribal differences eventually must be overcome if the African countries are to acquire a reasonable degree of economic integration and development. Of course this is true, but the argument here is that there is no point in meeting these difficulties unnecessarily, or unnecessarily early in development. It is difficult to see how the development of small-scale units, based upon more homogeneous groupings and providing a nursery for large-scale development, could be other than helpful in the following stage of national integration also.

Trading and Speculation. Given the African desire for independence, personal identification, and the present weakness of business talent, it seems true to say that in many cases the real alternative to the development of small-scale industries would not be the development of large-scale in- dustries but rather the development of trade and more speculative activities. To that extent, productivity comparisons between investment in large-scale and small-scale industries seem to be somewhat irrelevant. The true com- parison should be between development of small-scale industry, on the one hand, and trading and speculative activities, on the other. Although some economists have attributed very high development value to trading— and it is certainly valuable in transforming subsistence economies into money economies, in creating a demand for merchandise, and in forming capital—this consideration is also bound to shift the balance toward smaller- scale industries.

Self-employment. In small-scale industries, especially of the more rural type (cottage industries), there is an element of self-employment in the sense that employment of the owner and of his helping family members will be carried up to the point where marginal productivity of labor falls to zero —on the assumption that the alternative to this type of self-employment is nonvoluntary unemployment. By contrast, wage employment in large-scale units is only carried to the point where the productivity of labor is equal to the current wage. This means that with large-scale organization and wage employment and with excess labor supply, part of the labor force will remain unemployed unless there are adequate self-employment oppor- tunities. Hence, where there is a state of prevailing underemployment and lack of employment opportunities—this is particularly true of Africa in its present state of development—the principle of self-employment is better designed to maximize total production than the principle of wage employ- ment. This seems to me a good argument to promote small-scale industries with an element of self-employment as distinct from wage employment until employment opportunities have increased in the course of general economic development. The strength of this argument is of course diminished where there are ample land and no restrictions on land ownership so that those not accepted in wage employment can employ themselves on the land; but this situation is by no means universal in Africa.

Existing Small Industries. The development of small-scale industries in African countries has the advantage of building on something that already exists. The extent to which underdeveloped countries produce their own manufactures is often considerably underrated. This is also true of Africa. In nearly all African countries there are fairly widespread plants producing on a small scale, whether as urban or rural industry, such things as tiles, flour, pots and pans, brushes, pottery, paper, matches, glass, soap, beer, shoes, brasswork, leather goods, boxes, trunks, furniture, trinkets, and many other consumer goods, as well as simple capital goods—spades, hoes, ploughs, harnesses, hand tools, etc. To develop something that already exists is easier than to build up something entirely new. Among the existing small-scale industries, there are already a number of successful producers who have proved their ability and who can be encouraged to expand and a number of skilled persons who can be encouraged and aided to set up on their own. There is also a great deal of experience to be drawn upon as to the situations, incentives, and obstacles involved in the enlargement of the scale of existing units. This would make major mistakes and loss of investment less likely if large-scale units were developed out of smaller-scale units. The development of existing units, within limits, also has notoriously more favorable capital/output ratios than the establishment of new units.

The Chaos of Trading Areas. One of the great needs of Africa is the formation of new common market and trading areas. The present orientation of African economic relations is based more on history than on economic rationale. The present political boundaries are also very often drawn without regard to economic requirements. It is clear that any rational development of African countries will have to cope with these two problems. However, this will take some time; very complex and difficult policies and economic readjustments are involved. The main focus of the problem will be the establishment of large-scale industries serving markets larger than, or at any rate different from, the present country boundaries. A race by African countries toward large-scale industrialization based on present national markets could conceivably do great harm and turn out to be very wasteful in the light of the subsequent development of new and more rational economic areas. There is, therefore, a case for delaying such irrevocable decisions—at least in doubtful cases—until the underlying problem of rational trading areas has become clearer. This is all the more reason to push ahead as much as possible with the development of smaller-scale industries in which the question of reorientation of trade and redrawing of economic areas does not arise to the same extent.

An Open Future. This last consideration leads us to a more general consideration. The shorter gestation period of investment in smaller-scale industries will frequently have a particular advantage in the special circumstances of most African countries. Countries recently acceding to independence or countries awaiting early independence will be faced with much greater than normal uncertainties concerning their resources and requirements over the immediate future. Faced with such a situation, a rational technique of development planning is to allocate present resources with a minimum of prejudice to future decisions, i.e., retaining the greatest possible degree of freedom. There is no doubt that a number of smaller-scale units freezes future decisions to a lesser degree than the establishment of a large-scale unit. A large-scale unit will involve the growing up of subsidiary economic complexes and overhead investment around it and will require heavy investment in urbanization of a fixed pattern. The establishment of smaller-scale units keeps the situation much more fluid. There is no doubt that an industrial pattern based on large-scale industries and industrial complexes involves more irreversible decisions than does a multiplying of the development islands with emphasis on small-scale industries. Where the peculiar circumstances of African countries put a special premium on fluidity in development planning—and this seems to me the present situation—the balance should to that extent shift in favor of smaller-scale industries.

The Best Development Strategy. African countries are faced with specific shortages of indigenous administrators, especially technicians and economists. On the other hand, there is no doubt that the chosen route of development cannot be freewheeling growth but must be development planning. More than anywhere else the requirements for economic and social overhead capital—transport, power, housing, health facilities, educational assistance—will have to figure very largely. Hence, both with respect to the desperate shortage of capital and with respect to the great shortage of trained people to give attention to different sectors, there is a strong case for concentrating available resources in capital and trained manpower in these overhead sectors. This makes it all the more important to concentrate directly productive investment in those sectors where capital requirements are least and where results are least delayed.

Of the three sectors—agriculture, small-scale industry, and large-scale industry—it is small-scale industry, generally speaking, which seems to satisfy these two key requirements most frequently. An expansion in agricultural production is notoriously difficult, beset as it is not only with economic but also with social and institutional difficulties of all kinds. Moreover, in many sparsely populated areas of Africa it may have to be partly capital-intensive. The development of large-scale industry is mainly capital-intensive, particularly where machinery may have to substitute for skill as well as for simple labor. Besides, the gestation period is long, and the danger of major mistakes in African conditions is considerable. Compared with the two alternatives of agriculture and large-scale industry, therefore, investment in small-scale industry seems to have much to recommend it.

Fear of Unemployment. Perhaps the greatest individual obstacle to the improvement of economic efficiency in small-scale industries is the fear of unemployment. Although this fear may be more imaginary than real (in fact, improved efficiency in small-scale industries may lead to added employment rather than unemployment), this does not make it any less real as an obstacle to the development of efficient small-scale industries. It is probably for this reason that small-scale industries have become associated with suggestions of work making, traditional craftsmanship, and Gandhi philosophy rather than with efficient production. In those countries of Africa which are not overpopulated, this fear of unemployment is less marked than it is, shall we say, in India. Moreover, a generally vigorous development policy will also serve to hold fears of unemployment at bay.

The general conclusion would be that *efficient* small-scale industries are best developed as part of a generally vigorous and forward-moving economy.

WAYS AND MEANS

So far this paper has mentioned some of the reasons why the development of smaller-scale industries in Africa holds out some very special attractions and therefore probably deserves higher priority in our thinking than it has received so far. A few thoughts may be added about the ways of achieving this desired end.

One thought leads us back to the more political problem of the relationship of foreign capital and African capital, of foreign enterprise and African enterprise, which beyond doubt will be such an important determinant of African economic development. Large-scale investments will very often have to be foreign, and the establishment of a mutually satisfactory relationship between foreign investors and African governments and peoples will be a crucial problem. The best way in which such a harmonious relationship could be achieved would be for the larger-scale foreign firms not only to make a contribution to the development of domestic enterprise and domestic capital but also to be very obviously seen to make such a contribution.

This directs attention to the possibilities of organizing within the African countries a system of subcontracting and ordering by which the foreign firms could produce their requirements and components as much as possible within the country in which they were located. There will be limits to this process, particularly at the beginning, but it seems to be a good line of general policy to hew to in everybody's interest. The kind of system one would like to see develop in African countries is that wherein the larger-scale foreign firms (which might also themselves enter into some kind of partnership with local governments and local businessmen) would range around them and nurse along with them smaller-scale African firms. The techniques of doing this will be in need of further study and will need adaptation to special African conditions, but it seems a problem to which students of African development problems might well devote attention.

A second thought is suggested by Japanese economic history. In Japan, the economic take-off was not based on displacing small-scale or rural industries. On the contrary, it was accompanied by development of subcontracting by the larger firms and of a system based on village specialization. These experiences also might provide valuable guideposts for African development.

In the case of Japan, the geographical compactness of the country made it easier to diffuse new ideas and skills through the countryside and thus draw small-scale industries quickly into the production system.[1] This situation of compactness is not frequent in Africa now. It seems a little paradoxical to find compactness put forward as an argument in favor of small-scale industries, since generally it is exactly the sparseness of population, isolation of local markets, and high transport costs which are considered to be the best breeding ground for small-scale industry. The fact of the matter is probably that if other prerequisities for the development of small-scale industries are available (in terms of skills, finance, etc.), small-scale industries will draw strength from, and will adapt themselves to, diverse economic conditions.

Indonesia also provides interesting examples of village specialization in such things as ceramics, furniture, umbrellas, etc.; in given villages these articles or parts of them are produced in many homes or in small workshops.[2]

A third method for the development of efficient smaller-scale industries is the establishment of trading estates. On these trading estates smaller-scale industries can be given the kind of services they need—power, transport, maintenance, etc.—as well as general technical assistance and such aids to business management as training in accounting, etc. Perhaps even more important, by provision of buildings and equipment on a hire-purchase basis or on a rental basis, the overhead costs of starting smaller industries can be reduced and converted into running costs. Such trading estates could be deliberately used as a nursery for smaller-scale industries. New firms would be encouraged to set up on their own, to make room for new growth on the trading estate as soon as they extended beyond a certain size and proved their economic viability; and not only the successes but also the failures should be moved out from the estate in good time. The financing of such trading estates *cum* pilot projects *cum* training facilities would also be the kind of project which might attract aid from abroad.

---

[1] See W. W. Lockwood, *The Economic Development of Japan*, Princeton, Princeton, N.J., 1954, pp. 213–214.

[2] See K. N. Rao, "Small-scale Industry and Economic Development in Indonesia." *Journal of Economic Development and Cultural Change,* January, 1956.

Another method of small-scale industry development of interest to Africa should be the tradition of the central workshops—the *Centraals* developed by the Dutch government and the *Induks* developed later by the Indonesian government—in Indonesia. These central workshops provide a good focus in which to bring together government promotion, finance, and cooperative elements. The central workshops carry out those operations which are more efficiently carried out on a relatively large scale and provide financial and advisory services of all kinds, while grouping around them clusters of small-scale or home industries drawing their supplies from, and turning in their products to, the *Centraal* or *Induk*.[3]

[3] *Ibid.*

18

The African Development Bank

The idea of creating an African Development Bank goes back to a resolution which was unanimously passed by all the African countries in the United Nations Economic Commission for Africa about two years ago (1961). Since then the plan has been explored in several ways typical of UN procedures, ranging back and forth between Secretariat studies, panels of private experts, panels of governmental experts, consultants, ECA committees, private as well as official consultations. The project has so far emerged from all these various methods of examination, not indeed unchanged from its original conception, but still appearing to the African countries as a desirable and feasible goal.

ROOTS OF THE IDEA

The need for additional capital in Africa is undeniable if the continent is to join in the great ascent toward economic development. So are the need for cooperation between different African countries and the need to overcome some of the national and regional divisions which have marked the present history of the continent and the emergence of African countries into independence.

For established international financing and banking institutions, especially those located in the United States, Africa is a difficult area in which to operate, for lack of knowledge, lack of data, lack of contacts, and lack of tradition. The new African countries themselves are often new and inexperienced in dealing with the established sources of finance. Similarly, as far as aid is concerned, even though there is no fixed yardstick of what is a "reasonable" or "fair" distribution of aid, it is clear that the flow of aid to Africa from the United States, for instance, has been equally hampered by institutional factors and lack of contact points.

This article, originally prepared for publication in "Revue de Science Financière," was then used for information material circulated by the United Nations in connection with the establishment of the African Development Bank. Since writing this article, the African Development Bank has been established at a Conference of African

The idea of an African Development Bank also received undeniable impetus from the successful establishment of the Inter-American Development Bank, which caters to the Latin American continent. Although the situation of Africa differs, both in the absence of a single concept corresponding to the Alliance for Progress and also because of the greater homogeneity and longer history of regional cooperation in Latin America, yet the African countries may be readily forgiven for seeing a valuable precedent in the Inter-American Development Bank.

Of all the roots previously mentioned, the need for cooperation of African countries with each other is perhaps the most striking argument for creating instruments of regional cooperation in financing, although by no means in financing alone. If we leave out the United Arab Republic at one end of the continent and the Union of South Africa at the other end, and if we further take out Nigeria, which is the one example of a larger country in tropical Africa, what are we left with? We are left with about forty countries or countries-to-be, averaging perhaps 4 million people per country. On the average, of the 4 million people perhaps half are at present completely outside any contacts with the market economy, living in self-contained and often inaccessible tribal communities or jungle villages; they are at present beyond the scope of any orthodox financial approach to development. The remaining half, i.e., 2 million people with some varying degree of contact with the market economy, have an average cash purchasing power corresponding perhaps to one-twentieth of that of a European. Thus they represent a cash market equivalent to a moderate-size European town of about 100,000 people (but by contrast they are spread out, often over a wide area). Evidently, it does not make sense in Europe to have separate plans and separate financing institutions for each individual town of 100,000 people, regardless of what goes on in the next town. By the same token, a purely national approach to planning and financing economic development in Africa does not make much sense.

The present countries of Africa not only are too small, in the sense of present cash markets, to form economic units of development; also, their borders are determined by political and diplomatic history rather than by economic sense. Thus their present borders cut across natural river-valley development units, mineral deposits often extend across the frontiers, the natural outlet of one country is through another country, no rational transport network could be developed on a national basis, etc.

It is against this background that the idea of creating an African Development Bank should be understood. The background explains the in-

---

Finance Ministers held in Khartoum, Sudan, in the summer of 1963. The agreement establishing the Bank has now been signed by virtually all African countries and ratified by quite a number of them.

terest with which this idea has been greeted and supported by the African countries.

SPECIFIC GAPS TO BE FILLED BY THE AFRICAN DEVELOPMENT BANK

From the very beginning attention was focused on seven different types of projects which a fully developed and mature African Development Bank should specifically undertake. These are as follows:

(1) Regional projects
(2) Promotion of inter-African trade
(3) Promotion of exchange economies
(4) Fulfilling the needs of newly independent countries
(5) Education and training
(6) Promotion of small-scale African industrial enterprise
(7) Development plans: long-range support

The need for regional projects in Africa arises from the fact that individual African countries are often too small to be the right economic units for balanced economic development planning; moreover, the national boundaries are often in the nature of administrative lines rather than boundaries defining economic units. Examples of regional projects for which a need has already been established are health and locust control, higher education and technological research, transport projects, large-scale industries, irrigation projects, hydroelectric projects, river-valley development schemes, and migratory-labor links. Emphasis on regional projects will call for the formulation of general principles as to how the political and economic problems arising are to be tackled.

The promotion of inter-African trade is closely linked to the need for regional projects. It arises from the fact that in the past the trade of individual African countries has been developed almost entirely with an orientation away from inter-African trade. The need for inter-African trade also arises from the small size of African countries, from their diversity and possible complementarities, and from the requirements of efficient large-scale production and specialization. In many cases, this means that even though the project itself might not be regional in nature, yet its markets or sources of supply should be regional; and the development of related projects of this kind would require regional understandings and regional cooperation. Here again, an African Development Bank may suggest itself as a necessary focus for such a regional approach. The promotion of inter-African trade may also open up opportunities for the constructive use of local currency contributions.

The promotion of an exchange economy and national integration in African countries is an essential step in their economic development. In its turn, it presupposes a development not only of internal transport but also of domestic entrepreneurship. The creation of domestic capital markets and money markets is also an essential part of the creation of integrated exchange economies. To this whole complex of interrelated problems an African Development Bank could conceivably bring a special orientation and a special expertise.

The viability of newly independent countries may well become a special concern of an African Development Bank. This also will call for further establishment of guidelines. Even the type of financing may have to be specially adjusted. "The wisdom of burdening some of the newly independent African nations with external debt at this stage of their struggle for survival is also questionable."[1] If the Bank were limited to hard loans, " . . . the newly independent countries whose credit is not yet established and whose domestic resources are in some cases extremely limited, would be in a bad way."[2] The principle of special international assistance to newly independent countries has been recognized by the United Nations and also by individual countries in their bilateral or multilateral arrangements.

The limited economic and budgetary capacities of African countries make it difficult for them to carry the burden of the recurrent as well as capital expenditures on essential developmental services. Among these, education and training have come to be recognized as being particularly fundamental for African countries. The Conference of African States on the Development of Education in Africa which met in Addis Ababa from May 15 to 25, 1961, drew up and approved a plan for educational development of the African countries as a whole for the next twenty years.[3] It was estimated that the cost of realizing this plan would amount to approximately 590 million dollars in 1961, rising to 1.16 billion dollars in 1965, 1.88 billion dollars in 1970, and 2.6 billion dollars in 1980. On the assumption that the African countries would find it possible to devote to this shares of their national income ranging from 3 to 4 per cent between 1961 and 1965, increasing to 6 per cent by 1980, it was calculated that they would be able to find, unassisted, 450 to 700 million dollars during the first five years of the projected plan, reaching 870 million dollars in 1970 and 2.2 billion dollars in 1980. This would leave a gap to be filled from outside which was estimated to amount to about 1.3 billion dollars for the first five years of the plan (an average of 260 million dollars a year), rising to 1.01 billion dollars in 1970 and decreasing to 400 million dollars in 1980. An educational program of the magnitude envisaged in this plan could not possibly be financed entirely from the recurrent revenues of the African

[1] Robert E. Asher, *Grants, Loans and Local Currencies*, Brookings, Washington, D.C., 1961, p. 97.
[2] *Ibid.*, p. 99.
[3] Final conference report, UNESCO Document ED-181.

governments, and there would undoubtedly be a recourse to loan financing. This is an area in which the resources of an African Development Bank could conceivably be advantageous.

For many reasons, the promotion of small-scale African industrial enterprise also plays a fundamental role in African economic development.[4] This also raises a number of special problems, and an institution like an African Development Bank could conceivably be a good solution. In this area of operations, the need would particularly strongly arise to work with and through national institutions. The establishment of trading estates in selected locations throughout Africa which would become focal points of African enterprise and industrialization might conceivably be an important part of these activities.

Finally, it may be noted that many African countries are in an extreme state of underdevelopment. The formulation of long-range development plans for them is particularly important and also particularly difficult. Much of the developmental assistance must be of a very long-term nature, must be given on very flexible terms, and may take a considerable time to show results. These special conditions may also conceivably make it seem desirable to create an institution which can offer such long-range support in a way particularly adjusted to African conditions.

While the above seven areas, as tentatively defined, seem to open up possibilities for an African Development Bank, it must also be recognized that the arrangements which suggest themselves for dealing with each area are by no means identical or even similar. This brings home the point that the provisions made for the financing and mode of operations of an African Development Bank would have to depend on which of the various purposes or gaps it might fill was emphasized.

THE PRINCIPLE OF ADDITIONALITY

Also from the very beginning it was visualized that the African Development Bank could be justified only if it introduced new elements and tapped new sources of finance rather than replaced existing sources or undertook familiar functions. The seven specific gaps described in the previous section themselves go a long way toward mapping out a field of operation for a new type of institution.

As far as resources are concerned, the principle of "additionality" might be satisfied in a variety of ways: (1) if the African countries could be induced to devote to the African Development Bank resources which would otherwise not be devoted to developmental purposes or would be less effectively used for developmental purposes; (2) if the Bank could help

[4] See the preceding chapter, "Small-scale Industry in African Economic Development."

African countries to develop their own internal capital markets so as to promote a more satisfactory flow of potential savings into potentially productive investment; (3) if sources of finance outside Africa would be willing to channel through the Bank resources which otherwise would not be made available to Africa; (4) if the Bank, through its contacts, projects, and advice, would create a more satisfactory liaison between the potential borrowers in Africa and potential lenders or investors outside Africa; (5) if the African Development Bank could help to prepare projects which otherwise would remain general potentialities rather than concrete financing propositions and could pinpoint specific investment opportunities and bring them to the attention of potential investors, both African and from outside Africa.

It will be seen that even an elementary analysis of the ways in which additionality could be achieved already directs the mind to a variety of functions which an African Development Bank could carry out, either individually or in combination. To the extent that the Bank by its guarantees or otherwise could improve the terms and conditions by which African countries can obtain capital and thus could reduce their balance-of-payments burden, there would again be additionality. The absorptive capacity of African countries for capital is increased by an amelioration of the terms on which they can obtain it.

QUESTIONS OF CAPITALIZATION AND MANAGEMENT

Once a project of this type is being thought about and discussed in more detail, hundreds of questions arise to which answers must be found— answers which must be consistent with each other and many of which may lead to new questions. Foremost among such questions, perhaps are the closely related questions of capitalization and management.

In the early stages of the project, it was pictured that the legal capitalization might be partly African, partly non-African. This was largely based on the precedent of the Inter-American Development Bank, where the legal capitalization is partly from the Latin American beneficiaries and partly from the North American donors. In the case of the African Development Bank, however, it became clear quite soon that such an arrangement would lead to great difficulties.

How to ensure that the African capital contributions would not be hopelessly swamped by larger non-African contributions? How to ensure African control and African top management of the Bank in such circumstances? How to parcel out the non-African capital subscriptions among East and West, among former colonial and noncolonial countries? Whom to admit to capital subscriptions and whom to exclude?

The solution which on subsequent reflection proved superior was to limit the subscription to the legal capital of the Bank, and hence participation in the top Board of Governors, entirely to African countries. This had the inevitable consequence that the legal capital of the Bank had to be kept comparatively small. If the Bank really wanted to attain the scale of activities of the Inter-American Development Bank (for a continent and population of comparable size), it would be necessary mainly to rely on additional resources outside the legal capital. At one point compromise suggestions were made to have two types of capital subscriptions, African subscriptions of A-shares with full voting rights on the Board of Governors and non-African subscriptions of B-shares with limited or no voting rights. These compromise solutions however, also turned out to be unsatisfactory, and would in fact have created new difficulties of their own.

But even when the principle of purely African subscriptions had been settled, many subsidiary questions remained to be answered. Should all African countries contribute the same sum regardless of size, population, and wealth? This would throw a great burden on the smaller and poorer countries, although to this argument it could be objected that after a certain time all countries would be net gainers from the activities of the Bank, the poorer and smaller countries perhaps even more than the others. If unequal subscriptions were introduced, what should be the basis of subscriptions: size of population, national income, size of the government's budget, or a combination of all these? It should be remembered that for many African countries there would be no authentic base for determining a contribution, even the size of population not being accurately known. If subscriptions were unequal, should voting in the Board of Governors be proportionate and weighted according to each country's subscription? Should it be based on the principle of "one country, one vote"? Or some combination of the two? It will be seen that many of these issues are not capable of any scientific answer on strictly economic grounds and might in fact be divisive among the different African countries when the purpose of the Bank is to bridge existing divisions.

A special problem was raised by the existence of countries still in a state of colonial dependency, such as (at the time) Kenya, Northern Rhodesia, Angola, and Mozambique. Should such areas become members of the African Development Bank? Should the Bank operate in the areas of not yet independent countries? What would be the relationship of the metropolitan countries governing these areas to the African Development Bank? This is by no means an exhaustive list of the questions arising.

It is a remarkable sign of African willingness to compromise and to achieve the ultimate goal of setting up an African Development Bank that these and many other questions relating to the capitalization of the Bank were settled, without any hard fighting and dissensions which would leave bitterness behind.

Similarly, questions relating to the management of the proposed Bank, however intractable, were solved in principle to everybody's satisfaction at this preliminary stage. The picture clearly emerging is that of a Bank in which the Managing Director, his deputy, and the Board of Directors are all African. Underneath this top echelon of management, there would be a senior layer of management in which expertise and competence would be the governing criterion and non-African expertise and competence would find its place. Underneath this senior echelon, there would be a junior echelon which again would be wholly or predominantly African. This would be the place where younger Africans would be trained in the arts and sciences of banking, to take their place in later years either in the senior management echelon of the African Development Bank or in the service of their own countries.

Throughout the discussions, the African governments showed full awareness that a management which inspires confidence abroad is an essential precondition for the attraction of non-African capital in any form, which in turn is an essential precondition for operations on a really significant scale and for satisfying the principle of additionality. On the other hand, there was a strong determination that the Bank should be a thoroughly African institution. The present proposals are designed to reconcile these two principles. They are probably the best or only way in which this can be done. It is a good omen for the future that on this and other matters it was possible to reach agreement.

This does not mean that the establishment of the Bank will be easy or that it will follow the present plans in every detail. Very likely it will have to start off in a modest way, perhaps for a year or two more as a "task force" to study investment opportunities and a collecting point of financing for worthwhile projects on an *ad hoc* basis. But whatever happens, the evidence of African agreement and unanimity is impressive. Wherever the consulting groups of the ECA committee (charged with the preparatory work for the Bank) went in Europe, Asia, and North America in order to discuss the plans for the proposed Development Bank, everybody they met was deeply impressed by the fact that here perhaps for the first time in the history of the world, was a negotiating group representing the whole of Africa.

In fact it is possible that the very modest start of the institution may serve to demonstrate both to the African countries and to those eager to assist African countries from abroad its potential usefulness in a more convincing manner than if the Bank would spring fully-grown into life. There are still many areas of doubt to be overcome. Prominent among them is the problem of convincing African countries which are the beneficiaries and heirs of certain historical associations with important financial counterparts that they have much to gain and little or nothing to lose from the creation of an African Development Bank. Another of the problems is to gain gradually the confidence of potential investors from outside Africa. Both these problems can best be solved from a modest starting position.

In any case, little is lost by a modest start, since the African Development Bank would by no means be the only or even the main answer to all African development problems. This will be clear to anybody even remotely familiar with the situation on the continent. Nor is the creation of an African Development Bank in any way inconsistent with continued and even strengthened historical and financial associations.

But where the Bank has its great importance is in introducing a new idea, a new line of attack, into a picture from which this particular line of approach to Africa's problem has so far been sadly missing. This is the idea of cooperation at a truly regional level, cutting across, where this is needed, the more artificial groupings based on history and politics. On occasion the African Development Bank could ultimately even be the focus of cooperation on a fully continental scale, although one imagines that those occasions would be comparatively rare. It is no accident that the idea of an African Development Bank has its genesis in the United Nations, which embodies this new line of thinking in African affairs.

It may be reckoned as a further advantage that the history of the Bank has been the subject of the cautious checks and counterchecks by all sorts of committees and expert bodies and the numerous consultations that are characteristic of United Nations procedures. This means that the many problems and difficulties involved have been repeatedly brought to the attention of governments and others concerned. The adjustment and compromises made are the more solid for having been worked out often by the method of repeated approximations. The draft statute which is now emerging for the consideration of the United Nations Economic Commission for Africa—and later on adopted by a conference of finance ministers—is therefore not a rash venture.

No doubt life, which has its own way, may still give the idea of an African Development Bank all sorts of new and presently unforeseen twists and turns. But whatever happens, whatever the timetable and shape of developments may be, it may be safely predicted that the idea of an African Development Bank will not die again.

PART 6

Problems and Experience:
Northeast Brazil

19

Factors in the Lack of Development of the Brazilian Northeast and Their Relative Importance

Directly Demographic Factors. In the Northeast, 60 per cent of the total population over ten years of age is actively employed, as compared with 62.9 per cent in the whole of Brazil, including the Northeast. These are 1940 figures, the latest available, but there is no reason to assume that the relationship of the 1950 figures will differ significantly. The figures have been obtained by deducting from the total population of ten years and over the categories of *condições inactivas* (inactive conditions) and *condições ou actividades mal definidas ou não declaradas* (conditions or activites not well defined or not declared). Also excluded are *actividades não comprendidas no demais ramos* (activities not covered in other categories).[1] The difference between the Northeast and the whole of Brazil is due partly to a higher percentage of population under ten years of age and partly to a higher proportion of population listed as in inactive condition, presumably including, specifically, a higher proportion of persons unemployed and in ill-health. Since of any 100 persons in the Northeast only 60 are actively employed, including domestic work and education, as against 62.9 in the whole of Brazil, this factor accounts for a deficit of 4.6 per cent in per capita income in the northeast $(60/62.9 = 0.954)$.

Smaller Area of Land per Person in Agriculture in the Northeast. In the whole of Brazil, the area under cultivation for twenty-nine principal crops per person engaged in agriculture was 1.487 hectares in 1948 and 1.523 hectares in 1949. The corresponding figures for the Northeast were 1.049 hectares in 1948 and 1.083 hectares in 1949. In the Northeast the amount of land per person employed in agriculture was 70.6

[1] Agriculture, extraction, industry, commerce, transport, administration, defense, liberal profession, social services, domestic activities, and school activities.

The section on the economic development of Northeastern Brazil which begins with this chapter was written after a visit to the area in 1953. It has been published as a book in Portuguese by the Economic per cent of the national average in 1948 and 71.4 per cent in 1949. Thus we can take an average of 71 per cent for the two years. These two years were not drought years.

This means that each worker in the agricultural sector of the Northeast had 29 per cent less land than in the whole of Brazil; and even if output per hectare had been the same in the Northeast as in the whole of Brazil, output per person in agriculture would still have been 29 per cent less. The proportion of agricultural output in the total national income of the Northeast can be estimated as very close to 50 per cent. This follows from the computations on the employment structure of the region and the relative productivity in each sector subsequently dealt with in this report. Therefore, 29 per cent less of agricultural output due to land shortage, compared with the whole country, is equivalent to a reduction in the income of the Northeast by 14 per cent.

The two factors so far discussed may be brought together as "demographic factors." The first is directly demographic in the sense that it is based on the structure and other characteristics of the population. The second is indirectly demographic in that it indicates pressure of population on the land in the agricultural sector; but it is also largely economic in character, since it indicates inability, due to lack of equipment and other factors, to extend the area under cultivation. Together the two demographic factors account for a per capita deficit in the Northeast of 18 per cent ($100 \times 0.95 \times 0.86 = 82$).

Smaller Output per Hectare in the Agricultural Sector of the Northeast. The value of output for the principal agricultural crops per hectare of cultivated land in the nine states of the Northeast was 1.557 cruzeiros in 1948 and 1.743 cruzeiros in 1949. These figures constitute 73.6 per cent and 74.3 per cent respectively of the corresponding figures for the whole of Brazil, including the Northeast. Thus, it may be said that the relative value of production per hectare in the agricultural sector in the Northeast is 74 per cent, or 26 per cent less than for the whole of Brazil.

The above figures relate to nondrought years. For the whole of 1947–1951, i.e., including drought years, the figure for the Northeast is 69.8 per cent, or a difference of 30 per cent.[2] If the figure for the whole of 1947–1951 is used, i.e., 30 per cent less output per hectare in the Northeast, it follows that the total reduction in per capita incomes due to this factor

Development Commission of Pernambuco (Comissão de Desenvolvimento Econômico de Pernambuco), Recife, Brazil, 1962, under the title *A Study on the Economic Development of the North-East* (*Estudo sôbre o desenvolvimento econômico do Nordeste*).

[2] Data derived from speech by João Cleophas, Minister of Agriculture, in the Câmara dos Deputados, on May 7, 1953, mimeographed and published by the Serviço de Informações Agrícolas, p. 12.

is about 15 per cent, since the agricultural income of the Northeast represents just over one-half of its total income. In nondrought years the reduction is less.

When small cultivated area per person and small output per hectare are considered together, it will be seen that their combined effect, i.e., small output per person in agriculture, is such that output per person in the agricultural sector of the Northeast is only 50–55 per cent of the Brazilian average. In 1948, cultivated area per person was 70.6 per cent of the national average and output per hectare 73.6 per cent of the national average, so that output per person was 52 per cent of the national average ($100 \times 0.706 \times 0.736 = 52.0$). In 1949, output per person in agriculture in the Northeast was 53 per cent of the national average, the amount of land per person being 71.4 per cent and the amount of production per hectare being 74.3 per cent of the national average ($100 \times 0.714 \times 0.743 = 53$). Thus, productivity per person in the agricultural sector in the Northeast is a little over one-half of the Brazilian average in nondrought years. In producing this difference, smaller amount of land per person and smaller output per unit of cultivated land are about equally important. It will be shown that this deficit in the productivity per person in the agricultural sector of the Northeast is greater than the corresponding deficit in its nonagricultural sector.

Smaller Output per Person in the Nonagricultural Sector. A comparison of the Northeast and the whole of Brazil in respect of output in industry, commerce, and services in 1940 shows that output per employed person in the Northeast was 58.4 per cent of the national average in industry, 65.8 per cent of the national average in commerce, and 44.1 per cent in services. This compares with the above corresponding figure of 52 to 53 per cent in agriculture. It will be seen that the disadvantage of the Northeast in output per person is greatest in services, next in agriculture, next in industry, and least in commerce.

If industry, commerce, and services are combined in an index of the nonagricultural sector, total output per person in the Northeast is 58.3 per cent of the national average.[3] This may be compared with a corresponding figure in the agricultural sector of 52.5 per cent[4] of the national average. Thus, it can be seen that the comparative disadvantage of the Northeast is greater in the agricultural sector than in the nonagricultural sector, although it is serious in both sectors.

Since the output per person in the nonagricultural sector in the Northeast is 42 per cent less than in the whole of Brazil and since the non-

---

[3] The figure is 58.2 per cent if industry, commerce, and services are weighed according to employment in the Northeast, 58.4 per cent if they are weighed according to employment in the whole of Brazil.

[4] Average of 1948 and 1949.

agricultural sector accounts for almost 50 per cent of the total income of the Northeast, it follows that the lower productivity per person in the nonagricultural sector in the Northeast lowers its per capita incomes in relation to the rest of the country by 21 per cent.

Smaller Nonagricultural Sector in the Northeast. Finally, account must be taken of the different employment structure of the Northeast. In the Northeast, 77 per cent of the total employed population is in the agricultural sector and 23 per cent outside. In the whole of Brazil, 67 per cent is in the agricultural sector and 33 per cent outside (1940 data). The effect of this different employment structure on the total per capita income of the Northeast may be computed as follows: To equalize the employment structure of the Northeast with that of the whole of Brazil, 10 per cent of the Northeastern population would have to be shifted from the agricultural sector to the nonagricultural sector. The income per person in the nonagricultural sector is 210 per cent of the average income for both sectors. Thus, to move 10 per cent of the population to the nonagricultural sector would add 21 per cent to total incomes. On the other hand, account must be taken of the loss in production resulting from the withdrawal of the 10 per cent from the agricultural sector. Since per capita income in the agricultural sector is 51 per cent of the average income in all sectors, the withdrawal of 10 per cent of the population from agriculture would result in a loss of income of 5 per cent. Deducting the 5 per cent loss in the agricultural sector is 51 per cent of the average income in all sectors, the we obtain, from the transfer of 10 per cent of the population out of the agricultural sector, a net gain of 16 per cent in the total regional income. Thus, the different employment structure of the Northeast accounts for a deficit of 14 per cent in per capita income ($100/116 = 86$). It may be seen (Table 1) that the structural factor, i.e., the smaller nonagricultural

Table 1. *Poverty Factors in the Northeast (percentage by which per capita incomes in the Northeast are reduced below the national Brazilian average, including the Northeast)* [*]

Lower percentage of population actively employed:	Lower productivity per person in agricultural sector:		Lower productivity per person outside agriculture:	Smaller percentage of population in nonagricultural sector:
5	26		21	14
	Less land per person: 14	Less output per unit of land: 15		

[*] Each figure shows the effects of the factor listed in isolation. The effects of two or more factors combined will be less than the sum of the individual factors stated. The combined effect of all factors stated, acting jointly, is to reduce per capita incomes in the Northeast by 53 per cent below the Brazilian average.

sector, is about as important as each of the two agricultural factors separately, i.e., small amount of land per person and small amount of output per hectare. It is much less important than the agricultural factors combined, i.e., low output per person in agriculture.

Summary. In this chapter the lack of development of the Brazilian Northeast, compared with Brazil as a whole, is allocated among the following factors:

1. The small proportion of the Northeastern population actively employed. This factor (the directly demographic factor) accounts for a difference between the Brazilian Northeast and the whole of Brazil of 5 per cent in per capita incomes.

2. The smaller cultivated area per person actively employed in the agricultural sector. This factor (the indirectly demographic factor indicating land shortage in the agricultural sector) accounts for a difference between the Northeast and the whole of Brazil of 14 per cent.

3. The lower output per hectare in the agricultural sector. This accounts for a difference between the Brazilian Northeast and the whole of Brazil of 15 per cent.

4. Lower productivity per person employed outside agriculture, i.e., in industry, commerce, and services. This accounts for a difference of 21 per cent between the per capita incomes of the Brazilian Northeast and the whole of Brazil.

5. The large proportion of population in the low-income agricultural sector in the Northeast and the corresponding small proportion in the higher-income nonagricultural sector (the structural factor). This accounts for a difference of 14 per cent.

Table 2. Derivation of Northeast per Capita Income as Percentage of Brazil per Capita Income

	Per cent
Per capita income of Brazil, including the Northeast..............	100
Application of Northeast poverty factors:	
1. Smaller proportion of actively employed population..........	95.4
2. Smaller cultivated area per person in agricultural sector......	81.7
3. Smaller output per hectare in agricultural sector............	69.4
4. Lower productivity per person in nonagricultural sector......	54.8
5. Smaller proportion of population outside agriculture.........	47.1
Per capita income of the Northeast............................	47.1

Thus, of the five factors listed above, factor 4 (lower productivity outside agriculture) is the most important individually, accounting for 21 per cent. If the agricultural factors of small output per unit of land and small amount of land per person are taken together in the form of small agricultural output per person, they are more important combined (26 per cent) than factor 4 or factor 5. Lower productivity in the agricultural sector is more important than lower productivity outside agriculture but not very much so (26 per cent as against 21 per cent). The different structure of the Northeast, compared with the whole of Brazil, accounts for two-thirds as much as the lower productivity outside agriculture.

The directly and indirectly demographic factors taken together account for an 18 per cent income deficit of the Northeast compared with the whole of Brazil. They are less important than low productivity outside agriculture but more important than the different structure of employment with an unduly small nonagricultural sector. The two demographic factors are more important than small output per hectare in the agricultural sector.

In the course of this study, it is shown that the per capita productivity of the Northeast relative to the whole of Brazil is higher in the non-agricultural sector (about 58 per cent of the Brazilian average) than in the agricultural sector (52 per cent). The difference is greatest in services, next in agriculture, next in industry, and least in commerce.

If the factors reducing the Northeastern standard below the Brazilian average are successively applied, it is found that the per capita income in the Brazilian Northeast is 47 per cent of that of the whole of Brazil. This agrees well with the national income statistics to be analyzed in the next chapter.

20

Estimate of Capital Requirements for the Economic Development of the Brazilian Northeast

There are three basic reasons for venturing an estimate of capital requirements:

1. No other estimates exist, and in view of the multiplicity of sources of finance and fields of activity, it is essential to obtain a consolidated picture of the approximate orders of magnitude of the problem.

2. An estimate of this kind may serve as a starting point for investment programs based upon more technical data compiled from field experience. Such subsequent adjustment of estimates arrived at in a global manner is not too difficult if the assumptions on which the global estimates are based can be properly taken into account and adjusted in the light of whatever data become available by experience from actual investment in the region.

3. The basic data required for these computations have already been prepared, largely through the work of the Vargas Foundation. If these basic figures were worth computing, there must be a presumption that they might be of direct use in formulating policies. Since the statistical overhead expense had already been incurred, the output/capital ratio of this further work appeared favorable.

The procedure adopted was as follows: The data used were the estimates of national incomes by states prepared by the Vargas Foundation and presented in *Trends in Economic Development of Brazil*. No independent check of these data could be undertaken for the purposes of this report. These data may exaggerate the income deficit of the region in 1950, since profits of corporations making their income tax declarations in the Federal District and São Paulo are shown in those areas, but it is noted that the introduction to the report from which the data were taken states that ". . . although further detailed investigations might lead in a few cases to somewhat more accurate results, the estimates used in analysing the trends in economic development can be considered as adequate for this purpose." Although this is not expressly stated, the data relate to national incomes at factor cost. They include the effects of changing production trends as well as those of changing terms of trade.

From these data, together with the known figures of distribution of population over the various states, two basic figures can be computed:

1. The shortfall in total income in the region as a whole and the individual states, compared with the "fair share," i.e., with what incomes would have been if the region, or each state within the region, had had in 1950 the average per capita income of the whole of Brazil (see below).

2. The shortfall in income attributable to the deterioration in the relative position of the region from 1939 to 1950, i.e., the shortfall compared with what incomes would have been if the region had maintained the same rate of growth as the whole country from 1939 to 1950, while keeping unchanged the relative poverty of the region as of 1939 (see the second section of this chapter).

TOTAL INVESTMENT BACKLOG OF THE REGION

The global results are given for three areas: (a) the administrative Northeast, comprised of the states of Pernambuco, Rio Grande do Norte, Paraíba, Ceará, Alagoas, Maranhão, and Piauí, (b) drought states in the administrative Northeast, i.e., the above states except for Maranhão, which is not in the polygon of drought, and (c) all drought states, i.e., the states included in (b) and also Bahia and Sergipe, which are partly within the polygon of drought, but not Minas Gerais, the proportion of which within the polygon is insignificant.

The total deficits in incomes of the areas in 1950, compared with the Brazilian per capita average of the same year, are set out in Table 3. The results are also set out by individual states, in Table 4. It should be emphasized that the deficit figures would have been considerably higher if the standard of comparison had not been the Brazilian average, which includes the Northeast, but rather the per capita average outside the Northeast. The latter deficits can also be readily computed if required.

The figures in columns 1, 2, 3, and 5 are in 1950 cruzeiros. High as they are, they would have to be increased by about 40 to 41 per cent if expressed in current (January, 1953) cruzeiros.[1] The percentages in columns 4 and 6 are not affected by the changes in price levels when considered as a historical picture of the situation in 1950. When considered as a current estimate, the percentages in columns 4 and 6 would be higher or lower depending on whether the rise in the real income and real investment of Brazil since 1950 has been smaller or greater than the relative deterioration of the Northeast since that date. In view of the effects of the drought

---

[1] Both the wholesale price and the cost of living indices rose by 40 to 41 per cent between the average of 1950 and early 1953.

Table 3. Income Deficits of Northeast, 1950, Compared with National Average, and Estimated Investment Required to Raise Incomes to 1950 National Average in 20 Years (in million cruzeiros—1950 purchasing power)

Area	Actual income 1950	Hypothetical 1950 income if area had same per capita income as Brazil as a whole	Deficit	Deficit as % of 1950 Brazilian national income	Investment required to remove deficit compared with 1950 Brazilian average	Annual investment required to remove deficit compared with 1950 Brazilian average in 20 years as % of total 1950 Brazilian investment
	(1)	(2)	(3)	(4)	(5)	(6)
a. Administrative Northeast..........	24,082	49,392	25,310	12.4	61,750	7.2
b. Drought states in Northeast (excluding Maranhão)............	22,104	42,795	20,691	10.3	51,310	6.1
c. All drought states (plus Bahia and Sergipe)............	33,258	64,499	31,241	15.3	75,950	9.0

and the deterioration of the internal terms of trade of the Northeast, it is likely that the percentages in columns 4 and 6 understate rather than overstate the present position.

The last two columns of Table 3 require an explanation. In column 5 it has been assumed that the lasting addition of one unit to all future national incomes requires the present investment of 2.4 units (a capital/output ratio of 2.4). This is a low rate, indicative of fairly high productivity or a capital shortage. It is widely believed to reflect the national average and also marginal product per unit of capital. It is possible that this ratio, low at it is, could be lowered in a national investment program in the Northeast.[2] This report will later deal with approaches which could lower this ratio in the specific case of the Northeast. The figures in column 3 would be directly increased (or decreased) in proportion to the fall (or rise) in productivity of new capital in the Northeast compared with the figure of 41 to 42 per cent (1:2.4) here assumed.

Subject to the assumption made in the preceding paragraph, the meaning of column 5 of Table 3 is as follows: Investment of the sums of 62, 51, and 76 billion cruzeiros (1950 purchasing power) respectively in the three areas identified would have been required in the past on the assumptions stated in order to bring the per capita income level of the areas to that of the national average. This, of course, did not take place. This statement assumes that the lacking investment could have been absorbed by the region and would have resulted in a development comparable to similar investment in South Brazil.

Column 6 transforms the estimate of the investment backlog in the region to a forward-looking investment program—here, a twenty-year program—designed to remedy the 1950 backlog. This "special backlog investment program" would require 3¾ billion cruzeiros of 1950 purchasing power annually in the whole drought region (3 billion in the Northeast) over twenty years. For comparison, the 3 per cent appropriation of Federal tax revenue to drought areas, at 1952 levels of revenue, amounts to about 500 to 600 million cruzeiros of 1950 purchasing power. It should be emphasized that the data in Table 3 refer to the investment requirements not only of the polygon but of the drought states as a whole. On the other hand, the income deficiencies were computed before the cumulative effects of the drought were felt.

The total special backlog investment required in the Northeast and the drought states is also a multiple of the 17 billion cruzeiros of domestic resources estimated to become available to the Banco Nacional do Desen-

---

[2] According to data of the United Nations Economic Commission for Latin America, the capital/output ratio for Brazil was as low as 1.76 during 1947–1952. If this could be achieved for investment in the Northeast, the backlog investment would be reduced by over one-quarter.

volvimento Econômico (National Bank of Economic Development) over the five years 1952–1956, particularly when it is remembered that the estimates in Table 3 are in 1950 purchasing power. The special backlog of investment in the drought states of the Northeast alone would be satisfied to the extent of about one-fifth only, even if the total domestic resources of the Banco Nacional were concentrated there.

Column 5 of Table 3 is not an estimate of the total investment required in the region. In the first place, it does not include the investment required to provide for the increase in population in the Northeast over the twenty years during which the special backlog investment is assumed to take place. In the second place, in the light of recent trends, the national Brazilian average per capita real income would itself move upward during the twenty years, so that at the end of the twenty years the 1950 average would be reached but the region would still be a relatively depressed area.

As for the increase in population, the available data indicate that over the eleven years from 1939 to 1950 investment in the region was just sufficient to maintain per capita income. This was derived from data contained in *Trends in Economic Development of Brazil* by applying the shares of various states and regions of the net national income in 1939 and 1950 to the national product in constant prices in the two years.[3] This procedure disregards changes in internal terms of trade of the region between the two dates, but the improvement in external terms of trade and the relatively mild external overvaluation of the cruzeiro in 1950 could approximately cancel out during that period. The rate of population increase in column 4 of Table 4 has been obtained by adding one-tenth to the known population increase between 1940 and 1950.

If the conclusion derived from Table 4 that past investment has just been sufficient to maintain per capita income is accurate, it follows that the special backlog investment would have to be entirely *additional* to the rates of investment prevailing during 1939–1950, which were only just sufficient to deal with the increase in population at the decennial rate of 26.9 per cent. If the population increase should accelerate, either because of a decline in death rates or because of a reduction in emigration from the region (whether autonomous or as a result of the backlog investment program), further investment would be required. If the national capital/output ratio of 2.4 can be assumed to have obtained in the region from 1939 to 1950, an annual increase in population of 2.5 per cent would require an annual investment of 6 per cent of the regional income. The actual income of the administrative Northeast in 1950 having been 24,082 million cruzeiros, 6 per cent of it would be an annual investment of 1,445 million cruzeiros of 1950 purchasing power.

This investment of 1,445 million cruzeiros would be additional to 3,037

[3] *Trends in Economic Development of Brazil,* table VIII.

Table 4. Changes in Real Income in the Administrative Northeast, 1939–1950

State	1939 income, million Cr.	1950 income, million Cr. of 1939 purchasing power	1950 income as % of 1939	1950 population as % of 1939	1950 per capita income as % of 1939
	(1)	(2)	(3)	(4)	(5)
Pernambuco............	1,821	2,295	126	131	96
Rio Grande do Norte....	428	604	141	131	108
Paraíba...............	714	966	135	124	109
Ceará................	928	1,510	163	134	122*
Alagoas..............	500	544	109	118	92
Maranhão............	571	544	95	133	71
Piauí................	357	362	101	133	76
Total region.........	5,319	6,825	128	128	100

* This increase in the per capita income of Ceará is surprising, but it should be noted that Ceará showed a very heavy fall in absolute and per capita income from 1950 to 1951. The fall in per capita income amounted to 10 per cent, according to data in *Revista brasileira de economia*, December, 1952. This decline is in money terms. In real terms the decline would be about 25 per cent. This would bring the per capita income of Ceará approximately back to the 1939 level. Paraíba, which is also shown with a higher per capita income in 1950, also suffered a reduction in real income per capita of approximately 10 per cent from 1950 to 1951. The 1951 figure would again be roughly the same as for 1939. On the other hand, of four states which are shown to have suffered a decline in per capita income up to 1950, three increased their real income per capita (Maranhão, Pernambuco, and Alagoas) by about 3 to 4 per cent, and in Piauí it remained approximately constant. Thus, from 1950 to 1951 there seems to have been a tendency of approximation toward the 1939 level, and the 1951 figures would be closer to 100 per cent.

million cruzeiros a year required for the special backlog investment program over twenty years. If the above estimates are approximately correct, 6 per cent of the original income would also in fact have been the actual rate of investment in the region over the period from 1939 to 1950.

Thus the total investment required in the region in order to bring up per capita income to the 1950 Brazilian average within twenty years may be estimated as follows:

Table 5. Estimated Annual Capital Requirements of the Administrative Northeast
(in million cruzeiros—1950 purchasing power)

Special backlog investment per annum (for 20 years)	Investment for increase in population per annum	Total investment required	Estimated present (1939–1950) rate of investment	Additional investment required per annum	Present rate of investment as percentage of required rate
3,037	1,445	4,482	1,445	3,037	32.2

If the Table 5 is approximately correct, it follows that investment in the region would have to be tripled from its current (1939–1950) level in order to reach the 1950 Brazilian per capita average in twenty years.

Table 6 shows the distribution of the total backlog investment among the various states. Column 1 is in million cruzeiros of 1950 purchasing power. The percentage distribution of column 2 indicates the geographical distribution of any investment program arranged to be proportionate to the total investment backlog. A comparison of the geographical distribution of actual investment with the distribution shown in column 2 of Table 6 would indicate in which state the investment backlog of 1950 is more rapidly tackled than in others.

Table 6. Special Backlog Investment Requirements in 1950 by States
(in million cruzeiros—1950 purchasing power)

State	Investment deficiency (1)	Per cent (2)
Pernambuco	12,970	15.2
Rio Grande do Norte	4,380	5.1
Paraíba	7,890	9.2
Ceará	12,710	14.9
Alagoas	5,610	6.6
Maranhão	10,440	12.2
Piauí	6,750	7.9
Bahia	22,270	26.1
Sergipe	2,370	2.8
Total	85,390	100

Table 7 shows the distribution of population in 1950 between the polygon of drought and the areas outside the polygon. If per capita investment within and outside the drought areas were the same, this would describe the distribution of the investment program as between the dry zone and the areas outside. This assumption does not, of course, in any way imply an economic argument that investment should be distributed in this fashion between the two areas.

Table 7. Distribution of Population inside and outside Polygon, 1950

Area	Inside polygon, %	Outside polygon, %
Administrative Northeast	61.7	38.3
Drought states in administrative Northeast	68.6	31.4
All drought states (including Bahia and Sergipe)	43.8	56.2

In conclusion of this part of the estimate of capital requirements, it may be stated that an attempt to deal with the whole accumulated investment backlog of the region even over such a long period as twenty years would require massive investment of a magnitude not so far considered as feasible. This is the case as long as massive global investment of the same productivity as that obtaining in the rest of the country is considered the key to the problem. It follows that, unless the position of the area can be improved without investment or by investment of much greater productivity than assumed in the above calculations, the aim of an investment policy should be more modestly defined. This is done in the following section, in which the goal is defined as the elimination of the investment backlog accumulated since 1939 only, not the elimination of the total accumulated investment backlog.

An investment program of the type described above, i.e., designed to wipe out the total accumulated investment backlog of the region in twenty years, would have to raise the per capita income of the region by a little over 100 per cent. This may be inferred from Table 3, where it may be seen that the administrative Northeast in 1950 had less than half the per capita income of the whole of Brazil in 1950. This would involve a rise in per capita income over the twenty years of $3\frac{1}{2}$ to 4 per cent per annum, which is a very high rate but still lower than the recent (1947–1952) rate of growth of per capita output of the entire country.

Thus, the investment program outlined above would leave the region in twenty years time in the same or a worse position relative to the rest of Brazil, when compared with 1950, but with much improved absolute position. If the rate of growth of per capita output for the whole of Brazil over the twenty years should fall to a more normal rate of 2 per cent per annum, the relative as well as the absolute position of the region would improve.

ELIMINATION OF INVESTMENT BACKLOG ACCUMULATED SINCE 1939

A more modest target for an investment program in the Northeast would be to restore to the region the proportion of the 1950 national income which corresponded to the share of the region in 1939. In other words, the target would be to reverse the relative deterioration in the position of the region between 1939 and 1950. This deterioration has been considerable. The share of the administrative Northeast in the national income of the country fell from 14.9 per cent in 1939 to 11.3 per cent in 1950. Including the drought states of Bahia and Sergipe, the deterioration was from 21.2 per cent to 16.5 per cent of the national income.[4]

____

[4] As will be shown later, this relative deterioration continued from 1950 to 1951.

This more modest target has the advantage of not being based on such an abstract target of per capita incomes of the region as a national average, but rather on a condition actually achieved by the region in 1939. It is therefore a target which has been demonstrated to be within the possibilities of the resources endowment of the region within the recent past. All that it requires is the assumption that the resources of the region, with sufficient investment, would have enabled it to progress from its actual 1939 level at the same rate as the country as a whole during the eleven years from 1939 to 1950. This more modest target has also the advantage of requiring resources for investment in the region that are more in keeping with present feasibilities.

Table 8 shows the estimated investment required to remove the income deficiencies accumulated in the region between 1939 and 1950 as a result of the relative deterioration during the period. The data are presented for the three groupings in Table 3. They also correspond to the data in Table 3 in that they are based on assumed productivity of new investment of 41 to 42 per cent per unit of capital and are expressed in cruzeiros of 1950 purchasing power. It will be seen that the removal of this specific backlog in twenty years would require between 700 million and 1 billion cruzeiros annually (according to definition of the region) at 1950 prices, which are about 40 per cent more in current cruzeiros. It will also be seen that the additional investment required is of the order of magnitude of two-thirds of the estimated present rate of investment of the region. As indicated in Table 3, the estimated requirements would be lowered in the same proportion as it is found possible to raise the output/capital ratio above 41–42 per cent, and vice versa.

Table 9 shows the investment requirements on the more modest target (column 2) compared with those of the first target (column 1). It will be seen that the investment requirements on the more modest target are between 27.3 per cent and 30.5 per cent of the larger requirements computed in the preceding section for the region as a whole (according to the definition of the region used). For the administrative Northeast the percentage is 30.5 per cent.

Table 9 also shows that the relation of the two targets varies considerably from state to state. As is indicated, however, in the footnote to Table 4, this apparent discrepancy would have partly disappeared if 1951 had been taken instead of 1950. In this case, the geographical distribution of investment between states would not have been very different according to the two targets.

Table 9 also shows that the recent accumulation of an income backlog in the region has been very rapid. Almost one-third of the total historical backlog accumulated up to 1950 has occurred in the eleven years prior to 1950.

Table 8. Investment Backlog, 1939–1950 (in million cruzeiros—1950 purchasing power)

Area	Actual 1950 income	Hypothetical 1950 income if area had maintained 1939 share in Brazilian national income	Income deficit since 1939: (2) minus (1)	Estimated total investment required to eliminate 1939–1950 income deficit	Annual additional investment if program is executed in 20 years	Estimated present (1939–1950) rate of investment
	(1)	(2)	(3)	(4)	(5)	(6)
a. Administrative Northeast..........	24,082	31,755	7,673	18,415	921	1,445
b. Drought states in Northeast........	22,104	28,235	6,131	14,474	724	1,326
c. All drought states (including Bahia and Sergipe).....	33,258	41,786	8,528	20,467	1,023	1,896

Although the computations presented are based on 1950 data, it can in fact be shown that the backlog continued to accumulate from 1950 to 1951 at the same rate as from 1939 to 1950. According to data on net national income computed by the Vargas Foundation and contained in *Revista brasileira de economía,* December, 1952, the share of the administrative Northeast in the national income declined from 11.25 per cent in 1950 to 10.78 per cent in 1951. If the drought states of Bahia and Sergipe are added, the deterioration is from 16.46 per cent to 15.89 per cent. The

Table 9. *Investment Backlog, 1939–1950, as Percentage of Total Investment Backlog Accumulated to 1950 (in million cruzeiros—1950 purchasing power)*

State	Total backlog (1)	1939–1950 backlog (2)	(2) as per cent of (1) (3)
Pernambuco	12,970	6,620	51.0
Rio Grande do Norte	4,380	990	22.6
Paraíba	7,890	2,070	26.2
Ceará	12,710	510	4.0
Alagoas	5,610	2,600	46.3
Piauí	6,750	2,030	30.1
Drought states in Northeast	50,310	14,820	29.4
Maranhão	10,440	3,690	35.3
Total Northeast	60,750	18,510	30.5
Bahia	22,270	4,650	20.9
Sergipe	2,370	1,000	42.2
All drought states	74,950	20,470	27.3

money income per capita in the region increased only by 8 per cent (administrative Northeast) and 8.8 per cent (including Bahia and Sergipe), compared with the Brazilian average of 12.8 per cent. This is a deterioration by 4–4.8 per cent in regional per capita income compared with the national average.

Since the increase in the Brazilian average represented an increase in the gross real per capita product of 4.6 per cent between the two years,[5] it follows that in the Northeast region and the drought states real per capita gross product would have remained virtually constant. This is in agreement with the results for 1939–1950 shown in Table 4. Since the Brazilian average increased at a rather high rate, above the 1939–1950 average, it follows that the relative deterioration of the Northeast region continued

[5] According to data of the U.N. Economic Commission for Latin America, *Economic Survey of Latin America,* 1953.

at least at the same rate as between 1939 and 1950. Hence, the estimates of capital requirements contained in Tables 8, 9, and 10 should be raised by about 10 per cent if the backlog is computed for the years from 1939 to 1951.

Table 10 shows a summary of the results reached on the 1939–1950 basis. It indicates the number of years in which the two targets we have discussed could be reached by the annual investment of given sums of current (1953) cruzeiros in the administrative Northeast on the assumptions already stated.

Table 10. Number of Years in Which Additional Investment in 1953 Cruzeiros Would (Target A) Raise per Capita Incomes in the Administrative Northeast to the 1950 Brazilian Average or (Target B) Raise per Capita Incomes to the 1939 Level, Improved by 11 Years Progress at the Same Rate as Brazil from 1939 to 1950 (Restore 1939 Share in National Incomes)

Additional investment in Northeast, million cruzeiros	No. of years to reach target A	No. of years to reach target B
500 (+25%)	169	55
1,000 (+50%)	85	27
1,500 (+75%)	56	18
2,000 (+100%)	42	13
2,500 (+125%)	33	10
3,000 (+150%)	28	9
4,000 (+200%)	21	7
5,000 (+250%)	17	5

SUMMARY

The first section of the chapter estimates the magnitude and considers the implications of a program to eliminate the total investment backlog of the region in twenty years. It is found that investment in the region would have to be tripled from its present level, which is estimated to be just sufficient to keep per capita incomes constant.

It is estimated that if the productivity of investment in the region is the same as in the whole of Brazil, such an investment program would require an annual investment of 3,037 million cruzeiros of 1950 purchasing power in the administrative Northeast alone.

This investment program would raise the region, on the assumption estimated, to the 1950 Brazilian average level of per capita incomes but would still leave it at a level inferior to that of the rest of the country at the end of twenty years of investment.

The second section of the chapter estimates the magnitude of a program to eliminate the investment backlog accumulated in the region since 1939. It is found that the investment required would be about 30 per cent of the sums required to eliminate the total investment backlog. Such a program would require an addition of about two-thirds of the estimated present rate of investment. The twenty-year program would require the additional annual investment of 700 million to 1 billion cruzeiros.

It is found that the relative deterioration in the position of the region continued from 1950 to 1951 at the same or higher rate than during the period from 1939 to 1950. Summary Table 10 indicates the estimated number of years to reach the two targets assumed in this chapter with the annual investment of given sums of current (1953) cruzeiros in the region.

21

Investment Problems in the Development of the Brazilian Northeast

ECONOMIC JUSTIFICATION FOR AN INVESTMENT PROGRAM

The terms of reference for my studies do not include the feasibility of diverting resources, to a greater extent than hitherto, from other purposes into the development of the Northeast. Such a discussion would involve more detailed work on the relative resource endowment and prospects of the various regions of Brazil; it would involve the formulation of views on general objectives of development and general policies. All these are beyond the scope of this chapter. My terms of reference are merely to assume that certain resources are available for investment in the Northeast and to develop possible criteria for their best use in the region. However, the forms which investment in the region will take are inevitably interlinked with the reasons why investment is undertaken at all. The first part of this chapter tries to set out the economic basis of an investment program in the Northeast in a form which may lend itself to the derivation of investment criteria, and points out the criteria thus derived.

Correction of Unbalanced Development. Economic development is not a question of national averages. Such averages are in the nature of abstract concepts. Economic development is not an abstract concept but an improvement in the standard of living and comfort of life of the people of a country. Thus, economic development requires a dual test: (1) the test of national averages, and (2) the test of the degree in which improvements have spread among the people of a country. By the first test, development in Brazil has been rapid and practically continuous in recent years. By the second test, it has been much less satisfactory. The benefits of development have been concentrated in one part of the country. The preceding chapter has shown that the Northeast region stood still from 1939 to 1951, while the country as a whole was advancing steadily.

Moreover, the people who were thus excluded from the benefits of economic development do not form a diminishing proportion of the national population. In spite of some internal emigration, in spite of con-

240

centration of immigration from abroad in the more southern part of the country, such is the force of natural increase of population in the Northeastern region that its share in the national population has been maintained. It is quite possible, in fact, that the natural trends of population would create a condition in which the population thus excluded from economic progress forms an increasing part of the national population.

Thus, one of the purposes of an investment program in the Northeast would be to spread development more widely.

The corresponding criterion of investment would be that *investment in the Northeast should be of a type which has a broad and direct impact on the poverty of the existing population.*

It may also be argued that regional lack of balance in economic development poses dangers for the future, particularly if not accompanied by a concentration of population in the developing regions. The concentration of investment in one region may create conditions of diminishing returns, labor shortage, and bottlenecks in that region, and the "overflow" of development from one region might, with mutual advantage, be diverted into other regions. When certain stages in development are reached, the developed regions may also be hampered by lack of markets, and the lack of development of other regions may then become a drag on the national economy as a whole. The second problem, however, is in the relatively distant future in the case of Brazil; the first problem is more important. *To some extent it may even now be advisable to think of the development of the Northeast, particularly in the nonagricultural sector, as a method of relieving bottlenecks and overloads on existing capacities in other areas.*

Instances are not unknown where the development of more retarded units combined with more developed areas has been stimulated or initiated by such overflow functions.

Existence of Social and Economic Overhead Capital in the Region. The Northeast is an old, fairly densely settled area, in fact the oldest economic region of Brazil. In some ways the economic development of an old and settled area is more difficult than that of a new area of settlement. However, these difficulties are more in the field of social and legal institutions than in the field of economics. Economically, if the institutional problems can be solved, the development of a settled area tends to be cheaper than that of a new area, provided that the natural-resources situation in the two cases is reasonably similar.

It is true that the economic and social capital of the Northeast—in particular, railways, ports, roads, housing, and land improvements—is often of poor quality. But whatever their deficiencies, their improvement and the filling in of gaps in them is cheaper than the creation of an entirely new system of such overhead facilities. Some of the public utilities in the area, e.g., certain railways, are distinctly underutilized. Others are already well adapted for the needs of the region and capable of greater use, e.g., many roads.

The Brazilian economy is stretched to the limit in many respects. There is very little reserve of unutilized social capital in the rapidly developing regions of the country. Hence the existence of a framework of social capital on which to build is of great importance. The investment criterion to be derived is that *the development in the region should be to the greatest possible extent based on the existing public utilities and overhead capital.*

The social productivity of new investment can be very high where it results in the preservation and reasonably economic operation of an existing block of social capital which might otherwise have to be written off and abandoned.

Artificial Causes of the Decline of the Northeast (Transfers). The failure of the region to keep in line with the more southern parts of Brazil is not due—or at least is not entirely due—to reasons inherent in its natural-resource endowment and "natural" productivity of new investment. A process of transfer from the region to other parts of Brazil has operated. Such elements of transfer can be classified as (1) unfavorable internal terms of trade, (2) fiscal transfers, (3) the draining of the human resources of the region, and (4) the transfer of capital through migration.

The quantitative importance of the transfer under these four headings is difficult to estimate, but it is certain that the combined effect has been very appreciable. To that effect an investment program in the region could be considered as compensatory in nature; i.e., it would restore rather than upset the "natural" distribution of investment, in line with resource endowments and inherent economic productivity.

The criterion to be derived from the above considerations is that an investment program for the region need not necessarily be conceived in terms of specific projects within the region. Rather, the general economic policies or tendencies which now lead to transfers from the region and departures from the natural distribution of investment might also come under review. In each case, the relative advantages of compensatory investment as against modification of the original policies leading to internal transfers would have to be weighed. There is a general presumption that the social productivity of such compensatory investment would be high, since it would restore the natural distribution of investment, in accordance with resources and productivity.

As to internal terms of trade, it is remarkable that the deterioration in regional terms of trade has more than offset the improvement of the price relations of primary products to manufactured products which has recently occurred. Taking 1948 as 100, the domestic wholesale prices for manufactured goods in Brazil were 162 in 1952, and appreciably higher than that at the end of the year. At that time, the export value in dollars (i.e., converted at the unchanged official cruzeiro rate) was only 111 for cocoa, 112 for sugar, and 157 for cotton. The dollar prices of nearly all vegetable oils were actually below 1948 levels. To the extent, therefore, that the region exports primary products and obtains in return cruzeiros based on the official exchange rate while paying for its imports of manufactured or other goods from the other parts of Brazil at prices reflecting the much lower internal exchange value of the cruzeiro, the terms of trade of the region have severely deteriorated. It has been deprived of the potential benefits even of the temporary general upsurge of commodity prices in the early part of 1951 except perhaps in the case of cotton. The overvaluation of the external purchasing power of the cruzeiro must have had a considerable distorting and discouraging effect on new investment in the extension of production of export products in the region. An example is the direct decline in production of babaçú and oiticica in Piauí. Apart from such distorting effects on the benefit/cost ratio of investment, the resulting impoverishment of the region would have considerably discouraging effects on investments and improvements generally (with opposite effects in other parts of Brazil). It may be roughly estimated that the Northeast exports as much as 16 per cent of its total production if Bahia is included. This high figure reflects more the low level of income than the high value of exports in the region. If internal terms of trade deteriorate by 30 to 40 per cent after 1948 as the above figures indicate, this would represent a deterioration in the national income of the region of around 6 per cent, or as much as the annual estimated level of investment in the region. Some mitigation will occur insofar as the region imports directly from abroad rather than from the rest of Brazil, but from the figures it may be estimated that this would not offset more than perhaps one-third of the above-estimated loss.

Some further mitigation has occurred as a result of specific government stabilization policies, but this had only partial effects; and among the main products of the region, only sugar and sisal were affected.

As for the depletion of the human capital of the region, it is commonly known that some of the most successful entrepreneurs in other parts of Brazil have come from this region; at a more modest level, it is also universally agreed that workers from the Northeast often do very well as skilled workers in the South, even with comparatively short training. All this argues against the view that innate resources of the area are not capable of much higher development inside the area, given the right incentives. Of particular concern must be the effect of emigration on the age distribution of the population. The proportion of men between the ages of ten and twenty-nine years in the total population in the administrative Northeast diminished from 14.6 per cent in 1940 to 13.7 per cent in 1950. If Bahia and Sergipe are included, the drop is from 14.6 per cent to 13.5 per cent. Since young men are the most active elements in the labor force and also the nucleus of new skills and new techniques, this is a very serious decline, especially since it is superimposed on an economically unfavorable demographic situation of high birth rates and high death rates.

Since the emigration is internal, the age distribution of other areas becomes more favorable as that of the Northeast becomes less favorable, and no national net loss is involved. However, a vicious circle is set up in the Northeast. Poverty drives out the most skilled, the most enterprising, the young, and those without dependents. In doing so, it increases the poverty in the Northeast and thus acts as an additional deterrent to new investment. As a result of such a vicious circle, a region may decline much more than its "natural" conditions warrant, once a decline is started. An interruption of such vicious circles is recognized as a legitimate objective of compensatory investment and may be combined with methods of organizing emigration so as to make the emigrants more representative of the general population.

Finally, emigration involves a considerable though invisible export of capital. The Northeast has to some extent spent its limited resources, not in benefiting itself, but in benefiting other regions. The resources invested in food, clothing, education, and provision of other services for emigrants must have been a high proportion of the small share of a small national income available for the improvement of the region. This capital export would also create a presumption that compensatory investment might be justified, inasmuch as the local resources available for improvement are artificially reduced below the natural availabilities in the region.

Some technicians who have investigated the problems of the region have arrived at the conclusion that the resource problems are man-made rather than natural to a greater extent than is commonly assumed. This statement may be amplified in that the weakness of financial resources available to the region is also to some extent man-made and below its natural level.

Under the present circumstances, the Northeastern region appears to get the worst of all worlds.

1. The natural rate of population increase is high, higher than the national average and among the highest in the world. This reduces per capita income, in view of scarce investment funds.

2. This high rate of population increase is brought about in the economically most wasteful manner, by a combination of extremely high birth rates and high death rates, resulting in large-scale malinvestment and waste through the premature deaths of children and persons in young, productive age groups. This further drains the resources available for productive investment.

3. Emigration is fairly substantial and so further removes invisible and human capital from the region.

4. Emigration is unorganized and removes the young, the producers, the skilled, and the educated, thus further weakening the resources and investment opportunities of the region.

5. Yet at the same time, emigration is not sufficiently large to reduce the rate of population increase in the region below the national average. Its main effect is the deterioration of the composition of the population in respect of economic quality, without affording a relief in numbers compared with the rest of the country.

It may be noted that the share of the Federal revenue collected in the Northeast has considerably increased in the decade from 1941 to 1950, while the share of the region in the country's national income has steadily declined.[1] This trend is largely due to the shift from import duties to consumption taxes in the structure of Federal revenue. The increased incidence of taxation on the Northeast has to some extent offset the provision of allocating 3 per cent of the Federal budget, since it has resulted in a net transfer of 1.2 per cent of the Federal budget out of the region. This was equivalent to a transfer of 380 million cruzeiros in 1950, or 500 million cruzeiros per annum at current (1953) prices.

It can also be shown that the financial weakness of the states and *municipios* (small districts) in the Northeast results in declining shares of state and *municipio* expenditures in the Northeast yet at the same time constitutes increasing relative burdens on the declining income share of the Northeast. The financial weakness falls with full weight on the more "constructive" types of expenditures, particularly development, industrial services, and public utilities. In all these fields expenditure per capita in the Northeast is only a small fraction of the national average and even disproportionately small in relation to income.

It is a striking fact for an outside observer to notice that no Federal fiscal inducements exist at present to make investment in the Northeast attractive and to offset the above-mentioned fiscal and other transfer. In dealing with the not dissimilar problem of the "depressed areas" (called later the "special areas" and still later the "development area") in Great Britain, fiscal inducements played a considerable part, including remission or mitigation of profit taxation for new firms and for new branches of old firms, as well as goverment subsidization of proceeds of local taxation in order to strengthen the financial position of the poorer local authorities in the stricken areas.

Some Harmful Effects of Internal Migration. It has been pointed out above that for the country as a whole (as distinct from the Northeast) internal migration cannot have harmful effects on the age distribution or economic quality of the population, and also that there is no contradiction between organized (as distinct from the present antiselective) emigration and a national investment program in the Northeast. This, however, does

[1] See the section on fiscal problems of the Northeast in Chap. 22.

not mean that internal migration has no harmful aspects for the country as a whole. In the first place, the effect on efficiency of labor must be considered. Where internal migration is temporary and migrants return to their original states, their acquisition of skill and the inducement of employers to give training and provide capital will be reduced; the return flow of migrants to the Northeast has not stopped, although it has declined compared with earlier periods. In the second place, it may be considered that if productive employment were provided in the Northeast, employment opportunities would arise in the South of the country for immigrants from abroad who could be selected so as to improve the age distribution and economic quality of the population. In this indirect sense (by reducing the scope for immigration from abroad), internal migration may in fact be said to have an effect on the age and other composition of the population for the country as a whole.

Existence of Many Growing Points in the Northeast. The picture of the Northeast as a uniformly declining area would be very misleading. To the outside observer, at any rate, it is surprising to what degree the economy of the Northeast reveals a fluid structure with many sectors of the economy rapidly developing. The picture of general stagnation is not due to the absence of developing sectors within the Northeastern economy. Rather, it is due to the fact that the development in some sectors of the North-eastern economy is offset by decline or stagnation in other sectors (apart from the fact that development is so largely absorbed by the rapid population increase). This fluidity of the economy seems a hopeful sign. An investment program could be directed toward strengthening the already developing sectors in the Northeastern economy, and so could enable them to maintain their growth. It does not necessarily have to create *new* "growing points" in the economy.

Among the existing growing points there may be mentioned the great increase in the cultivated area of the Northeast (from 2.3 million to 4.3 million hectares from 1941 to 1950).[2] The increase in cultivated area is far above the increase in population, and if it were possible to restore the earlier yields per hectare, an appreciable impact on the problem would be made. The fluidity of the economy also shows in the rapid rise of new crops, such as sisal. It further shows in considerable shifts of crops between different states within the Northeastern region and in the effectiveness of the price mechanism in inducing changes in the crops grown. The population of the Northeast is sensitive to relative prices in a degree rare in areas of such low income. Fluidity is also evident in the readiness of people to move both within the area and outside it.

[2] Data from *Apreciação preliminar dos problemas da agricultura brasileira,* U.N. Economic Commission for Latin America, E/CN. 12/307, p. 29. According to the same source, this increase continued from 1950 to 1951 except for crops particularly affected by external factors arising from the overvaluation of the cruzeiro, such as cocoa, castor oil, and carnauba wax.

Inspection of the available data also shows that for almost every crop some states in the Northeast have yields which are considerably higher not only than those in other states in the Northeast but also than the national average. This is true even though the average yield in the Northeast is uniformly lower than the national average. This clearly suggests that possibilities exist for increasing output partly by a degree of specialization within the Northeastern region and partly by approximating within other states in the region the conditions already obtained elsewhere in the region. No doubt in many cases the better results (better than national as well as regional) in some states are due to special circumstances which cannot be reproduced elsewhere, or they may be due to concentration of specific crops on the best land. It is, however, suggested that a case-by-case examination of individual products would reveal possibilities of bringing the average conditions in the region closer to the best results obtained in the region. At this moment the spread between the average of the region and the best of the region is particularly wide.

Thus, considering only crops occupying considerable acreages in the individual states mentioned, yields per hectare are above the *national* average as follows (data for 1948–1950) :

Pineapples
  Paraíba
  Pernambuco
  Alagoas
Cotton
  Ceará (in 1950)
Rice
  Ceará (in 1949 and 1950)
  Paraíba
  Alagoas
  Sergipe
Bananas
  Maranhão
  Ceará
  Rio Grande do Norte
  Paraíba
  Alagoas
  Sergipe
  Bahia
Sweet potatoes
  Paraíba
  Sergipe
Potatoes (batata ingleza)
  Paraíba (in 1948 and 1949)
  Sergipe
Coffee
  Paraíba (both per hectare and per
    tree)
  Pernambuco (per hectare only)

Sugar
  Ceará
  Rio Grande do Norte
  Paraíba
  Alagoas
  Sergipe
  Bahia
Coconuts
  Maranhão
  Rio Grande do Norte
  Paraíba
Beans (feijão)
  Sergipe (in 1948 and 1949)
Beans (favas)
  Paraíba
  Bahia
Tobacco
  Sergipe
Oranges
  Maranhão
  Piauí
  Paraíba
  Sergipe
Castor oil
  Paraíba
  Alagoas
  Bahia
Mandioca
  Bahia

Only in the case of corn (maize) are yields uniformly bad and also little different between states. In all the cases in the above list, the states indicated show averages much above the rest of the region as well as above the national average.

Even in 1951, which was a drought year, of the seven states in the Northeast, the following states had yields per hectare above the national average:

Sugar
    Rio Grande do Norte
    Paraíba
    Alagoas
Castor beans
    Paraíba
    Alagoas

Sweet potatoes
    Paraíba
Fruit
    Paraíba
    Alagoas
Bananas
    All except Ceará

In the case of cotton, sisal, beans, coffee, and mandioca, however, yields in the Northeast were uniformly bad in 1951.

The fluidity of the economy of the Northeast is also shown by the existence of good patches and successful developments throughout the area. The Pesqueira development in tomato growing, the Baixo Verde, near Natal, where the use of deep wells has transformed the region into one of the principal cotton centers of the state, and the Cariri region in Ceará may all be mentioned.

The diversity of the Northeast precludes any general statements about its suitability or unsuitability as a field for investment. The Northeast is in fact an economic world of its own, and the varied conditions within the region seem to offer plenty of scope for productive specialization within it.

Cattle, long-staple cotton, carnauba, oiticica, and caroa seem to provide a natural economic basis for the economy of the *sertão*.[3] Food crops could be specialized more in the more humid areas, both coastal and *serra*.[4] Scope for some industrial development based on this agricultural specialization exists throughout the region. The integration of the dry areas with the rest of the zones would also increase the development of trade and port turnover on the coast. The economic basis of an investment program in the Northeast is certainly stronger than in a less varied region.

Specialization within the region, taking greater advantage of its variety, would presuppose population shifts within it. It has already been shown that unorganized emigration of an antiselective type has weakened the economic foundations of the Northeast. There is no contradiction at all between a program of organizing emigration from the region and investment within the region. Apart from emigration, however, population movement might be conducive to economic improvement in a number of ways.

[3] The arid interior of the Brazilian Northeast.
[4] Higher parts of the Northeast.

These are (1) movement of population from the dry polygon to the more humid parts of the Northeast, partly to the coast and partly to the fringe areas, such as Maranhão; (2) movement of population within the dry polygon to regions more suitable for new improvement, such as irrigation; (3) movement to areas of nonagricultural development, e.g., industries and minerals. A decision to invest in the Northeast by no means implies that the existing pattern of population in the Northeast should be accepted. In view of the existing diversity of conditions within the region, creating possibilities of an investment program in the region also means the need for mobility of population within it to take advantage of this diversity.

Existence of Underemployed Manpower in the Region. No one doubts that in years of drought underemployed manpower exists in the Northeast, particularly among landless tenants. To utilize this manpower would greatly reduce the true social costs of any investment undertaken in the region. This fact is already recognized both in the speeding up of public works in the region in time of drought and in the substitution of manpower for machinery in such public works. The existence of the latter procedure, i.e., the keeping idle of construction machinery in order to give employment to unemployed men, suggests that it would be possible with little further social cost to add to the investment program in times of drought by preparing sufficient projects to give employment to both the available machinery and the unemployed population rather than substitute one for the other.

There seems controversy whether underemployment exists to any appreciable degree in good years. While the Conselho Econômico (Economic Council) in its recent report has held that there is little agricultural underemployment, other observers have pointed to the seasonal nature of much of the work in the region. However, it seems that the seasonal occupations in the dry zones are now supplemented by other seasonal works or by more continuous work such as cattle raising. In normal years, the degree of direct underemployment, as distinct from underproductive employment, will not be high.

It is certain, however, that there is a good deal of underemployment in the towns. The data show that the percentage of the urban population throughout the Northeast has increased fairly rapidly. This is a perfectly natural occurrence in a normally progressive economy with rising per capita incomes. In the Northeast, however, as indicated elsewhere,[5] the level of real per capita output at best remains constant, and real income has deteriorated as a result of highly unfavorable terms of trade. A shift to urban population and out of agriculture in a stationary or declining community is evidence of underemployment in the towns. By all accounts, there exist now in the towns of the Northeast considerable reserves of underemployed

[5] Chaps. 20 and 22.

manpower, particularly in the suburbs and in the more rural fringes close to the coastal towns. These have been attracted to the towns by the urban amenities, higher minimum wages, prospects of intermittent work, and the difficulty of obtaining land or steady work in agriculture rather than by a genuine employment opportunity.

The utilization of the urban unemployment as well as the intermittent underemployment in periods of drought would greatly increase the productivity of new investment in the region.

Importance of Investment in Agricultural-surplus Region. In the past year, the direction of investment in Brazil has been in danger of frustration and distortion under inflationary pressure. Inflationary pressure has been unfavorable to agricultural investment, very specifically to investment in agricultural export crops, since domestic inflation was combined with fixed exchange rates. The answer to the danger of distortion perhaps lies not really in specific investment projects in agriculture or agricultural crops, although such projects (particularly in crops of growing importance such as sisal and fruit) would probably play a part in any program. The real rectification of the inflationary influence on the direction of investment would probably be a balanced program, i.e., a program including industrial as well as agricultural projects in a region which is naturally agricultural and productive of agricultural export crops. Such a balanced investment program in such a region would raise the general productivity and lower the real cost of agricultural exports and also provide the resources for natural capital formation on farms and in processing equipment. The past neglect of such capital formation has created some exceptional opportunities for high-yield investment, although in some cases the opportunity may already have been lost. Improvement in the quality of carnauba wax and reduction of waste in drying and threshing by means of better premises with walls and cement floors and mechanical extraction is a case in point: it is possible that by now the development of synthetic substitutes has gone too far to be reversed even by a great reduction in real cost of the natural product. At present, the rate of waste in drying and threshing alone may be estimated at 50 per cent.

If the argument for a balanced investment program in a main agricultural area with emphasis on export products is accepted, the Northeast would obviously come in for consideration. It is possible that a general investment program which raised all-round productivity, lowered real costs, and provided employment opportunities outside agriculture would be more effective in restoring export competitiveness than a series of projects specifically designed to deal with particular commodities. The latter are obviously necessary but not sufficient.

No Filtering Through from South Brazil. Even if the necessity of raising relative income levels in the Northeast is accepted, whether for welfare, social, or economic reasons, reliance might still be placed on "filtering through" of the benefits of the progress in the more advanced regions to the Northeast. There is no evidence that such filtering through has occurred. Since 1939, the position of the Northeast has deteriorated, while that of São Paulo and other such areas has greatly improved. At present, it seems that the disparity between the South and the Northeast is too great and that the links between the two economic areas are too weak to permit a process of filtering through.

One argument for an investment program in the Northeast may be that it will reduce the disparity and integrate the two economic areas to an extent sufficient to permit a more automatic filtering through of the benefits of the progress of the South to the Northeast.

Experience in the international field, between different countries as well as regionally within the same country, has shown that conditions may persist indefinitely under which developments in one country or one region, may lead to cumulative processes within it without any tendency to spread benefits to more retarded countries or regions. Experience has also shown that an initial investment program in such retarded countries and regions may place them in a position to participate in the benefits of development elsewhere. The case of Puerto Rico may be mentioned as an illustration, where an initial investment program has placed the island in a position to share in the progress of the continental United States economy.

MEASURES TO INCREASE THE PRODUCTIVITY OF NEW INVESTMENT IN THE NORTHEAST

Even the most preliminary analysis of the resources and present income levels of the Northeast indicates that a reasonably rapid improvement of the present extremely low income levels in the Northeast—which are similar to per capita incomes in some of the least developed countries—is dependent upon economizing capital, so that output per unit of capital available for investments in the Northeast would have to be raised considerably above the conventional 25 to 40 per cent yield per unit of capital. It may be observed that in normal development plans of underdeveloped countries yields higher than 30 to 33 per cent are not generally anticipated. Even with conventional yields it would indeed be possible to achieve reasonably rapid rates of increase in the national income of the Northeast, but this would involve such a heavy diversion of the total available Brazilian investment resources from other regions of Brazil that such a program would and should not be contemplated. Indeed, it may be estimated that to raise per capita income in the Northeast by 2 per cent per annum, given the present rate of population growth in the Northeast, would require *all* available Brazilian investment resources if the yield of capital in the Northeast were as low as 5 per cent. In view of the overriding importance of raising the yield per unit of capital in order to make any impact on the poverty of the Northeast, the following part of this chapter considers some possibilities existing in this direction.

The most obvious method of economizing in the use of capital is by improvements which do not require any investment at all. Such improvements would be particularly (1) to improve the institutions of the area, and (2) to reduce or eliminate waste of present resources, including capital resources. The first type of improvement without investment i.e., institutional reform occurs when, for instance, tenants are given greater security of land tenure so that cultivators have a greater incentive to undertake improvements—to erect fences, dig wells, use new methods to produce larger crops, etc. An illustration of the second type, i.e., reduction of waste of present resources, is the controlled use of water now provided by irrigation through public reservoirs, whether such better use is achieved by stricter enforcement of contracts with the owners of irrigated lands or achieved through economic inducements or penalties, such as differential water rates. The possibilities of improvement without investment in the Northeast deserve particular study. This report, however, is more concerned with the possibilities of increasing the yield of investment than with improvement without investment.

The following recommendations may be made, all designed to increase the yield of investment. They are listed not necessarily in order of importance. Time has not been sufficient so far to determine the relative importance of the various points listed.

Economy in Transport. The provision of new transport facilities is among the most expensive and capital-intensive aspects of economic development. In the Northeast, the transport system can be considered as roughly adequate for the present structure of the area. In fact, some of the railways in the area are among the least utilized in the world, and some duplication of road and railway has already occurred. It may be pointed out that where railways and roads have been duplicated in order to avoid loading and unloading of consignments, this is economically unjustified because reserves of manpower exist. Loading and unloading of freight adds considerably to cost of transport in the accounting sense, but where it can be done mainly by using underemployed manpower, its true cost is much lower than that of providing duplicate transport.

A good deal of past investment, especially through DNOCS (National Department of Works against Drought) and DNER (Department of Roads), has taken the form of provision of roads. The main reliance on roads and trucks (as well as on coastal shipping) for the movement of goods corresponds well to the economic needs of the region. In an investment program for the immediate future the cost of providing new means of transport should be a minor factor. This does not exclude the need for specific transport projects, especially where connecting links have to be provided or where transport forms a specific bottleneck, such as exists in gypsum production in Rio Grande do Norte, which could be doubled with transport rehabilitation. One can also foresee that in the case of closer economic integration of the area and specialization within the area, the volume of transport will increase, so that in the long run transport provision may have to occupy a more normal proportion of the total cost of investment. In the more immediate future, however, it should be possible to keep the cost of transport well below the normal proportions of a balanced investment program. The emphasis should be on maintenance and repair of existing roads and other means of transport rather than the provision of new ones. Where new roads are provided during periods of drought with otherwise unemployed manpower, the true cost of these roads is so small that the principle of economy of capital is not disturbed.

Considerable economies can be achieved in an investment program in this field. The postponement of major provision of new transport facilities has the additional advantage of determining at a later date the location and nature of the additional transport requirements in the light of whatever new patterns of trade and exchange may emerge from the economic development of the region.

Economy in Reservoirs. In the case of reservoirs, too, emphasis could be placed on maintenance, utilization, and completion of existing facilities. At present, the utilization of existing reservoirs is poor by all accounts. Agreement obtains that reservoirs take excessive time to construct and that an excessive proportion are therefore in a state of incompletion; that existing reservoirs are not linked with other reservoirs; that irrigation channels of existing reservoirs are not constructed; that the provision of electricity through existing reservoirs suffers from flood damages which could be reduced by means of watershed control upstream from the reservoir. All these cases point to types of investment which are likely to be highly productive, since they are based on better utilization of what already exists. High priority should be given to these projects, and the idea that development must necessarily be in the form of new structures should be resisted.

Improved Use of Irrigated Land. Irrigated land represents one of the most valuable, as well as expensive, resources of the region. Its better utilization would also be highly productive. To some extent this may be dependent on institutional reforms, such as better enforcement of contracts with landowners and extension of the system of public lands. Some of the uses of irrigated land may be positively harmful, e.g., where bananas are grown and their roots are allowed to destroy the irrigation channels. The control of crops on irrigated land to assure the best use of such land, particularly for food crops, will involve some investment. Expenditure for demonstration services on irrigated land, initial capital for setting up farms on new public land, inspection services to check water use and maintenance of irrigation channels, provision of seeds suitable for irrigated land and of tools needed in irrigated farming—all these will be required. Again, such investment ought to be given very high priority, since it is likely to be more productive per unit of capital than new structures or new projects would be. Purely financial investment, such as credit arrangements for farms on irrigated land, compensation arrangements for landowners, financial strengthening of available agricultural extension services, and subsidies of desired crops through free supplies of water or in other ways, may well be more productive in real terms than direct real investment in new projects. There may be a feeling that "financial investment ought to be avoided" and that "real investment is needed"; and in the ultimate sense, this is of course true. For a public investment program in the Northeast, however, I believe that good schemes of financial investment leading to increase in real output may be much more productive than new real investment.

Utilization of Underemployed Manpower. As indicated earlier, opinions differ as to what degree of underemployment exists in normal years in the Northeast. It is certain, however, that at the present time institutional factors limit the use of slack seasons for improvements in the land or the capital on farms and that no organized effort is made to utilize the free time of the rural population in the slack seasons for community development projects of direct benefit to themselves, especially the provision of water. If it were possible to emphasize in an investment program schemes which would result in the utilization of unemployed manpower with a minimum of materials and capital, the productivity of investment could be increased. Again financial investments, such as subsidization of community development schemes organized by the *municipios,* may well be more productive in real terms than any other form of investment. If it were possible to utilize the spare time and slack seasons for purposes of mass education and reduction of illiteracy, this could also be a highly productive method of investment. In view of the shortage of teachers of literacy and farming improvements and in view of the existence of a radio system, the systematic use of community radios for these purposes suggests itself. At present the radio system seems completely unutilized for any educational purpose. In Turkey, a successful attack on illiteracy and bad farming practices is made through the use of village institutes and the settling of teachers with some training in farming in the villages.

High Productivity of Local Processing. The productivity of local processing of materials usually is particularly high for the following reason: where processing is partly or wholly for the local market, it reduces the dependence of the raw material producer on exports abroad. In the case of the Northeast, exports are particularly fluctuating in quantity, partly because of the importance of commercial policy and partly because of the high cost of

Brazilian supplies in the world market; thus exports are more than proportionately affected by changes in demand. This applies to nearly all export commodities from the Northeast. Processing for the internal market will give increasing stability to production. The instability due to absence of processing facilities has often led to direct waste and abandonment of potential supplies. This has been true in the case of cocoa, sisal, carnauba, cotton, oiticica, and other major exports from the region. Thus, the presence of processing facilities will lead to an increased production of the primary raw material, without necessarily (in view of the specialization of resources) reducing the supplies of other commodities to anything like the same degree and without necessarily (in view of Brazil's marginal position in the world market) reducing exports of the crude material to anything like the same degree. Under such conditions, where the establishment of a processing facility results in increased output of the raw material without corresponding offsets, the true cost of the raw material is nil or very small. The increased production of the raw material should be counted as part of the productivity of the processing facility. This will increase the productivity of investment in processing very considerably and will in many cases more than offset any direct cost disadvantage of processing. It seems that an examination of possibilities in the Northeast in this direction, taking into account the increased and stabilized production of the raw material, could discover productive investments.

High Productivity of Removal of Bottlenecks. Where one single element of a combination of productive factors is lacking, its provision will be highly productive, since it will enable the other already available factors to be more fruitfully employed. Examples of this are the provision of power in the salt-producing area of Rio Grande do Norte, which might unlock latent opportunities for establishment of chemical industries, and the reduction in oiticica production in certain parts of Piauí because of the high trucking rates, which in turn are due not to the absence of roads but to their poor maintenance. This second example also illustrates the previously mentioned need for laying emphasis on maintenance and repair as distinct from new projects in a "cheap," i.e., high-yielding, investment program.

In many parts of the Northeast, port facilities are a bottleneck (almost literally). The removal of this bottleneck through port improvement can be productive in itself, particularly if it is combined with the abandonment of uneconomic ports. This could simultaneously (1) remove individual bottlenecks, (2) lower the cost of port operation through concentration on good ports, (3) assist in a new transport orientation of the whole area toward the good ports, and (4) be combined with a systematic use of empty trucks to carry as return loads from the port such bulky articles as bricks or cement needed in the interior for housing improvements, urgent hygienic improvements, and improvement in productive facilities. A number of such integrated schemes combining several high-productivity features could lower the cost of improvements appreciably.

High Productivity of Improvements of Existing Land. Advantage might well be taken of the fact that the Northeast is an area of old settlement with a comparatively dense population. Agricultural expansion in the form of colonization on new land has its advantages, particularly in the bypassing of social handicaps arising from ownership and existing institutions. However, this advantage is offset by the cost of opening up of new territory, which is expensive unless the new settlers are able to construct their own social capital as well as direct agricultural output. In the case of the Northeast, investment can consist mainly of the increase in output from existing land which can be made to move.[6] While land shortage is undoubtedly a problem in the Northeast, the raising of yields per hectare of actually cultivated land to the level of the rest of Brazil alone would raise the agricultural income of the region by almost 20 per cent and the total income of the region by almost 10 per cent, and might thus be considered one of the primary objectives. The other objective of reducing the land shortage is equally important, but might well be considered as secondary because of its probable higher cost.

Specialization between Various Parts of the Northeast. The productivity of new investment in the Northeast could be increased by projects which deliberately utilize the comparative advantages of the dry and the humid or irrigated areas of the Northeast. Such combined projects are likely to be more productive than projects which are confined to the characteristics of one particular climatic region within the Northeast. To illustrate, the dry zone is in great need of improved and selected seeds or plants naturally adapted to the dry zone—improved and selected for further development of their resistance and adaptation to drought. On the other hand, the development of such seeds can only take place on irrigated land because of the length of time required to develop the new strains of seed, during which the seed cultures need regular water. Thus, an investment project for the use of irrigated land for research and culture of seeds for crops to be grown in the dry area would be highly productive.

High Productivity of Purely Financial Investment. Reference has previously been made to the possibility of using additional finance in the region more effectively as a means of producing institutional change, giving inducements to desirable private activities, and serving as the equilibrating factor between the existence of administrative machinery for fulfilling certain functions and the lack of financial appropriations. In Piauí, to

---

[6] Moreover, in the only major new development area on the Piauí-Maranhão border, the cost of new development could be cheapened by provision of river transport on the Parnaíba River.

illustrate, the State Road Administration, which is charged with the maintenance of roads and has machinery in existence, is reported to be unable to maintain existing roads for lack of financial resources. In such a case, the appropriation of proper financial resources would be more productive than the undertaking of specific road projects by new agencies. I am greatly impressed by the possibility of additional finance for the region playing the role of a smoothing factor to enable necessary institutional changes to be made, to enable existing machinery to function properly, and to enable the right inducements to be given to existing agents of investment.

THE CAPITAL/OUTPUT RATIO IN CEARÁ

Agriculture: Computation A. In the Model Scheme below, the capital/output ratio in the Northeast was taken, on the basis of general data available, to be 1.74:1. This corresponds to a yield per unit of capital of 57.5 per cent per annum.

To test this assumption on the basis of more specific data, an inquiry was undertaken, based on the agriculture of Ceará. The data used are contained in *A estrutura da economía agropecuária do estado do Ceará.*[7] The data relate to 1940.

The procedure used was as follows: The difference between the capital employed per person on large farms (*em grande escala*) and on small farms (*em pequena escala*) and the corresponding differences in value of output per person were computed. For each of the three *tipos de exploraçao—agricultura* (agriculture), *agropecuária* (mixed), and *pecuária* (cattle raising)—the amount of capital[8] on large farms was computed (1) as it actually was, and (2) as the smaller amount it would have been if the large farms had had only the same amount of capital per person as the small farms; and the results for the three types of exploration were then aggregated. The same was done for the value of the output. Value of output was computed (1) as it was, and (2) as it would have been if output per person had been the same as on small farms. Thus it is possible to compute the additional output associated with the additional capital investment connected with the increasing scale of the agricultural establishment.

The result is as follows: The capital of large-scale establishments was 389 million cruzeiros larger than it would have been with the amount of capital associated with small units. The corresponding additional output was 222 million cruzeiros. This yields a capital/output ratio of 1.75:1, which is almost exactly the same as assumed in the Model Scheme.

If the value of land is excluded from the definition of "capital," the capital/output ratio is improved from 1.75:1 to 1.35:1. But this neglects

---

[7] Serviço Grafico, Instituto Brasileiro da Geografía Economía, 1952.
[8] Land, buildings and constructions, animals, equipment and vehicles.

(1) the improvements contained in the value of land which make land a part of capital, and (2) the real shortage of cultivated land, which makes land a limited resource in short supply, like capital. Hence, the first ratio of 1.75:1 seems more relevant.

The computed capital/output ratio of 1.75:1 represents a *marginal* ratio because it relates *additional* capital (on large farms) to *additional* output. It represents an *average* ratio in that it measures productivity of capital *over a broad sector*. It does not necessarily measure the productivity of selected investment in special agricultural projects. It is assumed that capital *outside farms* for large and small units is the same per person.

This may be interpreted as follows (assuming that the agricultural ratios can be applied to the economy in general):

MODEL SCHEME: THE BRAZILIAN NORTHEAST

Per capita income.	$75 at current prices
Estimated gross investment, including 3% appropriations.	7% of Northeast income
Estimated replacement.	3% of Northeast income
Estimated net investment.	4% of Northeast income
Rate of population increase per annum (1931–1940).	2.3%
Rate of growth of Northeast income (disregarding changes in its terms of trade).	2.3%
Rate of growth of per capita income (disregarding changes in terms of trade).	zero
Therefore, capital/output ratio (4%/2.3%).	1.74:1
Yield per unit of new capital.	57.5%

1. To achieve 2 per cent of growth of per capita income in the Northeast with present yield and population increase, investment would have to be increased from 4 per cent net to 7.5 per cent net, or by 1.75 billion cruzeiros.

$$(0.575 \times 7.5) - 2.3 = 2$$

2. A 2 per cent per capita growth with present investment and yield of capital would presuppose reduction in rate of population increase to 0.3 per cent, or emigration of 300,000 persons per annum (nonselective).

$$2 = (0.575 \times 4) - 0.3$$

3. A 2 per cent per capita growth with present investment and rate of population growth would require a raising of the yield of capital from 57.5 per cent (capital/output ratio 1.74) to 108 per cent (capital/output ratio 0.93).

$$2 = (1.08 \times 4) - 2.3$$

Agriculture: Computation B. The capital/output ratio in the agricultural sector of Ceará was computed above to be 1.75:1. This was based on a comparison of the smaller-scale and larger-scale units (as measured by their total volume of output, not necessarily by hectarage), and thus represented a *marginal* ratio (transition from smaller to larger volumes of capital per person).

An additional computation has now been made of the *average* ratio in the *agropecuária* (mixed) type of farms in Ceará. The data, like the previous data, relate to 1940.

The results are set out in Table 11. It was found that the ratio of capital (land, buildings, construction, equipment, vehicles and animals) to output was 2.07:1.

Table 11. Agricultural and Cattle-raising Establishments in Ceará

Area, hectares	No. of persons employed	Capital per person, Cr.$	Output per person, Cr.$	Capital/output ratio
(1)	(2)	(3)	(4)	(5)
Up to 1	25,281	329	157	2.10
1 to 2	15,063	356	235	1.51
2 to 5	38,021	302	226	1.34
5 to 10	47,183	347	262	1.32
10 to 20	75,934	501	292	1.72
20 to 50	123,886	522	318	1.64
50 to 100	105,231	768	356	2.16
100 to 200	92,746	772	371	2.08
200 to 500	84,648	1,018	409	2.49
500 to 1,000	31,197	1,155	405	2.85
1,000 to 2,500	14,099	1,330	445	3.00
2,500 to 5,000	4,201	2,030	413	4.92
5,000 to 10,000	2,287	1,298	337	3.85
10,000 to 100,000	1,801	1,433	289	4.96
Not declared	2,007	915	235	3.89
Total	663,585	684	330	2.07

The breakdown of Table 11 shows that this ratio reaches a low level for farms from 2 to 10 hectares, where productivity of capital is highest (although with a very intensive use of manpower per unit of capital and land), and then rises steadily up to 2,500 hectares. For farms above this size the ratio becomes irregular[9] but remains high.

[9] Possibly because of the small number of observations—only 235 establishments and only 1½ per cent of the value of output of all farms above 2,500 hectares.

The observed ratio is below the ratio of 2.4:1 obtained in much more aggregative United Nations Economic Commission for Latin America calculations, indicating a more favorable productivity of capital investment. Farms below 200 hectares had a more favorable ratio than 2.4:1. Farms from 200 to 500 hectares were close to that ratio. Farms above 500 hectares had a less favorable ratio.

Industry. The following data relate to 1940. They have been obtained from the Censo Industrial: Estado de Ceará.

When based on *net* output (value added), the capital/output ratio is 2.73:1, which is above that of agriculture in Ceará (2.07:1) but indicates a high yield of 37 per cent per unit of capital.

When based on gross output, the ratio is as low as 1.03:1, far below that of agriculture. It should be noted that insofar as the difference between *gross* output and *net* output is due to consumption of locally produced raw materials and insofar as it can be assumed that these materials would otherwise not have been produced for lack of a market, it is the *gross* output, rather than the net output, which measures the social productivity of capital Hence, the true social capital/output ratio of industry in Ceará will lie between 2.73:1 and 1.03:1, depending on the share of locally produced raw materials in gross output. (This could be determined by inquiry on the spot.) If half of the difference between gross output and net output is accounted for by domestic raw materials, the true ratio would be 1.88:1. This is close to the ratio of 1.75:1 previously computed by more aggregative measures (see Computation A).

If firms in Ceará industries are divided among *firmas individuals* (assumed to represent small scale), *sociedades de pessoas* (medium scale), and *sociedades de capital* (large scale), the following results are obtained (see Table 12 below):

Table 12. Capital/Output Ratio in Ceará by Scale of Industrial Units

Scale	Applied capital per person, 1,000 Cr.$	Gross output per person, 1,000 Cr.$	Net output per person, 1,000 Cr.$	Capital/output ratio On gross output	On net output	Persons employed per million Cr.$
Firmas individuals (individual ownership)............	5,029	7,729	2,663	0.65:1	1.89:1	187.7
Sociedades de pessoas (partnerships)...............	12,020	12,794	4,203	0.94:1	2.86:1	87.9
Sociedades de capital, mistas e outras (corporations).....	19,555	13,988	6,054	1.40:1	3.23:1	51.1
All scales...............	10,900	10,591	3,993	1.03:1	2.73:1	91.73

1. "Applied capital" per person increases steadily with scale, as expected.

2. Output per person (both gross and net) increases steadily, as expected.

3. The capital/output ratio increases steadily with scale (both gross and net).

4. The diminishing yield per unit of capital with increasing scale is matched by diminishing use of labor per unit of capital employed. The smaller units use less capital more productively with more lavish employment of labor, and vice versa.

22

Trade and
Fiscal Problems of the
Brazilian Northeast

ESTIMATE OF DETERIORATION OF TERMS OF TRADE, 1938–1952
AND ITS ECONOMIC SIGNIFICANCE

Export Surplus of the Region. The ratio of exports to the net income of the region can be established fairly closely. The total exports in 1950 from the ports within the Northeastern region amounted to 3,561 million cruzeiros, which is 12 per cent of the estimated income of the region of 34,836 million cruzeiros. The computation of exports from the main ports of the region represents a minimum figure for the following reasons:

1. Only the major products are included; an addition should be made for a number of minor products.

2. Exports from the region through ports outside the region should be added, such as export commodities brought by truck to Rio and other ports.

3. An addition should be made for exports from other regions which incorporate materials from the Northeast, such as vegetable oils refined in São Paulo or the Federal District.

4. Exports in 1950 from the Northeast were abnormally small. If 1948–1949 figures had been taken, a considerably higher export ratio would have been obtained. In 1951, the export ratio would have been higher because of higher prices.

In view of the foregoing, the export ratio of the region to net national income can be estimated as 15 or 16 per cent. This figure also agrees closely with data in *Apreciação preliminar dos problemas da agricultura brasileira.*[1] Total imports of the region from abroad in 1950 amounted to 1,656 million cruzeiros, or less than 5 per cent of the estimated national income. This leaves an export surplus of 10 to 11 per cent of the net national income. It will be noticed that the Northeast is a considerable foreign exchange earner; its imports from abroad account for less

[1] U.N. Economic Commission for Latin America, E/CN12/307, p. 29.

than half its total export proceeds. This export surplus is covered by net imports from other parts of Brazil. This is evident from the fact that both the coastal shipping balance of the region and the interstate commerce balance by road are heavily negative in relation to the rest of Brazil. These two negative balances virtually account for the export surplus.

Thus, the terms of trade of the region are largely determined by the ratio of the export prices obtained abroad for the products of the region to the prices paid for imports from the rest of Brazil. The impact of changes in the terms of trade on the national income of the region is determined by the ratio of the export *surplus* to the national income.

Terms of Trade. These terms of trade have deteriorated very heavily since 1948. The prices paid by the region in respect of its import surplus from the rest of Brazil have increased, from 1948 to 1952, by 62 per cent to 71 per cent, depending on whether the wholesale prices of manufactured goods or total wholesale prices are considered. The true index for the imports of the Northeastern region from the rest of Brazil will lie somewhere between the two limits. The export prices for the products of the region going abroad have increased much less or have actually fallen. The major export product of the region, cocoa, increased only by 11 per cent in unit value. Among the minor commodities, sugar and tobacco increased by 12 and 13 per cent respectively. Carnauba actually fell in export unit value by 2 per cent, sisal by 15 per cent, vegetable oils by 48 per cent, and hides by 44 per cent. Only cotton, which is exported in negligible quantities from the region, increased in price to a degree approximate to that of domestic wholesale prices (by 57 per cent.)[2]

Thus, the price index of goods imported by the Northeast from the rest of Brazil increased by 62 to 71 per cent. The index of prices of goods exported by the region to other countries actually fell by 1 per cent. The latter index has been obtained by weighing the 10 major export commodities of the region according to the value of their exports from the region in 1950. This index includes practically all the exports of the region. Thus, the terms of trade of the region, in the sense described above, have deteriorated by 39 to 42 per cent ($99/162 = 61$; $99/171 = 58$) in the four years from 1948 to 1952.

Effects on Income and Investment. If we apply this deterioration in terms of trade to the relative importance of the export *surplus* to other countries (and the import surplus from the rest of Brazil) in the net national income of the region, of 11 per cent, it is found that as a result of

[2] The data mentioned in this paragraph and used for the computation of the index in the following paragraph are directly based on Brazilian export unit values of cocoa, carnauba wax, sugar, and cotton. In the case of sisal, hides, and tobacco, they are based on United States import values. United States import unit values for coconut oil have been assumed to describe the price changes of castor oil, cocoa butter and babaçú from the Northeast.

the deterioration in terms of trade, the income of the Northeast has been reduced by 4 to 4½ per cent. It has previously been estimated that 6 per cent of the national income of the region is required to maintain per capita incomes and that the actual ratio of investment in the region is close to this figure.[3] It can now be seen that the deterioration in terms of trade of over 4 per cent within four years has wiped out over one-half of the minimum savings and investment funds of the region.

In an area with income levels as low as the Northeast, it is legitimate to assume that the incidence of a decline in real income due to deterioration of terms of trade will be mainly on savings and investment rather than consumption.

Hence, the conclusion is justified that if over the 1939–1950 period the rate of investment was barely sufficient to maintain existing conditions, the present rate of investment must be considerably below that level. This has been brought about by the deterioration in terms of trade due to the discrepancy between export prices and internal prices, and the peculiar balance-of-payments structure of the Northeastern region.

The income and investment deficiency of the Northeast as a result of the deterioration of the terms of trade of the region may be estimated to be at least 1.5 billion cruzeiros at current prices (1953).

The above data do not include the reduction in the real income of the Northeast because of falls in the quantity of exports, also due (like the deterioration of terms of trade) to the discrepancy between the external and internal purchasing power of the cruzeiro. Thus, the export of carnauba wax from the Northeast fell from 9,292 tons in 1948 to 7,196 tons in 1952. Reduction in export quantum also occurred in other major items. It may be estimated that such reductions in export quantum reduce the real national income of the region by at least another 2 per cent, or an estimated 750 million cruzeiros of current purchasing power.

FISCAL PROBLEMS OF THE NORTHEAST

One of the fiscal developments which has led to transfers from the Northeast in recent years has been the increasing importance of consumption taxes and the decreasing importance of import duties in the structure of the total receipts of the Union. In 1941, import duties and consumption taxes were about equally important, accounting for 22.2 per cent and 24.9 per cent of the Federal revenue respectively. In 1950, import duties had declined to 8.8 per cent of the Federal revenue. The Northeastern region paid, in 1950, only 5.6 per cent of all import duties, but 9.7 per cent of all consumption taxes. The low share in import duties was due to the small imports from abroad of the Northeastern region, leading to the considerable export surplus described at the beginning of this chapter. It is

[3] See Chap. 20, and Table 4.

notable that the Northeast, which in 1950 had 16.5 per cent of the total national income of Brazil, paid 9.7 per cent of all consumption taxes. This shows that in spite of the fact that real incomes of the Northeast were only a fraction of those of the rest of Brazil, the share in income paid in consumption taxes was only moderately lower. The relative burden on the much lower incomes of the Northeast is greater than the relative burden on the higher incomes in the rest of the country.

The shift from import duties to consumption taxes has resulted in an increase in the proportion of the total fiscal revenue of the Federal government collected from the Northeastern region, as was to be expected. The share of the Federal revenue drawn from the Northeast increased from 6.5 per cent in 1941 to 7.7 per cent in 1950, even though at the same time the share of the Northeast in the total national income declined heavily.

In 1941 the contribution of the Northeast to the Federal revenue of the Union was less than one-third of what would have corresponded to taxation proportional to income (21.6 per cent of national income; 6.5 per cent of Federal revenue).

In view of the very low incomes in the Northeast, this share could not be considered as unduly low. Yet in 1950 the contribution of the Northeast had risen from less than one-third of its proportional income share to almost one-half (16.5 per cent total income; 7.7 per cent of total revenue). In this sense there has been a clear tendency toward fiscal transfers added to unfavorable changes in internal terms of trade.

It is noteworthy that the increase in the share of the Northeastern region in the total Federal revenue came to 1.2 per cent of the total Federal revenue, amounting to 380 million cruzeiros in 1950, or the equivalent of 500 million cruzeiros at current prices. This transfer of 1.2 per cent of the Federal revenue goes a considerable way toward offsetting the effects of the constitutional provision of spending at least 3 per cent of the Federal revenue in the drought areas.

While the share of the Northeast in the Federal revenue increased, it is noteworthy that the share of the fiscal revenue received by the states in the Northeast declined quite sharply, from 13.45 per cent of the national figure in 1941 to 11.29 per cent in 1950. This indicates the increasing financial weakness of the Northeastern states. Per capita of population, the income of the states in the Northeast was 38 per cent of the Brazilian average in 1941, but had declined to 33 per cent in 1950. On the other hand, even the declining share of the income of the Northeastern states involved an increased relative burden on incomes in the Northeast, in view of the even steeper decline in the share of the national income in the region. Thus, in 1941 the Northeastern states received, in proportion to incomes in the region, about 60 per cent of what would have been the proportionate figure in Brazil as a whole; in 1950, this proportion had increased indicating a greater relative fiscal burden. Similarly, the share in receipts of the *municipos* in the Northeast declined between 1941 and 1950, and yet the decline was less steep than the decline in national incomes, indicating greater fiscal burdens. From Table 13 it may be seen

Table 13. *Fiscal Shares of Northeast (Including Bahia and Sergipe), 1941–1950, Compared with Shares in Population and National Income, as Percentages*

	1941	1950
Share in Federal revenue............	6.5	7.7
Share in receipts of states...........	13.5	11.3
Share in receipts of *municipios*........	17.4	15.8
Share in population................	35.0 (1940)	34.6
Share in national income...........	21.6 (1939)	16.5

that the *municipios* in the Northeast in 1941 received on a per capita basis just under one-half of the income of *municipios* in Brazil as a whole, but that in 1950 their per capita income had declined to 45 per cent of the national average. In relation to incomes in the region, however, the receipts of the *municipios* in 1941 were about 20 per cent less than in Brazil as a whole, whereas in 1950 they were almost in the national proportion to the regional incomes (less than 5 per cent below the national proportion)—a relatively much heavier burden, in view of the lower income. The share of the Northeastern *municipios* in receipts is greater than the share of the Northeastern states, but this is partly explained by the fact that the Federal District is treated as a state in the statistics.

The decline in the total receipts of the states between 1941 and 1950, in relation to the rest of Brazil, is only part of the story of fiscal weakness. Further analysis shows that of the small receipts of the states in the Northeast, a more than average share is retained for such purposes as general administration, debt service, etc. A less than average share of state expenses goes into the more "constructive" services such as education, public health, economic development, industrial services, and public utilities. The exception is the Public Health Service, on which state expenditures in the Northeast amounted to 15.8 per cent of all health expenditure by states in 1950. While this reflects the greater need for such expenditure and a disproportionately heavy burden on the small state receipts, it still represents less than half of the per capita expenditure in the rest of Brazil. Per capita state expenditure on education is less than one-third of that in the rest of Brazil. The real burden, however, of the low state revenues in the Northeast falls on development, industrial services, and public utilities. State expenditure on these three services only amounts to 9.1 per cent, 7.6 per cent, and

6.6 per cent of the corresponding figures for the whole of Brazil; this expenditure not only is as low as one-fourth to one-fifth per capita but also is only around one-half of the proportionate income in the region. The smallness of these percentages shows the degree in which the burden of financial weakness falls on such productive residual expenditures rather than the more general overhead expenses.

Summary. It is shown that the share of Federal revenue collected in the Northeast has considerably increased in the decade 1941–1950 while the share of the region in the country's national incomes has steadily declined. This trend is largely due to the shift from import duties to consumption taxes in the structure of Federal revenue. The increased incidence of taxation of the Northeast has to some extent offset the provision of allocating 3 per cent of the Federal budget, since it has resulted in a net transfer of 1.2 per cent of the Federal budget out of the region.

It is also shown that the financial weakness of the states and *municipios* in the Northeast results in declining shares of state and *municipio* expenditure in the Northeast while at the same time constituting increasing relative burdens on the declining income share of the Northeast. The financial weakness falls with full weight on the more "constructive" types of expenditures, particularly development, industrial services, and public utilities. In all these fields expenditure per capita in the Northeast is only a small fraction of the national average and even disproportionately small in relation to incomes.

Table 14. State Expenditures in the Northeast (Including Bahia and Sergipe) as Percentage of Total State Expenditures in Brazil

All state expenditures	10.1
"Constructive" state expenditures	9.7
Other state expenditures	10.6
Public health	15.8
Education	11.3
Development expenditures	9.1
Industrial services	7.6
Public utilities	6.6
Share in population	34.6
Share in national income	16.5

23

Economic Impressions
of the Brazilian Northeast

The national income figures with which we have been operating, based on the work done in the Vargas Foundation, would place the Northeast somewhere halfway between the more prosperous parts of India-Pakistan (such as the Punjab) and Turkey; my impressions confirmed this expectation. Perhaps the national income figures are slightly understated and the general levels would be closer to Turkey; my impressions may be due to the fact that the observations were made during the period immediately following the rains. Perhaps more striking than the general income level of the region, however, are the great disparities to be observed within the region. Taking Turkey as a standard, I should say that economic levels in the larger towns are distinctly above the levels of Turkey, as long as attention is focused on the more directly productive machinery rather than on specific social problems such as health and housing. On the other hand, conditions in the agriculture of the Northeast are distinctly below Turkish levels and roughly similar to those of the Punjab. The discrepancy between the towns and the countryside is greater than I have ever seen before. This confirms the previous findings from statistical data that the disadvantage of the Northeast is greater in agriculture than in industry and commerce.[1] My estimate would be that the per capita income level in the towns is five to six times higher than in the agricultural sector of the Northeast generally (the corresponding ratio for Brazil as a whole is also very high, about 4:1). This is not incompatible with the observation that even within the larger towns the social conditions of large numbers of people, particularly in health and housing, do not correspond to the comparatively high productivity levels reached there. This is only partly due to considerable inequality of income distribution within the nonagricultural sector, which in turn is presumably largely caused by the excess population in agriculture and the downward pressure on wages caused by low agricultural living standards and the influx into towns.

[1] See Chap. 19.

To a large extent I felt that the observed disparity in the towns between economic and social standards must be attributed to a noneconomic lag. To a surprising degree, workers and similarly placed groups in the towns living in extremely bad health and housing conditions seemed to have possession of such articles as bicycles, sewing machines, good radios, reasonably good furniture, and similar indications of moderate comfort which seem to be out of line with their state of health and housing.

To sum up, I found the standard of productivity and economic levels in the towns higher than I expected but the standards in the countryside and the social standards of large groups in the towns rather worse than I expected.

INDUSTRIAL PROBLEMS

Businessmen in the Northeast. Even after allowing for a process of natural selection by which there is a tendency for the visitor to be more in contact with more progressive and more prominent businessmen and even after allowing for some conspicuous exceptions, I was impressed by the high quality and competence of a number of the businessmen and industrialists, reflected also in the efficient organization of a number of the factories seen.

Furthermore, I was struck by the disparity between the often efficient, progressive, and clean conditions in the factories, including social services provided in a number of the larger factories, on the one hand, and the home conditions of the workers, on the other. Some of the social service provision seen would rarely be equaled in the United States or in England. There are conspicuous exceptions—one or two of the factories seen would remind one of the worst features of the early industrial revolution.

I believe that the businessmen of the Northeast tend to suffer from three main weaknesses and that efforts at improvement in the towns might well start off from these three sources of weakness:

1. A mania for "keeping the business in the family." I have never before seen this carried to such length. The system will sometimes accidentally give good results. In one case, a ceramics factory, the various members of a family had specialized in various types of technical studies, had gone to various countries such as the United States, England, Germany, and France for studies, and had formed a complementary and obviously effective team. This, incidentally, was an aristocratic family in a declining industry (sugar) who quickly saw the possibilities inherent in the new discovery of high-grade kaolin deposits in the Northeast for porcelain manufacture and deliberately and efficiently shifted the production facilities and the accumulated family wealth to the new line of production, later extending to new fields, such as tiles, factory bricks, etc., by the utilization of ploughed-back profits.

Generally speaking, however, the family nature of enterprises is a great weakness. Usually the activities of the firm, even a large firm, rest on one or two individuals. There is a reluctance to utilize outside credit and a resulting limitation of finance. It is remarkable that the reluctance to draw in outside sources of finance, even by borrowing, should have prevailed over the incentive to borrow which one would normally expect as a result of inflationary experience.

2. Reluctance to seek outside advice or assistance. This is presumably related to the tendency to keep the business in the family.

There is a tendency to do everything within the factory. I was struck by the enormous development of workshops right in the factory for the production of spare parts and even whole pieces of new machinery. An extraordinary number of these factory workshops had their own foundries. Owners of plants evidently take great pride in their workshops. I heard of a particular case—this is not based on direct observation—of sugar mills having workshops producing their own transportation equipment as well as machinery and spare parts.

This development of factory workshops probably has a harmful effect on the development of a specialized engineering industry. It was notable that in Campina Grande, where smaller specialized engineering workshops exist, the tendency toward expanding workshops in the factories was considerably less marked. I should say that in these expanded factory workshops there exists considerable unutilized engineering capacity. The possibility of utilizing such capacity in activities of more general interest might be considered. Very few of these factory workshops seem to take in any outside orders.

It is difficult to say whether this tendency of doing everything in the factories is a cause or a result of the absence of more specialized facilities. Presumably a vicious circle is at work. In the case of power facilities, however, the tendency for factories to provide their own power is clearly a result of the shortage of public power which is discussed below.

In the same direction, a tendency could be observed for firms to try to solve their technological problems themselves, without outside advice. Again, it is difficult to judge how far this is the cause or the result of absence of technological institutes, research laboratories, etc. It is extraordinary that towns like Campina Grande or Fortaleza should not have engineering schools or technical institutes or even higher technical-training facilities.

The reluctance to seek outside technical advice, combined with the tendency to keep things in the family, does give the conduct of industry in the Northeast a curiously amateurish tone, with empirical rather than scientific solutions of technical problems prevailing. The amateurish tone of business is reinforced by the fact that a number of businessmen tend to invest their profits in other enterprises only indirectly related to their original enterprise. To illustrate this point, the owner of a considerable-sized tannery also manages a large-scale farm in the neighborhood, with the use of by-products and waste from the tannery as fertilizer on the farm serving as a tenuous link between the two enterprises.

It is my impression that a movement in the direction of greater specialization and integration of business with research and outside experimentation could be highly beneficial. Even the training of mechanics and similar highly skilled workers was often undertaken in the same factories, although sometimes the services of Senai (Government Training Institute) were utilized. It was noteworthy that employers seemed to be satisfied with the skill of workers trained in their own factories and also with those trained by Senai.

3. Neglect of the human factor in production. The third blind spot among the businessmen seems to be their surprising indifference to social conditions of their workers.

The cost of ill-health, ignorance, and illiteracy in terms of productivity must be very considerable, but in contrast to American or English employers, very few employers in the region seem to be conscious of the connection. I was continually struck by the contrast between the pride of businessmen in their workshops, their side lines, or some mechanical improvement, on the one hand, and their lack of interest in the social conditions of their workers, on the other. I even had the feeling that the provision of special social factory services was more a result of legal requirements or a showpiece than evidence of social concern.

Power Shortage. Power failure (*falta de energia*) was a universal problem, although in various degrees. Not all of the effects of *falta de energia* seemed to be inevitable. In several towns, power is cut off without prior warning, at irregular, unpredictable times and for irregular, unpredictable intervals. It would obviously be preferable for the cutoffs at least to be regular and predictable, and there seems no reason why this should not be accomplished.

In the second place, industry does not seem to receive any priority over domestic consumers, even where the factory district is well separated from the other consumers and priority could easily be given. This is clearly wrong in an area so poor, where productivity should have priority over domestic consumption. The failure to give priorities to industries may be related to the low tariffs paid by industries in several towns—often lower than domestic consumers and some among the lowest in the world. This means that for the sake of a penny's revenue, a pound of production is lost (milreis of revenue, cruzeiro of production). Since it is the job of finance to "see that nothing is done on financial grounds which should not be done on real grounds," it would be preferable either to readjust the tariff differentials so that there is an incentive to differentiate in favor of industry or else to subsidize or compensate the power companies directly for any loss they may suffer by giving priority to industry.

Workers are paid for idle hours due to shortage of electricity, since nearly all workers are on time rates. In any case, earnings are so low that payment of workers for lost time is inevitable. This means, however, that the power shortage adds to cost of production, resulting in an inability of industries to afford their own power supply (especially when the reluctance to borrow outside funds for this purpose is remembered). In this way, a vicious circle is created, and the power shortage becomes chronically worse. Moreover, since it is the larger firms which have their own power supply, the shortage operates particularly against the small plants or workshops and more particularly against the small shop which is trying to increase its output. In view of the desirability of encouraging scattered growth and small-scale industries, this is an especially deplorable effect of the power shortage. Moreover, many other possible technical improvements are not undertaken because output could not be increased for lack of power anyway.

Where firms have their own power supply, they often prefer to rely on public power when available (because it is cheaper) and use their own plant as a stand-by. This is wasteful. It intensifies the power shortage for the (smaller) plants which have no power of their own and results in idle capacity of power equipment. In some cases, there is waste for the opposite reason: firms are so reluctant to rely on public power and risk interruption that they duplicate their own power equipment and have their own stand-by. Firms which have their own power should utilize it fully and sell any surplus to the public system. This is now rarely done.

To sum up, even granted the power shortage, much could be done to mitigate its effects.

Small-scale and Cottage Industries. Many industries in the Northeast would automatically come under the heading of small-scale industries. The typical unit is very small. A number of small-scale industries have naturally grown up, for instance, repair and servicing facilities for trucks as a result of the development of roads and trucking. As far as the scope for promotion of small-scale and cottage industry is concerned, my impression is not encouraging as far as concerns the growth of nonagricultural activities carried out directly in the countryside and as a complement to agricultural work.

For work other than handwork, the lack of power is a constant obstacle. The population in the countryside is very scattered, which makes cooperative or contract systems difficult to operate. Educational levels are low. On the whole I felt that educational improvement and improvement of agricultural practices should take priority over attempts to develop cottage industries. The absence or low development of a cooperative system in the Northeast would also be an obstacle.

However, exceptions exist. In Ceará, for instance, the embroidery of

cloth and also production of hammocks is already farmed out by manufacturers to people to do the work in their homes. The Fortaleza District is
renowned for its high tradition of embroidery and similar work. Some research on the possibilities of home use of tree cotton and also caroa might be
worthwhile. The weaving of palm products for mats, shoes, etc., could be
extended. I cannot, however, see more than a subsidiary role for such development in the Northeast.

I would expect more from another development which seems to be
beginning. As a result of the improvement of roads and the development
of airplane transport, the *sertão* has now become much more accessible from
the coastal towns than used to be the case. This has evidently increased
interest in the setting up of farms and also of industrial branches in the
industrial and commercial circles of such towns as Fortaleza. Some of the
surplus funds in the towns which might previously have gone elsewhere
are now employed in such developments. With the development of roads,
the *sertão* has ceased to be a mystery and romance and is being looked
at as an economic proposition. If the power problem could be solved, some
decentralization of industry from the towns might result. I feel such decentralization would be more important than the installation of cottage
industries. It is true that much has been done through cottage industries in
India and other countries of Asia, but the circumstances in the Northeast
of Brazil seem to me different.

AGRICULTURAL PROBLEMS

Water and Politics. The two "great debates" in the Northeast are (1)
on the *açudes* (reservoirs) and in particular on the relative roles and merits
of the large systems and the small reservoirs built under the system of
cooperação,[2] and (2) on the relative places of deputies and technicians in
deciding the location of the *açudes* and the general conduct of irrigation
policy. To my mind, these two questions are interlinked, as I shall explain.

The debate on small or large *açudes* seems to be meaningless. I
formed the impression that these must be considered at quite different
levels. The large systems are part of the *economic development* of the area
and, I believe, an essential part of it. The small reservoirs are a matter
of *social relief* for the distress created by droughts. It follows that the large
systems ought to be determined entirely by long-range and technical considerations and governed by a picture of possible developments in the
area as a whole. In the case of the small reservoirs, there seems no harm
in political determination, since deputies and representatives will presumably
reflect actually felt social needs at least as well—if they are true representatives—as technicians or officials, and the need for technical study hardly
exists. I have arrived at the conviction that a good deal of the mistakes and

[2] Constructed with private cooperation.

confusion of the past have arisen from a hopeless attempt to combine the two—large systems and small—in one single mechanism and procedure. A separation of the two seems to me essential.

The large systems ought to be in the hands of a technical organization which has the facilities for the required technical studies, which is not pressured into premature construction before the technical studies have been completed, and which receives its funds, not for specific projects with prescribed locations and sizes, but for general expenditure in the light of the technical studies and the general development picture for the area. None of these conditions has been satisfied in the past.

The Drought Department (DNOCS) has never had the necessary technical staff; it has never had the required time for research and preparation; it has been under detailed nontechnical instruction of where, when, and how to construct; and it has been under constant pressure to start new constructions rather than to complete existing ones. The root of the trouble has been that the determination of its work has not been a matter for the Department under the control of the competent Minister (in this case, of Public Works) responsible to Parliament. Appropriations have been made in such a way that in fact the determination of the work has been divorced from technical considerations. At the same time, while the technicians have been nontechnically controlled where they should have been free, they have been free where they should have been controlled and guided. They have had to operate on an *ad hoc* basis without control by the existence of a development picture for the area which could have given them the necessary yardsticks for the interpretation of technical data. In the absence of such guidance, decisions have been made on technical grounds which should have been made more on the basis of general economic considerations. At the same time, decisions were made on nonrelevant grounds under parliamentary direction, without the necessary technical data. At best, the projects were determined on grounds appropriate to the small *açudes* and their social objective. At worst, they were determined by political bargains or oratorical persuasiveness.

For a non-Brazilian unfamiliar with the country's institutions and traditions, it is difficult to recommend a solution. One possible solution would be a movement in the direction of the practice, similar to the practice in England and a number of other countries, of giving the Ministry and the Drought Department more administrative discretion within the framework of their appropriations. This would be subject to the publicity and debate of Parliament and under the direction of the President's general policy, but giving free appropriations not tied to specific projects. Another possible solution would be to convert DNOCS into an *autarquia*,[3] which would remove it from detailed parliamentary prescription. But in the light

[3] An independent public corporation.

of what has been said above, I feel that in that case the new *autarquia* might well be confined to the large systems and the small *açudes* left in the Ministry of Public Works, with or without a separate department. Another possibility would be for the work of preparing and building of some of the larger systems to be undertaken by some new entity not subject to the same pressures, such as a public bank. The latter course, however, would raise the problem of duplication of the technical services, since undoubtedly the technical services of DNOCS should in any case be strengthened, especially in the direction of economics and geology.

In the case of the large *açudes*, the overriding purpose must be irrigation—the earliest and fullest utilization of the irrigation potential. *Vasantes*[4] culture, fish culture, fixation of population, provision of water for man, cattle, and industry, and even provision of power are all subordinate, and have come to play a disproportionate part in the justification for the construction of *açudes* as a reflection of the failure to utilize the irrigation potential. Having been too much conceived as a multipurpose project, the *açudes* are in danger of becoming no-purpose projects unless full irrigation is immediately laid on. Any necessary research and study should have been done before construction, and cannot serve as an argument for delay in completing irrigation. Perhaps there is also a case for a different kind of *açude*, quite separately conceived in connection with local industrialization projects, with primary emphasis on power and water for industrial and human use.

If a technical agency is set free to deal with the problems of large *açudes* without detailed political prescription and without troubling about the small *açudes*, as is here suggested, no rapid expenditures should be expected or failure to spend rapidly made the ground for reducing allocations of funds. It may well be that actual expenditures would for a time be less than now, with the emphasis on completion and particularly on research and study. Time and resources spent on study will be highly productively employed, not wasted. The present lack of research and the political pressure for quick "results" (not increased output, but construction) reminds me strongly of the atmosphere surrounding the ill-fated groundnuts scheme in Tanganyika. By "research" is meant study of the economics, agronomy, and geology of such a complicated and differentiated region rather than the engineering problems involved in construction.

Perhaps such necessary research facilities need not be part of an agency directly operative in the engineering sense, but might be attached to a more general institution, such as the Bank for the North-East, or be organized as a separate institute. On balance, however, I feel that more might be lost than gained by such a separation. The separation required is not between research and operation but between economic development

[4] Cultivation on the humid margin of reservoirs.

and social relief. The former requires research and operation, the latter only operation.

Irrigated Land. Inspection of the statistics at one of the larger reservoirs (Engineiro Arcoverde) indicated that on the public land in the irrigation basin output per hectare was 40 per cent higher than on the private irrigated land, while consumption of water per hectare was 25 per cent lower. This would indicate that twice the production was obtained on the public land per unit of water used. This estimate is based on one individual case and on rough figures of combined tonnages of crops. It is possible to undertake more thorough comparisons based upon all major reservoirs and standardizing the data for the different crops. All the data necessary for such a study exist in the files of the Serviço Agro-Industrial of DNOCS in Fortaleza. Such a study would throw valuable light on one of the most important aspects of economic development in the Northeast—an aspect which is now approached more on political than on technical grounds.

If the result obtained in this one case should be confirmed or even approximately confirmed, it would establish an urgent case for a policy of acquiring land publicly as a part of all irrigation projects or at least an urgent case for the passing of the long-delayed irrigation code providing for proper control of the use of irrigated land. The cost of expropriation of land would add about 10 per cent at most to the cost of a reservoir-irrigation scheme; and if the benefits could be doubled or even approximately doubled, that would make a vital difference to the economics of irrigation in the Northeast.

The main factors to which the higher output on the public land were attributed were (1) proper leveling of the land, (2) crop specialization, and (3) better seed selection. A more detailed and refined statistical analysis of the data in Fortaleza could also throw light on the causes of the differences in production. The technicians seemed to be agreed that private owners often consider irrigation as a substitute for fertilization, and are satisfied with the increase in output due to irrigation ("We are well off now; why go for more?"), whereas the best benefit can only be derived from irrigation when it is combined, *for all crops,* with fertilization.

Density of Population Which Can Be Supported in Irrigated Land Near Reservoir. The difference in output between public and private land (and hence presumably also between rationally used private land and badly used private land) may explain some of the divergent estimates as to the capacity of irrigated land to sustain population. This is one of the key questions for the Northeast. Since there seems agreement among all concerned that the area suitable for irrigation from reservoirs in the real drought zone is about 200,000 hectares (Mr. Berredo's figure, subsequently accepted and used generally), the population that can be provided for by reservoir irrigation depends entirely on the density per hectare. Here we have divergent views, ranging from 2 persons per hectare (Mr. Berredo), to 7 per hectare (Professor Robeaux), to even 15 per hectare. If the low figure is accepted, reservoir irrigation would appear as only a minor contribution to the problem of the Northeast (400,000 people, or less than 10 per cent of the population of the *real* drought area, for the polygon is larger). If the higher figure of 7 is true, reservoir irrigation could be vital (1,400,000 people, or one-third of the population affected by droughts).

Part of the difference may be due to different assumptions as to standards of living in the irrigated areas. Here we must guard against a confusion. Some of the estimates say, "We must assume a decent standard of living, higher than the present." But it does not seem legitimate to assume *present* levels of production on irrigated land and a *higher* standard of living. When standards of living on irrigated land rise, this would be associated with higher production on the irrigated land (both as cause and consequence). There is no reason to think that the standards of production on irrigated land are less capable of subsequent improvement than any other standards of production. All experience elsewhere is to the contrary. Hence, in computing the capacity of irrigated land in the Northeast to sustain population, I have assumed the present standard of living in the Northeast as the initial figure—Cr.$ 3,000 per capita per annum at present (1953) prices. This is, of course, a very low standard of living which should be raised as quickly as possible. But I assume that production in irrigated land would increase *pari passu,* so that capacity to sustain population would not be reduced.

On the basis of statistics of the Serviço Agro-Industrial of DNOCS, I have computed the capacity of 1 hectare of irrigated land to sustain population at this level (Table 15). This computation is based on gross

Table 15. Crops and Number of Persons They Can Sustain
per Hectare at Cr.$ 3,000 per Annum

Rice	2.3
Maize (corn)	1.3
Sweet potatoes	4.0
Mandioca	5.3
Tomatoes	3.6
Oranges	2.7
Bananas	4.7
Simple average	3.4

production per annum minus costs for materials needed for irrigation, fertilization, and insecticides. The cost of outside transport and of machinery used in leveling, terracing, etc., should also be deducted, but could not be isolated from personnel costs of this kind. Hence, the figures are maximum figures. Perhaps as much as 5 to 10 per cent should be deducted to allow for the above items, according to crops. The data refer to 1952.

It will be noticed that the figures vary greatly between crops, as was to be expected. The simple average is 3.4 persons per crop per hectare, or 3 persons if the overstatement contained in the data is remembered. This figure of 3 persons per hectare could be increased if the irrigated land could be specialized on mandioca, bananas, and sweet potatoes. It would be reduced if specialization were on maize and rice. In no case could it approximate 7 persons per hectare, let alone 15.

In actual fact, the average would be likely to be less than the simple average of the seven crops. Maize, which has the lowest population-sustaining capacity, occupies at present more hectares in the drought states than all the other crops combined.

It may be concluded that irrigation by reservoirs cannot be the main solution of the problem, although it may contribute more than some estimates would allow for.

The Public Reservoirs. I acquired great admiration during my visit for the quality of the work done at and around the greater reservoirs and the caliber of the technical staff. Most of the staff seem to maintain their work at personal sacrifice in terms of both money and comfort. It should be remembered that the opportunity of spare-time work or outside consulting work does not exist in the Northeast as it does in Rio. Salaries which are adequate in Rio only because of the possibilities of supplementation are inadequate in the Northeast. The public reservoirs and the *postos* (reservoir-based stations) appear a veritable oasis, humming with life and activity while the surrounding country is dead.

This is precisely my criticism: that while the *postos* are wonderful, they do not seem to me to penetrate into the life of the region. "C'est magnifique, mais ce n'est pas le développement." A place like São Gonçalo is a world in itself, with its employment queues, farms, brickworks, housing developments, production of tiles, sales of seedlings and plants, water supply, tractor station, training shop, hospital, roads, etc. But just outside the limits of São Gonçalo life goes on unchanged. Admirable and invaluable as all this is, unless there are the money and, more specifically, the staff to have fifty São Gonçalos in the Northeast—which certainly there are not—its impact on the life of the region is limited. The work is in danger of becoming an end in itself. Demonstration becomes the oasis.

I cannot say whether it is a criticism of the approach of the *postos,* or whether it is a reflection on the low level of education or unwillingness to accept changes in technique on the part of the agriculturists. My impression is that the fault lies more with the agriculturists than with the officials, and that the officials, frustrated in their primary function of demonstration, have fallen back upon and developed the secondary function of an oasis. I regret very much that in building up an "oasis," the *postos* should not also have branched out into the field of adult education and new schools of their employees and others.

The only literacy course for adults which I came across was in Campina Grande. I was told that the demand for this course was great and that from two to three hundred adults participated. (Unfortunately, the intervention of a holiday prevented me from observing this course and talking to the participants.)

Insecticides. I saw the Northeast after the "winter" (rainy season). Moreover, the preceding year generally had been a year of fairly normal rainfall, although it failed to make up for the two previous years of drought. Much of the distress seen among the people driven from their land seemed to arise from the ravages of caterpillars. It seems especially hard that the effects of the drought should thus be aggravated by the much more avoidable effects of insects and that people who have clung to their land through the drought should be thus forced out. The complaint was made that it is the larger farmers who have the money, the access to the trade, the credit, and the spraying equipment which enable them to obtain and use insecticides. The small man cannot get them. There seems to me a very special case for the provision of spraying equipment and giving or supplying on credit of insecticides by the government to drought-stricken small farmers. Alternatively, the trade might be induced to extend its services and extend in drought years the same kind of credit facilities which would be extended in good years. There seems a strong case for some kind of public guarantees of credits granted for insecticides and equipment.

Special thought might be given to the supply of insecticides to tenants of large owners. The supply of insecticides could be considered a function of the owners, but the incidence of the drought is so hard on the tenants that their inclusion in any scheme for the supply of insecticides in drought areas might be considered.

Stability in Markets of Drought-resisting Plants. Another productive drought-relief measure which might be considered is some support of drought-resistant crops, for instance, caroa. Caroa is drought-resistant; but on the other hand, one of the chief uses of caroa is the packing of cotton, and since cotton output is reduced by the drought, the market for caroa is also affected. Thus, the drought does indirectly what it cannot do directly. In the circumstances, this seems to be a good case for production support and government-financed stockpiling. The social value of drought stability would seem ample to justify small public losses in any such support schemes.

In the case of carnauba wax, public support might well take the form of technical improvements and subsidies for research in drying, threshing, extracting of wax, utilization of by-products, and perhaps also domestic industrialization of wax. In tree cotton, public support might be directed toward creating a regional demand for this high-grade product by developing the production of fine yarns and high-grade cloth in the Northeast. In sisal, the main need seems for development of decorticators (locally produced). The development of multipurpose machinery suitable for the processing of both sisal and caroa and perhaps even cotton would also be advantageous and might be made a subject of special research.

A TENTATIVE DEVELOPMENT OUTLINE FOR PERNAMBUCO

The "Northeast region" is an abstraction. This is true both because of the variety of the different zones within the region and because of the different nature of the economic interrelations between the different zones in the various states and parts of the region. I do not think that there could be or should be a single development approach for the whole Northeast. Rather, there should be studies of the economic relationship within smaller regions, sometimes parts of states. This study should lead to the definition of key factors in the economic improvement of these smaller regions.

As an illustration of this isolation of key factors and the formulation of a development approach based on them, there follows a tentative scheme of this kind for the state of Pernambuco. Lack of time has prevented similar studies for other parts of the region.

Moving inland in Pernambuco, we have first the city of Recife, with an excellent port and great industrial opportunities. Recife is also the terminal of one of the main transmission lines from Paulo Affonso, on the São Francisco River. Nearby, in Olinda, there are also newly discovered phosphorite deposits of great economic importance. (It is worth noting that these deposits were discovered, not as a result of a systematic geological survey, but accidentally, while looking for limestone for the production of cement.)

Next to Recife, there is the *zona da mata*,[5] where sugar production is concentrated. Further inland, there is the *agreste*,[6] fairly heavily populated and with much production of food crops. Next, there is the *sertão*, with more specialization in cotton and some dry crops. At the back of it all, there is the great São Francisco River.

The power from Paulo Affonso would be used to produce fertilizers in Recife, both nitrogenous and phosphate. While some of this fertilizer no doubt would be exported to other states and some would also be used in the *agreste* and the *sertão*, it is suggested that one of the primary markets for this product might be the sugar zone.

In the *zona da mata*, the yield of sugar per hectare has been steadily

[5] Humid coastal zone.
[6] Intermediate zone between the humid coastal zone and the arid interior.

declining. As a result, the sugar industry of Pernambuco has been in rapid economic deterioration relative to São Paulo. It is a moot point how far this deterioration is due to the purely physical factors of declining yields and how large a part the price policy of the Institute for Sugar and Alcohol has played. We shall leave aside the question of possible review of the price policy of the Institute as part of a development scheme for Pernambuco. The declining yields of the sugar land are due to soil exhaustion. Much of the sugar land has now been worked for centuries without sufficient rest, recovery, or fertilization. Deterioration of the Pernambuco sugar industry is also, of course, due to other factors such as lower productivity in processing of sugar, labor problems, and so forth; but these other factors are partly secondary and partly the result of the lack of profit and resources caused by the declining yields of the land. Declining yield can therefore be designated as the key factor in the decline and hence in the recovery of the industry.

The application of fertilizer and resulting recovery of yields in the sugar land would, in turn, enable the sugar zone to resume its traditional role of offering employment opportunities and supplementary incomes to the population in the *agreste*. The sugar harvest in the *zona da mata* is at a different season from the harvest in the *agreste*. Hence, mobility of population between the *agreste* and the *zona da mata* was very important and beneficial in solving the labor problems of the sugar industry and also the problem of poverty and overpopulation in the *agreste*.

The decline of the sugar industry has made it impossible for the industry to offer the wages which would attract the labor from the *agreste* at harvest time. This creates a vicious circle for the industry and for the population in the *agreste* alike. The additional income earned in the sugar zone by the population of the *agreste* would enable the population in the *agreste* to afford the additional equipment and also insecticides and fertilizers required to raise food production in that zone. It would also make the *agreste* into a market for the manufacture of consumption goods produced in Recife (and of course elsewhere).

In addition, the *agreste* would become a better market for the meat and cattle of the *sertão*. Thus, economic improvement, based on the use of Paulo Affonso power for fertilizer production, would work inland through the various zones. However, this process would not be automatic; it would have to be directed and promoted by policy measures. For instance, the increase in food production in the *agreste* would presuppose agricultural extension services in that area. Furthermore, the process of filtering through of benefits from the coast to the *sertão* would not in itself be sufficient to provide the required degree of development to the *sertão*.

For this reason, the use of Paulo Affonso electricity for purposes of irrigation of the land along the São Francisco River is advocated as an additional and second key factor in the economic development of Pernambuco. This would set in motion economic forces of improvement which would operate outward toward the coast, i.e., in the opposite direction to the first chain of improvement.

The two developments would thus supplement each other. The land along the São Francisco River is fertile (alluvial), and irrigation, although costly, could have a high productivity. Moreover, the population of the *sertão* would be enabled, partly by colonization along the São Francisco River and the higher incomes on the irrigated land there and partly through the increased sales of its products to the other zones, to afford the increased application of fertilizers, insecticides, and equipment to the land of the *sertão*. This would also result in projects of high productivity. Although easily exhausted and subject to droughts, the soil of the *sertão* is considered by the agricultural experts as inherently superior to and more responsive to fertilization than much of the land in the *agreste*. In fact, the development scheme outlined here would ultimately result in a certain redistribution of population away from the *agreste* and into the *sertão*. The bulk of the population increase, however, would no doubt be attracted to Recife.

In conclusion, it should be emphasized that this scheme is tentative and based on only initial impressions. It is put forward as an illustration of the kind of study of economic interrelations within the region that leads to an isolation of key factors, rather than as a final product. In other areas, different conditions and different relationships exist, and hence different key factors would emerge from analysis.

SUMMARY

To sum up, I would venture to make the following suggestions as a result of my observations in the Northeast:

1. Greatly extended research and study of the land problems of the region, specifically in the direction of economics and geology, both of which are now badly neglected in comparison to engineering and agronomy. A geological survey is a primary requirement. Study of economics of irrigation on the basis of the experience of the Serviço Agro-Industrial of DNOCS.

2. Establishment of technical control of new larger reservoir projects by reviewing the appropriations procedures of the DNOCS or establishing the Department as an *autarquía* or transferring the works to an independent institution of the development-bank type.

3. Passing of the irrigation law and/or transfer of irrigation basins into public land. Finance of required compensation in the latter case. Completion of irrigation systems of existing reservoirs.

4. Encouragement of technical research, subsidies for technical improvements, and market stabilization for sisal, caroa, carnauba, oiticica, and tree cotton.

5. Development of fertilizer industries (nitrogenous and phosphates) and high-grade textiles based on long-staple cotton as first priorities. Utilization of existing workshop facilities.

6. Establishment of technological institutes in Campina Grande and Fortaleza.

7. Educational improvements and extended activities of social housing in the rural parts of the Northeast.

8. Distribution of insecticides and spraying equipment to smaller farmers.

9. Strengthening of the demonstration activities of the agricultural services and state services.

10. Irrigitation along the São Francisco River and in the dry river valleys.

11. Preparation of a public works program for the next drought period with emphasis on the improvement of railways—straightening, new roadbeds, etc.—rather than of roads.

A FINAL IMPRESSION

I have formed, as a result of my studies and my observations in the Northeast, a definitely favorable impression of its development potential. I should say that, while not ideal, it may be rather better than the average of underdeveloped countries.

The natural conditions are not unfavorable. The climate is remarkably good for an equatorial region, and the variety of landscapes and zones offers scope for specialization. By all accounts the population, although badly neglected in health and education, is inherently intelligent, hardy, and adaptable. Rainfall is abundant in part of the region and will be sufficient in all of it as soon as the one single problem of maldistribution can be solved by storage, retention, and pumping. An urban civilization and a money economy already exist. There are no holy monkeys or cattle money.

The region has at least one splendid port. The sea has an abundant supply of fish which would make possible the year-round operation of fishing and canning plants.

The mineral resources of the region are also remarkable when it is remembered that no systematic survey has been undertaken. Salt from the sea, as well as rock salt; abundant clay and excellent kaolin; limestone; excellent phosphate deposits in extremely favorable locations and conditions; tungsten, magnesite, and other nonferrous metals; copper. All this adds up, not exactly to a magnificent, but to a good resource endowment.

In many respects, the resource endowment is complementary to that of the rest of Brazil, especially in metals.

The soil of the area, even in the *sertão*, is often naturally and chemically fertile. While it may need more rest and more fertilization than most soils in temperate zones, it also responds better to such treatment. Crop periods are much shorter of course. The dry zone itself has important specialized products which are drought-resistant.

The power supply of the area will be revolutionized through the development of Paulo Affonso. Practically the whole Northeast is within the reach of potential transmission from Paulo Affonso.

Over the area as a whole, there is a good balance between population and natural resources once irrigation is developed, with the population neither too thin nor too dense. However, the extraordinary rate of increase is a great danger for the future.

An adequate road system and an almost adequate railway system already exist. An urban business class with surplus funds also exists. Last but not least, the area is part of a larger entity and enjoys free access without tariff or currency barriers to the much more highly developed and expanding South Brazil, to which the region could be complementary both as a market and as a source of supply.

No doubt it would be possible to draw up a similar list of weaknesses and obstacles. But on the strength of the above-mentioned assets, I have no hesitation in saying that the region should be as capable of development as São Paulo.

24

A Development Outline
for the Brazilian Northeast

The following development outline is an "empty box." It has to be filled with technical substance before it has meaning. It should be emphasized, however, that the outline has been drawn up after consulting with technicians and obtaining their advice as to what kind of outline would be feasible and most helpful to them.

The outline takes as its starting point the actual position in 1950. It has been assumed that present investment in the Northeast and present resources are just about sufficient to cater to the natural increase in population at the same rate as in the past. It is assumed that this will continue to be the case and that therefore the increase in population can be neglected as long as the discussion is conducted in terms of the *additional* investment required—the investment over and above that which is now being made. Two things should be remembered, however: (1) The rate of population increase may speed up in the initial stages of development, since death rates may well be lowered and emigration may fall or cease. No provision is made for this possibility. (2) While present resources are sufficient to provide for the population increase at existing low standards, future provision at higher standards would require correspondingly greater resources.

While the following discussion takes the position in 1950 as a starting point, the money figures used are in terms of current (mid-1953) cruzeiros. The Northeast has been defined as the eight states of Piauí, Ceará, Rio Grande do Norte, Paraíba, Pernambuco, Alagoas, Sergipe, and Bahia. These states seem to share the main economic characteristics associated with the term "Northeast."

In 1950 this region contained 16.6 million persons, of whom approximately 5.5 million were workers (in the sense of persons employed in the direct earning of incomes). Of the 16.6 million persons, about 12.8 million were in the agricultural sector and about 3.8 million outside agriculture. Comparing the region with the whole of Brazil, including the Northeast itself, we may say that in proportion to population there was an excess of agricultural population of 14.9 per cent in the Northeast. Yet, in spite of this excess labor force of 14.9 per cent, the agricultural sector of the Northeast produced 14.1 per cent fewer agricultural goods and services per capita of total population than the whole of Brazil.

The nonagricultural sector of the Northeast had a relative population deficiency of 30.3 per cent and produced 44.8 per cent fewer nonagricultural goods and services in relation to total population than the whole of Brazil.

It will be observed that although the deficiency of production of the Northeast is greater in the nonagricultural sector than in the agricultural sector, the *per capita deficiency* is greater in the latter;[1] 14.9 per cent more people producing 14.1 per cent fewer goods in the agricultural sector of the Northeast amounts to a per capita deficiency of 26 per cent, while 30.3 per cent fewer people producing 44.8 per cent fewer goods in the nonagricultural sector amounts to a per capita deficiency of only 21 per cent.

Let us consider the agricultural sector first. Let us set as the target for a development program the maintenance of the present total agricultural production (still 14.1 per cent below the whole of Brazil), but without the excess population in agriculture. In other words, the target is to withdraw the relative excess population in agriculture in the Northeast amounting to 1.7 million people without affecting total output. It should be emphasized that this is an initial assumption for expository purposes only. It will be shown that in actual fact the agricultural excess population cannot be withdrawn from the agricultural sector. But the assumption of such a target provides a convenient starting point for establishing a development outline.

The removal of the excess 14.9 per cent of the agricultural population of the Northeast without reduction in total output would require an increase in per capita production in agriculture of 17.5 per cent, other things remaining equal. This is so because 851 persons will now have to produce as much as 1,000 persons produced before.

Let us assume that this increase in agricultural production per capita will be brought about entirely by irrigation (or that methods other than irrigation would be as expensive as irrigation). From the productive capacity of dry farming and irrigated farming respectively,[2] it may be estimated that a 17.5 per cent increase in per capita output would require 8 per cent of the total agricultural population transferred from dry land to irrigated land. It should be emphasized that this figure is based on the assumption that output on irrigated land will reach the level presently achieved on the public irrigated land in the Northeast, directly worked by the Serviço Agro-Industrial. This presupposes either public ownership or public control of irrigated land.[3]

Eight per cent of the total agricultural population after removal of the

---

[1] This was stressed in Chap. 19.
[2] From data obtained from the Serviço Agro-Industrial of DNOCS.
[3] See Chap. 23.

excess population in the Northeast would be 890,000 persons; their transfer from dry land to irrigated land would require the irrigation of 300,000 hectares.[4] Technically this is an entirely feasible target. It has been estimated that large reservoirs in the three states of Ceará, Paraíba, and Rio Grande do Norte alone could irrigate 200,000 hectares.[5] Adding to this pump irrigation of the banks of the São Francisco River, small reservoirs, and possibilities in the other five states not covered by the above estimates, another expert has estimated the total possibilities over the wider areas as about 1 million hectares.[6] Hence, the transfer of the excess population would not seem to be a technically unrealistic target even if it had to be entirely achieved by irrigation within the framework of a possible ten-year program, from 1955 to 1965.[7] To the extent that the improvement in per capita production stipulated in our target is achieved by methods other than irrigation, the acreage to be irrigated would be correspondingly reduced.

The cost of irrigation at present prices may be estimated at Cr.$ 20,000 per hectare. This would include the total costs of construction as well as irrigation. In detail the figure is higher for irrigation from large reservoirs and lower for river irrigation and pumping subsoil water. Thus, the exact figure would depend on the proportion of large reservoirs and other forms of irrigation; Cr.$ 20,000, however, seems a reasonable standard to take. Thus, the irrigation of 300,000 hectares (or other corresponding measures) would cost approximately 6 billion cruzeiros.

Turning now to the nonagricultural sector, we may take as our starting point the increased power supply from Paulo Affonso which will be available in the Northeast by 1955. This allows for 3 units, or about 180,000 kilowatts. It is assumed, however, that when this additional hydroelectric power is available, a certain proportion of the present thermal power will become obsolete.[8] It is assumed that the total power supply to the area will be almost doubled by 1955. This is a revolutionary change for the Northeast. But it is an indication of its present low power consumption that even with this increase, the Northeast will have less than its per capita share of the total increase in power availabilities for the whole of Brazil between 1950 and 1955.

Calculations based on the number of jobs per unit of power in European countries have been made. It has been assumed that little of the

---

[4] This allows for a density of 3 persons per hectare of irrigated land. For details of this calculation also see Chap. 23.

[5] Estimate by Mr. Berredo.

[6] Guimarães Duque, *Solo e água no polígono das secas Fortaleza* 1953.

[7] This would be true even remembering the need for considerable detailed study and research emphasized in Chap. 23.

[8] All these data are based on *Paulo Affonso é a expansão econômico do Nordeste,* Cia. Hidro Electrica S. Francisco.

additional power available would be used for consumptive purposes or for improvements in urban transport, etc. It is assumed that after making some allowance for use of power for irrigation purposes, the bulk would be available for industrial expansion, or, more generally, the creation of nonagricultural employment. It is assumed that about half of the additional power would be required by large power-consuming industries, especially those making fertilizers and caustic soda and additional cement plants. Another part would be used in the expansion of employment in less power-consuming industries such as textiles, food processing, etc. Of course, this calculation is rough and was made merely to supply an outline in general accord with reasonable technological conditions. On the basis of such rough calculations, it is estimated that the additional power supply would make it possible to create employment for 300,000 workers in the Northeast, outside the agricultural sector.

If we may assume that the present limiting factor in nonagricultural employment in the Northeast is the lack of power and that the nonagricultural sector would in fact expand in proportion with the new power facilities, it would be possible to find employment for 300,000 workers, or approximately 1 million persons, in the nonagricultural sector. If we assume that the provision of nonagricultural employment costs 110,000 cruzeiros per worker,[9] the total costs of the provision on nonagricultural employment at the rate indicated would be 33 billion cruzeiros.

If we take stock of the position presently reached, we have transferred 1.7 million people out of agriculture without loss of output (at a cost of 6 billion cruzeiros invested in agriculture). We have provided employment for 1 million persons in the nonagricultural sector (at a cost of 33 billion cruzeiros). At this point, we have reached the following position, comparing the Northeast with the whole of Brazil:

1. The reduced agricultural sector (11.1 million people) produces 14.1 per cent fewer goods in relation to total population and also per capita.

2. The old nonagricultural sector (3.8 million persons) produces 21 per cent less per capita than the corresponding sector for the whole of Brazil.

3. The new nonagricultural sector (1 million persons) produces, it is assumed, as much as the Brazilian nonagricultural average.

4. Another 700,000 persons, at present in agriculture, produce only about 15 per cent per capita of what their counterparts in the whole of Brazil produce, since these counterparts are in the nonagricultural sector.

It follows that at this point (which we may call 1965, assuming a ten-

---

[9] This figure is based on the present average amount of capital employed per worker in the nonagricultural sector of the Brazilian economy as a whole. If capital-intensive industries predominate in the development of the Northeast, the figure may well be higher.

year program starting from the availability of power in 1955) the North-east would still have a per capita income about 20 per cent below the Brazilian average. This would be an improvement in per capita income of about 80 per cent from the present level which is 55 per cent below the Brazilian average.[10]

It is now obvious that the remaining 700,000 persons should be provided for in agriculture, i.e., not transferred as provisionally assumed. Considering that the per capita income in the region, even after this development program involving a total expenditure of 39 billion cruzeiros, would still be about 20 per cent below the present Brazilian average, it would be prima facie inconsistent to provide for a nonagricultural sector as large proportionately as in the whole of Brazil. The remaining task, therefore, would be to provide for these 700,000 persons in the agricultural sector. For purposes of calculation, we may visualize that this is also done by irrigation. On the previous standard, this would require the irrigation of a further 250,000 hectares or so, which would still be in the technically feasible realm. The total cost of this final program would be, also on the previous assumption, 5 billion cruzeiros. This would represent about 12.5 per cent of the 39 billion cruzeiros of additional investment previously allowed for, or perhaps 25 per cent of the additional income which the expenditure of the 39 billion cruzeiros would generate. If the marginal ratio of saving, i.e., retention of the 80 per cent increase in Northeast per capita incomes for new investment, could be made as high as 25 per cent, the sum required could be financed from the increasing domestic resources of the Northeast without further additional outside investment. Perhaps we may assume that at least a part, if not the whole, of this new requirement of 5 billion cruzeiros could be obtained from the increased internal investment potential of the Northeast and that whatever part was not covered in this manner might be covered either by emigration from the Northeast or else, conceivably, by a margin contained in the previous figures. It should be remembered that investment in the Northeast possibly can be kept cheaper than has been assumed and that the required increases in agricultural output in particular can be partly achieved by less expensive methods than irrigation.

The rough estimate of this total additional investment program then would be in the region of 44 billion cruzeiros, of which about 33 billion cruzeiros would be nonagricultural. Of this total, 4 billion cruzeiros would be found internally. It has previously been assumed for illustrative purposes that this program would be spread out over ten years from 1955 to 1965. This would require an annual additional investment from outside of about 4 billion cruzeiros. Considering that total Brazilian net investment is now in the neighborhood of 45 billion cruzeiros, this would mean the diversion

[10] See Chap. 19.

of about 9 per cent of total Brazilian investment from elsewhere to the Northeast. Present investment in the Northeast may be estimated at about 8 per cent of total Brazilian investment. Hence the development program would assume that 17 per cent of all Brazilian investment took place in the Northeast. Considering that the region contains over 30 per cent of the population, this does not seem a grossly unrealistic figure. With the additional power available from Paulo Affonso and assuming that it can be reserved for productive purposes, none of the studies undertaken indicates that the productivity of such new investment in the Northeast need be inferior to the present levels reached elsewhere.

It must be emphasized in conclusion, however, that this last statement is based on the present productivity of the very small amounts of capital presently employed in the Northeast. The increase in this capital to the level postulated here would have to be combined with advances in education and social conditions as well as technological facilities in order to maintain these levels of productivity with the larger amounts of capital. If this is not done or cannot be done, a program of this kind may turn out to be a national malinvestment, although perhaps still defensible from a social and from a balance-of-payments point of view.

Index